NEW FUTURES FOR SOUTH ASIA

This book is a comprehensive examination of the society, polity and economy of South Asian countries and their future trajectories. The chapters included in the volume present key insights into the geopolitical dynamics of the region.

New Futures for South Asia:

- draws on case studies from the region to discuss how democracy has fared in terms of state-society linkages, transformational possibilities and the globalization and radicalization of politics;
- studies possibilities of economic cooperation in South Asia, including common currency, regional imbalances and aid, transport connectivity and electricity consumption;
- examines the crucial role of SAARC and bilateralism in forging connectivities across the diverse geographies of the region.

A major intervention in re-shaping South Asian studies, this book will be a great resource for scholars and researchers of security studies, strategic affairs, international relations, development studies and politics.

Adluri Subramanyam Raju is Professor and former Head of the UNESCO Madanjeet Singh Institute of South Asia Regional Cooperation (UMISARC) and Centre for South Asian Studies and coordinator of the UGC Centre for Maritime Studies, Pondicherry University, India. He is the recipient of the *Mahbub Ul Haq Award* (Regional Centre for Strategic Studies (RCSS), Colombo, Sri Lanka), the *Scholar of Peace Award* (WISCOMP, New Delhi, 2002) and the *Kodikara Award* (RCSS, Colombo, 1998). He was also a Salzburg Seminar Fellow (2006). He received the National Best Teacher Award (C.V.S. Krishnamurthy Theja Charities, Tirupati, 2017) and Best Teacher Award twice (Pondicherry University, 2013 and 2018). He was previously a visiting fellow at the Bandaranaike Centre for International Studies, Colombo. He is on the editorial boards of five journals.

NEW FUTURES FOR SOUTH ASIA

Commerce and Connectivity

Edited by Adluri Subramanyam Raju

Routledge
Taylor & Francis Group

LONDON AND NEW YORK

First published 2020
by Routledge
2 Park Square, Milton Park, Abingdon, Oxon OX14 4RN

and by Routledge
52 Vanderbilt Avenue, New York, NY 10017

Routledge is an imprint of the Taylor & Francis Group, an informa business.

British Library Cataloguing-in-Publication Data
A catalogue record for this book is available from the British Library.

Library of Congress Cataloging-in-Publication Data
Names: Subramanyam Raju, A., editor.
Title: New futures for South Asia : commerce and connectivity / edited by Adluri Subramanyam Raju.
Identifiers: LCCN 2019032297 (print) | LCCN 2019032298 (ebook)
Subjects: LCSH: South Asia—Politics and government—21st century. | Democratization—South Asia. | South Asia—Economic conditions—21st century.
Classification: LCC DS341 .N476 2019 (print) | LCC DS341 (ebook) | DDC 330.954—dc23
LC record available at https://lccn.loc.gov/2019032297
LC ebook record available at https://lccn.loc.gov/2019032298

ISBN: 978-1-138-50645-9 (hbk)
ISBN: 978-0-367-41911-0 (pbk)
ISBN: 978-0-367-81682-7 (ebk)

Typeset in Bembo
by Apex CoVantage LLC

MIX
Paper from
responsible sources
FSC® C013985

Printed in the United Kingdom
by Henry Ling Limited

Dedicated to
UNESCO Goodwill Ambassador (Late) Dr Madanjeet Singh
Philosopher, Diplomat, Philanthropist, Writer, Artist
Founder, South Asia Foundation, New Delhi

CONTENTS

PART 2
Democracy in South Asia 63

PART 3
Economic cooperation in South Asia 129

PART 4
Connectivity in South Asia 175

TABLES

CONTRIBUTORS

Mahesh Bhatta, Program Manager, Centre for South Asian Studies (CSAS), Kathmandu, Nepal

Shibashis Chatterjee, Professor, Department of International Relations, Jadavpur University, Kolkata, India

Kamal Raj Dhungel, Retired Professor, Central Department of Economics, Tribhuvan University, Kathmandu, Nepal

Kithmina V. Hewage, Research Assistant, Institute of Policy Studies of Sri Lanka, Colombo, Sri Lanka

G. Jayachandra Reddy, Professor and Director, Centre for Southeast Asian and Pacific Studies, Sri Venkateswara University, Tirupati, India

Mahendra P. Lama, Professor of South Asian Economies, School of International Studies, Jawaharlal Nehru University, New Delhi, India

Rashmi Mahat, Research Scholar, Centre for South Asian Studies, Jawaharlal Nehru University, New Delhi, India

N. Manoharan, Associate Professor, Department of International Studies, Christ University, Bengaluru, India

Amena Mohsin, Professor, Department of International Relations, Dhaka University, Bangladesh

Indranath Mukherji, Former Professor of South Asian Studies and Dean, School of International Studies, Jawaharlal Nehru University, New Delhi, India

Smruti S. Pattanaik, Research Fellow, IDSA, New Delhi, India

Adluri Subramanyam Raju, Professor and former Head of the UNESCO Madanjeet Singh Institute of South Asia Regional Cooperation (UMISARC), Centre for South Asian Studies and coordinator of the UGC Centre for Maritime Studies, Pondicherry University, India

Ramakrishnan Ramani, Research Scholar, Department of Defence and Strategic Studies, University of Madras, Tamil Nadu, India

Praveen Tiwari, Research Scholar, Centre for International Politics, School of International Studies, Central University of Gujarat, India

Rahul Tripathi, Professor and Head, Department of Political Science, Goa University, India

Y. Yagama Reddy, Former Director, Centre for Southeast Asian and Pacific Studies, Sri Venkateswara University, Tirupati, India

ACKNOWLEDGEMENTS

We express our gratitude to the South Asia Foundation, New Delhi, for financial support to carryout academic activities at the UNESCO Madanjeet Singh Institute of South Asia Regional Cooperation (UMISARC) and the Centre for South Asian Studies, Pondicherry University. We express our gratitude to Prof. Anisa Basheer Khan, former Vice Chancellor (Officiating), Pondicherry University, for her support in organizing the seminar. We also express our gratitude to Prof. Gurmeet Singh, Vice Chancellor, Pondicherry University, for his constant encouragement and support to carryout academic activities at the institute and the centre. We would like to take this opportunity to thank all the authors sincerely for contributing their valuable articles to this volume. We also thank the anonymous reviewers for their valuable suggestions in improving the quality of the manuscript. It is impossible to produce a volume of this nature without editorial and administrative support, and so we thank all, particularly Dr S.I. Humayun and Group Captain R. Srinivasan, for supporting us in this regard.

INTRODUCTION

Adluri Subramanyam Raju

Introduction

South Asia represents one-fourth of the world's population with a low gross domestic product, low per capita income and low literacy rate coupled with high birth and high death rates. The region is afflicted by a number of social, political and economic problems. Disputes, mutual distrust, misunderstanding and suspicion remain in the region. The absence of collective identity and a lack of sense of belonging prevail in the region. Conflicts and disputes have pushed the region into backwardness. Though geographical continuity remains the greatest asset for the South Asian Association for Regional Cooperation (SAARC), the potential from it is not harnessed because boundaries are identified with national identity in the region. Further, cultural linkages between the countries are common and strong, but they cannot influence them to come closer.

However, South Asia is viewed as an important region in the world, and it is gaining identity across the globe. The SAARC has expanded its membership from seven to eight (Afghanistan joined in 2007 as the eighth member), and nine external and major states[1] joined as observers. South Asia is one of the fastest-growing economic regions in the world (six per cent growth rate per year). It is trying to integrate with other regions of Asia, which are expected to play a vital role in the global arena. Though there were no significant developments[2] in regional cooperation, the SAARC organization, established in 1985, is the only platform where the member states can debate and discuss various issues related to the region.

The SAARC's aim is to accelerate economic cooperation among the South Asian countries. It was agreed by the members of the organization that there shall be a meeting of heads of governments or states once a year. Though the SAARC has completed thirty-three years, only eighteen summits could be held.

Because of political instability in the host country or strained bilateral relations between some countries, the summits had to be either postponed or cancelled. As the SAARC charter stipulates that no bilateral issues are to be discussed at the regional forum, it has resulted in the rise of bickering among members and the cancelling of summits. Recently, because of strained relations between India and Pakistan, the nineteenth SAARC summit was cancelled. However, in the recent SAARC summits, the member states stressed the importance of addressing various issues, including promoting commerce and connectivity through regional cooperation.

New futures for South Asia

Improving infrastructure; making borders with minimal restrictions; ensuring access to technology; connecting maritime, air and roadways; promoting free trade; strengthening governance; eradicating poverty; improving education; and cooperating in energy, food and health sectors are some of the issues of focus for South Asian countries to move towards greater integration in the region. It is to be noted that South Asia's GDP was about twenty-five per cent of the global total in 1700. It was due to the trade links with common currency and common market that existed in the region. At present, the trade among South Asian countries is only five per cent, and a major causative factor is the insufficient trade facility measures. In 1947, trade among South Asian countries was around twenty per cent.[3] South Asia inherited and integrated the transport system from the British, but it was fractured by the partition and by its political aftermath. It needs to be reintegrated. Because of lack of integration of the transport system in South Asia, the logistic costs are very high and range between thirteen and fourteen per cent of GDP. Connectivity plays a significant role in enhancing commerce/trade. For instance, because there is no transit facility prevailed between India and Bangladesh, shipment of Assam tea to the West required it to be transported 1,400 kilometres to reach Kolkata port along the Chicken Neck. There is no agreement in existence for India to use the traditional route through Chittagong port, which would be shorter by sixty per cent. The southern border of Tripura state is only seventy-five kilometres from Chittagong port, but goods from Agartala are required to travel 1,645 kilometres to reach Kolkata port through the Chicken Neck. If transport cooperation were there, goods would have travelled 400 kilometres across Bangladesh to reach Kolkata.[4] Further, many people would benefit through the penetration of new technology, information, and communication. If people are connected, they are more productive.[5] According to the World Bank report, if transport networks improved, there could be $40 billion trade – twenty per cent of trade in South Asia.[6] There is a convergence of interests among the South Asian countries for cooperation in commerce and connectivity.

In the twelfth SAARC Summit, held in Islamabad in 2004, the member states agreed to strengthen transport, transit and communication links across South Asia. Through connectivity, the countries would enhance trade and reduce logistics-related expenditure. Later, the eighteenth summit, held in Kathmandu in 2014, envisaged three regional agreements for connectivity and integration – motor vehicle, rail and energy cooperation. However, these agreements are yet to be implemented.

The priorities of SAARC need to be changed, as the emphasis should be on development, and the member states must shift their focus from self-centred to regional cooperation. The SAARC should have institutional mechanisms to make it an effective body rather than acting as a consultative body. South Asia is a not a poor region, but the people of the region are poor because of the imprudent policies of the member countries. South Asian countries can work collectively to enhance the welfare of South Asians. Democracy has penetrated into all countries, and it is good sign for the countries to understand each other and focus on enhancing cooperation in the region.

The present volume is a collection of articles presented at the international conference on "Imagining South Asia in 2030: Emerging Trends, Challenges and Alternatives," organized by the UNESCO Madanjeet Singh Institute of South Asia Regional Cooperation (UMISARC) and Centre for South Asian Studies, Pondicherry University, Pondicherry, India, in March 2016. Experts from India and neighbouring countries in South Asia participated and debated in the conference on issues related to challenges and alternatives for constructing new futures for South Asia by focusing on commerce and connectivity.

Structure of the volume: The volume consists of four parts and fifteen articles.

Part 1 Emerging trends in South Asia

The five articles in Part I primarily address the potential and concerns in the South Asian region. Home not merely to a fourth of humanity, South Asia also has abundant natural resources and human potential. The rich biodiversity makes the region also home to flora and fauna that are unique. Its rich cultural heritage, the deep spiritual grain of the populace and exotic natural locales and manmade structures offer not just variety but immense tourism potential. In the decades following decolonization, the region's economic potential has grown, and a historical turnaround appears possible. Yet, the region is plagued by its own historical legacies. Border disputes, disputes over natural resource sharing, and an unfortunate religious divide bog the region down.

The leaders of the region remained mired in the consequences of three major armed conflicts until about 1975. Democratic governance took severe setbacks in India indirectly and Pakistan directly for a decade more. When globalization in the aftermath of Soviet collapse in 1991 set out its challenges, India, amongst others in South Asia, began a path of growth that has been sustained albeit inconsistently. In the case of Pakistan and Afghanistan, the challenges of the times mired them in conflicts and religious fundamentalism. Pakistan also took to fostering terrorism as a tool to resolve issues with India, which has consistently backfired, in general affecting the entire region. During the course of the 1980s and '90s, Sri Lanka also went through major challenges to its physical integrity, drawing India also into its fold of domestic conflicts. Bangladesh, which came into being as a result of Indo-Pak war of 1971, spiraled into military dictatorship and religious fundamentalism that took over two decades to show signs of relenting.

In the background of such incredible yet real challenges to security and peace in the region, integration and growth, both regional and domestic, were the victims of circumstances. Commencing with a plea exploring opportunities for a new horizon, the first part ends with a new vision for South Asia. Possible new scenarios promoting both bilateralism and regionalism are visualized by the authors in the hope that the future will afford opportunities to exploit them.

Mahendra P. Lama's article "Visualizing a New South Asia" explains that South Asia as a region with its distinct geopolitical advantages was expected to grow steadily and become a model for regional integration. South Asia could not make use of the opportunities, and it failed to capitalize on the institutions the region inherited. The article discusses the ways in which the countries in South Asia could come together and become a model of sustainable development.

Further, Mahesh Bhatta, in his article on "Challenges and Opportunities in South Asia", explains that South Asia is a region that is geostrategically located between Central Asia, West Asia, China, and Southeast Asia, which provides potential economic and strategic benefits. To reap the benefits, the countries in the region have to put aside their differences and work collectively. The article examines the challenges faced by South Asia as a region and the opportunities that await the region if it overcomes these challenges.

Y. Yagama Reddy, in his article entitled "Geopolitical Conflagration in South Asia Biased to Geographical Primacy and Historical Legacy," maintains that South Asia has a shared cultural heritage that can act as a pillar of support for regional integration. However, the political system in the region is immensely associated with the historical geographic and economic issues. The article examines the role of geographical determinism and historical legacy in South Asia and its influence on regional cooperation initiatives in the region.

Praveen Tiwari and Rashmi Mahat, in their article "SAARC Needs China or China Needs SAARC?," analyze the bilateral relations of SAARC member countries with China and focus on the latter's strategy behind its huge investment initiatives in the region. The article deals with the issue of whether to admit China as a permanent member of SAARC.

In his article "Bilateralism in South Asia: Future Scenario," Adluri Subramanyam Raju maintains that though SAARC was formed to achieve cooperation among the countries in South Asia, the member countries could achieve very limited goals for various reasons, including mistrust and a sense of insecurity among them. The article focuses on how bilateral relations between India and its neighbours would be strengthened in the near future. The author constructs eight scenarios to visualize South Asia in near future.

Part 2 Democracy in South Asia

In contrast to the UK or Denmark, where constitutional recognition of a particular religion exists, India and Bhutan, amongst the South Asian countries, have proclaimed themselves to be constitutionally secular. All other member states of the region are avowedly religious, whether it is the Hindu Nepal or Islamic Pakistan. While the separation of church from state is the foundation of secularism, even in secular India, there are allegations of political patronage for vote bank politics. Religion thus has a huge sway in the politics and, conversely, governance of the region. The religious diversity and its impact on the social-political fabric of the region therefore is a necessary ingredient for any study of the region.

The future of South Asia rests not on democratization but in transforming its diversities into strengths to lay strong foundations of good governance. The three subsequent articles look into this aspect from different vantage points, providing a platform for policy discourse.

The final article in this part examines the role media has to play in building trust among South Asia's most turbulent neighbours – India and Pakistan. Irrespective of all the initiatives taken multi-laterally and bilaterally between South Asia neighbours, each country in this region is aware that the way forward in regional dynamics and cooperation depends on the resolution of issues between Pakistan and India. Critical as it is to regional health, the formation of public opinion in the region, as well as the two countries, rests on how the media plays it out. The role of the fourth estate revolving around this question brings this part to rest, posing thought-forwards.

Shibashis Chatterjee's article "South Asia in Future: Democratization and the Politics of Transformation," maintains that it is impossible to prognosticate the actual shape the South Asian region will assume in the near future. The article looks into the democratization of South Asia and argues that the future of South Asia depends on how the democratic experiment unfolds in the region. It argues that based on the historical and political trends, the future of South Asia depends on what happens to the contradictions that define the region.

Amena Mohsin, in her article entitled "Globalization, Radicalization and South Asia: Bringing People In," explains that globalization as a phenomenon has brought within its fold increased challenges and opportunities for South Asia. The article examines whether a nexus exists between globalization and radicalization and the role of people in the region in tackling the challenges so that South Asia can be turned into a zone of trust and cooperation.

In her article "Challenges to the Democratization Process in South Asia: Looking at the Future," Smruti S. Pattanaik argues the problem of a weak institutional framework continues to threaten the nascent democracies in South Asian countries. The article examines the internal factors that have shaped the process of democratization in South Asia and analyzes what the future holds for the region.

Ramakrishnan Ramani's article entitled "Perception Building in India-Pakistan Relations: the Media's Agenda" argues that a country's perception of its neighbours is influenced by many factors, and the role of news media is very prominent in that respect. The article examines the news media's portrayal of India-Pakistan relations and proposes a few recommendations that the media and government could consider for better outcomes.

Part 3 Economic cooperation in South Asia

Globalization has brought about a new compulsion in South Asian countries. They have increasingly realized that domestic prosperity rests in cooperation and trade, which may as well provide the motive for setting aside their differences. The geopolitical differences need to be set aside in favour of economic and trade cooperation. While SAARC and BIMSTEC have taken many initiatives, the need to energize and adopt new paths is the need of the times. Taking this cue, the opening article in this part examines the prospects for cooperation and integration.

Taking perhaps a leaf from the European model, a common currency as a means of integrating the region is examined in the next article. The challenges to such an initiative are discussed, and a way forward is outlined. It may, at the outset, appear to be an idea that is based on idealism, a page out of the Odyssey. However, if one considers France and Germany, who were sworn enemies and who grew into the founding inspiration for the European Union (EU), a distinct possibility does exist in South Asia when India and Pakistan together set their shoulders to such a thought.

The part ends with the role India, the biggest economy in South Asia, can play in setting straight regional imbalances not out of Utopian considerations but its own needs to expand its economic milestones, bringing about regional prosperity.

Kithmina V. Hewage, in his article entitled "Re-energizing Economic Cooperation Through Regional Aid for Trade: Lessons from Europe," maintains that South Asian countries have to play a role in spurring regional integration and growth through developmental assistance that improves trade and cooperation. The article examines the prospects of improved regional cooperation in South Asia, drawing lessons from Europe with the new trends in trade and investment.

Rahul Tripathi's article titled "Common Currency in South Asia: an Optimalist Assessment," argues that the option for going for a common currency in South Asia is desirable, but the feasibility of such an initiative is still a question to ponder. Though introducing a common currency is seen as a logical step in cementing regional trade and investment, there are many hurdles that South Asia has to overcome in order to implement such a reform. The article discusses the practicality and various dimensions of a possible common currency regime in South Asia.

G. Jayachandra Reddy's article titled "Regional Imbalances and Implications for South Asian Economic Integration: an Outlook," analyzes regional and intra-regional disparities in South Asia that have been hindering the economic integration of the region. Being a regional economic power, the neighbouring countries expect India to play a greater role in the region's development. The article analyzes the issue of regional disparities and the means by which the countries can overcome such impediments of regional cooperation in South Asia.

Part 4 Connectivity in South Asia

The three articles in this final part focus on infrastructure and connectivity as a means of regional prosperity. China has taken huge steps under its ambitious OBOR initiative to connect with Central Asia and Southeast Asia. The economic advantages that accrue to its partners have come into both accolade and accusation. Notwithstanding, transport electricity and other natural resource sharing between the countries of its sphere of activities have increased, providing their own platforms for growth. Whether the South Asian region must, under the aegis of its existing charters as well as newer avenues of cooperation, explore this dimension is a question potent with more opportunities than pitfalls.

India already has such pacts with Bhutan and Nepal, which have benefitted all the partners. The new arrangement for free trade and comprehensive economic cooperation with Sri Lanka may prove to be yet another incentive towards regional cooperation in the coming decades. The articles envision these possibilities and address solutions for the challenges that lay hidden in the path of infrastructure sharing and cooperation.

Indranath Mukherji, in his article on "Transport Connectivity in South Asian Sub-region: Emerging Trends, Opportunities and Challenges," explains that transport connectivity is essential in South Asia, since it is expected to reduce the cost of movement of passengers and cargo and is instrumental in opening up enhanced opportunities for sub-regional trade and investment. The article analyzes the existing challenges and the future opportunities in the transport connectivity sector in South Asia.

An article entitled "Linkages between Electricity Consumption and Economic Growth: Evidence from South Asian Economies" by Kamal Raj Dhungel explains a majority of the population in South Asia lives without access to electricity. Most of the countries in South Asia obtain electricity from both renewable and non-renewable sources of energy, and all countries in the region are endowed with one source of energy or the other. The article analyzes the linkages between electricity consumption and economic growth in various countries in South Asia.

N. Manoharan, in his article "Connectivity between India and Sri Lanka: a Model for South Asia," maintains that India's free trade agreement with Sri Lanka demonstrates the extent of economic linkage between the two countries, which serves as a model for developing such arrangements in South Asia. The comprehensive economic cooperation agreement currently under negotiation between India and Sri Lanka will further boost connectivity between them. The article analyzes the connectivity initiatives between India and Sri Lanka, projecting it as a model for the whole region to emulate.

Notes

1 Australia, China, Iran, Japan, Korea, Mauritius, US, European Union and Russia.
2 There were some achievements made by the SAARC: SAPTA, SAFTA, Social Charter, approved setting up the South Asian Energy Grid, established the South Asian University and SAARC Development Fund and agreed to improve connectivity and transportation, transit and communication links across the region.
3 "Why is Indian FDI shying away from South Asia?" *East Asia Forum*, 12 September 2014, see www.eastasiaforum.org/ 2014/09/12/why-is-indian-fdi-shying-away-from-south-asia/ (Accessed on 10 May 2019).
4 M. Rahmatullah, "Transport Issues and Integration in South Asia", in Sadiq Ahmed, Saman Kelegame, and Egaz Ghani (eds.), *Promoting Economic Cooperation in South Asia: Beyond SAFTA*, New Delhi: Sage Publication, 2010, p. 178.
5 Kishore Mahbubani, *The New Hemisphere: The Irresistible Shift of Global Power to the East*, New York: Public Affairs, 2008, p. 25.
6 Rahmatullah, n.4, p. 175.

PART 1

Emerging trends in South Asia

1

VISUALIZING A NEW SOUTH ASIA

Mahendra P. Lama

Introduction

South Asia has been a highly endowed region and remains tightly integrated as an economic block and system. Given the varied geographies, rich socio-cultural heritage, extraordinary bio-diversity and natural resources, robust institutions and huge pool of quality human resources, this region at one point of time stood most promising in both terms of development status and regional power. For almost a century, the region's political system, economy, foreign policy and defence were treated as part of a composite unit. This unit began to disintegrate after the Second World War.

With all these distinct advantages, we would have expected it to grow steadily, making the region the first set of "flying geese" in Asia. We would have seen it as the region of efficiency, sufficiency and sustainability, and the world would have celebrated it as a sound model of sustainable development. We frittered away a plethora of opportunities, we failed to capitalize on the institutions we inherited and we could never think big and act out of the box. This turned the region into a mini-power and somewhat of a peripheral one.

It disintegrated because of various politico-historical reasons. We are now trying to reintegrate the economic strength, civilizational panorama and natural resources management primarily to promote sustainable development, consolidate socio-cultural heritage and practices and unitedly and collectively fight against newer threats and challenges. We are trying to re-emerge as an Asian power. Reintegration is always a cumbersome and daunting task, and any initiatives towards this would meet with unprecedented resistance, invisible road blocks and, more critically, a static mindset. This is what we have witnessed in the last four decades or so.

Cooperation always implies that certain resources are shared and thus, the national control over them. But the abandoning of national control in turn means a loss of national sovereignty. Therefore, states are reluctant to cooperate on merely economic grounds. The gas from Bangladesh to India, water from India's rivers to Bangladesh and hydel power from Nepal to India have to be shared under cooperation. And sharing means losing control, leading to the perception of erosion of identity and national sovereignty. Whenever these countries have felt like this, they have tended to withdraw from the regional cooperation process.

Such reactions largely depend upon the size of the country, political institutions and systems and development status of the country. Tackling this perception of national sovereignty itself is a major question, as it demands extending a new form of cooperation, sacrifice and contribution and an altogether different and matured outlook. And invariably the countries in the region lack this. That is why initiatives like the beneficial bilateralism of the Janata regime in the late 1970s and the "unilateral gestures" (Gujral doctrine of the mid-1990s) have really not worked in the case of the region.

The differences have been very visible in three aspects. On the economic development front, the differences in the size of the economies and the level of development between member countries and the nature of their economic relations with third countries and on the political front, the degree of political heterogeneity in the region, the level and stability of political will, the pattern of foreign political relations – especially with super powers and former metropolitan powers – the efficiency of institutions and the governance have been major hurdles in integrating the region.

In geo-strategic parlance, South Asia constitutes a geo-political sub-system where they do not share a common threat perception. We have seen asymmetrical models of security in South Asia, where India has been inclined to evolve a security framework in regional terms, whereas other states tend to be guided by intra-regional rivalries leading to trans-regional linkages. States have joined the global alliance system of the non-regional countries through military pacts, strategic consensus, and understanding on base facility. Pakistan's security framework is conditioned by its antagonism towards India. Nepal and Bhutan have the problems of weak buffer states sandwiched between two powerful states and yet linked traditionally to the dominant regional power in South Asia. India's very size and the fear of its dominance make South Asia divided and fragmented.

Conflicts, borders and borderland

These differences are avidly reflected in conflicts which have undergone large-scale transformation over the years. These conflicts have become fiercer and more recurrent and have killed many times more South Asians than the conflicts created by the geo-political rivalry or traditional forms of inter-state wars. These conflicts have a huge variety. Yet we hesitate to recognize and address these conflicts in our schematic and attempts to build peace and cooperation in the region.

Let us take an example of the nature, diversity, variety and depth of conflicts in India alone. When we were building the School of Peace, Conflict and

Human Security Studies in Sikkim University in 2008, many asked us why such a school is required in a relatively peaceful and stable state like Sikkim. We had to convince them by saying the following: Do not look at Sikkim alone. One could stand in Sikkim and just check the perimeter of 800 kilometres (kms). And you imagine of any genre of conflict one will get it here. Possibly nowhere else in the world do we find this concentrated location of conflicts in a specific geographical locale and politico-strategic context. We find inter-state and intra-state conflicts like the Sino-India War in 1962 just 60 kms away, the India-Pakistan War in 1971 (for liberation of Bangladesh) just 110 kms away, conflicts in Tibet and the exodus of Tibetans to India again 60 kms away in 1959; the naxalite movement of the 1960s and 1970s hardly 90 kms away, the exodus of Bhutanese refugees in the early 1990s, the Gorkhaland movement in Darjeeling for a separate state within the Indian constitution and the language movement of 1960–1992, the Maoist movement in Nepal of 1996–2006; water issues, including dam project disputes between India and Bangladesh and India and Nepal; conflict in the Chittagong Hill Tracts in Bangladesh and insurgencies, secessionism and terrorism in India's northeast region; and the Assam conflict on the issue of foreign nationals. Even the remnants of the Second World War remain in the war cemeteries of Nagaland. This means that except for nuclear war, we have seen all varieties of conflict. So we used to say in a lighter vein, then why study conflict in Delhi where conflicts are not visible and tangible at all except on the TV channels? Why not in Sikkim and the vicinity where conflicts always hover around?

Borders have been the core element in all these theatres of conflict. No politico-geographical region has such varieties of borders like those of South Asia. We have open, natural, fenced, porous, barbed wired, and concrete-built borders. Seventeen provincial states of India (out of twenty-nine) have international land borders. In places like Daoki in Meghalaya, the *chanawalas* and *jhalmuriwalas* who stand in the no man's land in Bangladesh are India's borders; heel and sole are in India when we put our feet on the borders.

In the northeast of region of India, ninety-nine per cent of its borders are with neighbouring countries and one per cent with the rest India. Border interactions are fast becoming critical. The character and contents of border regimes are changing. We are now propagating borders as opportunities and not orthodox sources of national security threats. Therefore, we consciously develop a narrative about "borderlands" and not "borders."

The paradigm of threats themselves are fast changing. In future, the conflicts will relate to natural resources, environmental dislocations, climate change and cross-border environmental injuries, disease transmission and bio-invasion and bio-piracy like those mentioned in the famous book of Chris Bright's entitled *Life Out of Bounds*. The likely impact of global warming on the glaciers and hydrological flows in trans-border river systems was raised in volumes like *China's Water Crisis* by Ma Jun; *China's Water Warriors* by Andrew C. Mertha and *Pakistan's Water Economy: Running Dry* by J. Briscoe and U. Qamar.

So by 2030, can we imagine a new course where we shall treat borders as opportunities rather than sources of national security threats only? This is where South Asian countries could launch a smart border plan. This plan would essentially comprise the following:

1   a seamless border for cross-border low-risk exchanges, including tourism, health and educational amenities, trade and commerce, energy exchange and transport and communication
2   a secure natural resources area to be covered by a regional convention and mutual harmonization of each other's regulatory regimes
3   a common space like an economic corridor
4   comprehensive connectivity for all purposes

Regionalism

The regional cooperation process has not made any tangible progress, as all the efforts towards this are thwarted by the mistrust, suspicion and inhibitions of at least some of the member countries. For instance, India-Pakistan relations have literally and symbolically become a snakes and ladders game. The only difference is in rolling the dice; instead of one to six numbers, in the India-Pakistan relationship related dice, one is written on all six sides. This means climbing the ladder is a one step by one step process (i.e., very incremental change in the relationship). It can never reach 100 because in 99, the snake head appears, and the moment it reaches 99 – symbolically Kashmir – it goes down to the very low number of 12. This means one has to restart from 12 once again. It is a never-ending game.

Though the SAARC was initiated with the objectives of "promoting the welfare of the people of South Asia and to improve their quality of life"; "to accelerate economic growth, social progress and cultural development in the region"; and "to contribute to mutual trust, understanding and appreciation of one another's problems", this regional grouping has shown no progress worth mentioning.

SAARC has initiated an Integrated Programme of Action (SIPA) consisting of seven crucial activities, signed several agreements and conventions, established a large number of regional centres and institutions, including a university and, more important, has crucial programmes like SAARC Development Funds and the free trade area. No conventions or agreements on terrorism, food security, poverty, trafficking of children, and so on have been ever implemented. However, the euphoria with which these activities are launched in SAARC summits dies down in no time because of both the absence of a proper monitoring and evaluation mechanism and also because of the virtual non-involvement of people and the non-governmental institutions in the entire exercise.

There is an increasing feeling that many of these activities are just initiated as summit rituals by the heads of the states and the governments. One can find an array of literature that calls SAARC "ritualistic" and criticizes it as a "magnificent paper tiger," "a political white elephant,"

> a talk shop of no consequence, suffocatingly slow, a military convoy in a mountainous region, a regional past time, a club of tongues, a bureaucratic den, and so on.

We are now clear that the SAARC model itself has very strong limitations. Despite strong dissimilarities with other regional blocs, like the European Union, and complex and contentious regional problems, we followed the conventional model where we start with phases and forms like a preferential trading arrangement (PTA) and then get graduated to a free trade regime (FTR) and then to customs union and common market and finally to economic union. This meant intra-regional trade and investment was the core of the entire SAARC development process. Unfortunately, even after thirty years of SAARC, intra-regional trade remains hardly six percent of the SAARC region's global trade. And despite a clear road map drawn by the Eminent Persons Group in 1998 to reach the final stage of South Asian Economic Union, we are still doubtfully hovering between the PTA and FTR.

More important, the SAARC has been designed to be an institution of the government, by the government and for the government. It is a victim of governmental lethargy, bureaucratic inhibitions and national prejudices. There are no space and scope for the private players, civil society, media, academia and, of course, the people of South Asia to play any role. How do we then expect to do regional good? Where are the equivalent of Mohamad Mahathir and Lee Kuan Yew of ASEAN and Helmut Kohl and Francois Mitterrand of the EU, who took regionalism as the single most pivotal instrument and mission of national and regional development. They became a regional power with a regional policy.

New regionalism

In 2030 in South Asia, the "new regionalism" would have overtaken the present garb and substance of regional cooperation. The alternative model of sub-regionalism would be the hallmark of a regional integration model. We feel sub-regional initiatives like Bangladesh, Bhutan, India and Nepal (BBIN); the Bangladesh, China, India and Myanmar (BCIM) conglomerate; the Bay of Bengal Initiative for Multi-Sectoral Technical and Economic Cooperation (BIMSTEC with Bangladesh, Bhutan, India, Myanmar, Nepal, Sri Lanka and Thailand); and the Mekong-Ganga Cooperation (with Cambodia, India, Laos, Myanmar, Thailand and Vietnam as members) arrangements will be much faster and more effective as an instrument of regional integration in South Asia.

Many significant developments are taking place around India and will create transformational changes in the geo-politics and socio-economic structures in this region and other connecting regions of India by 2030. For instance, even if SAARC has given observer status to China, the initiative the "Silk Road Economic

Belt and 21st-Century Maritime Silk Road," also known as "One Belt and One Road" (OBOR), of China would make it a very critical and transformational player in South Asia. The $46 billion China-Pakistan Economic Corridor linking Gwadar Port with Karakoram Highway is likely to change the face of Pakistan. China's most effective entry, penetrative practices and durable presence into the geographies, societies and economies of this region will begin here. It will provide newer platforms for India but could also inject newer varieties of vulnerabilities in India's neighbourhood.

It could trigger a "new regionalism" exclusively based on connectivity, communication and the related openness of geographies and people. This could even render regional organizations like SAARC ineffective.

Confidence-building measures (CBMs)

The CBMs we have addressed to in the past in South Asia themselves have to be re-evaluated, redesigned and rebuilt. So far, we have extensively depended on military and political CBMs. For the past fifty years, no political and military CBMs have been sustained. These CBMs were addressed only to those who were serious stakeholders in perpetuating the conflict and keeping it alive. This meant that the stakeholders thrived on the adverse situations. This, therefore, takes us to the domain of economic CBMs, where we consider business and other economic cooperation (Track III diplomacy) and the participation of other non-state actors as a strong measure.

The economic CBMs with neighbouring countries, including Bangladesh, Bhutan, Nepal, Sri Lanka and more recently China have worked effectively. India and China started with $40 million trade in 1990, and despite serious disputes on the border and borderlands, trade volume has reached over $68 billion. All Indian gods and goddesses are made in a communist country now which sells calculators and watches in terms of kilograms. There have been serious political crises these countries have faced vis-à-vis India, but they have been remarkably momentary and have shown urgent recovery mainly because of the large-scale economic stakes on both sides of the border.

Could we then have economic CBMs that ultimately lead to comprehensive economic partnership arrangements? For this to happen, we must have economic channels and corridors at the local, broader national and larger regional levels. This also means giving considerable autonomy to the federal units like Punjab, Chennai, Bihar, Gujarat, Rajasthan, Maharashtra and Jammu and Kashmir; Northeast states on the Indian side; and Lahore, Karachi, Phunsoling, Ilam, Sylhet and other provinces of neighbouring countries to locally integrate in terms of trade, education, health, agricultural practices, investment, tourism and other cultural and economic exchanges.

This is what the Chinese have done with almost all their neighbouring countries in Jilin province and Kunming and with the Greater Mekong sub-region countries in Southeast Asia. The more the local areas are integrated, the softer the border.

When the borderlands become more vibrant, borders become a little secondary. Once the border becomes softer, orthodox military-centric treatment of borders actually transform into opportunities galore, which in turn could lead to resolutions of many political problems. A soft border creates its own interest groups, pressure agencies and an array of institutions that promote multiple cooperation and development ventures. This is what happened after the re-opening of the Nathu La trade route in Sikkim to the Tibet Autonomous Region of China after 44 years in 2006. Today, the route is being used for the Kailash Mansarovar pilgrimage *yatra*.

Therefore, the idea should be to do something big, transformational and far reaching. And in areas where there are public concerns, people are directly touched and the national prejudices and traditional discourse are set aside.

Sustainability issues

South Asia 2030 will have several issues of sustainability. Once, we were a symbol of sustainability with communities well integrated with natural resources management; social practices and religious beliefs harmonized with the production and consumption patterns; and traditional institutions coordinating delivery systems and disaster management and, more important, technology on which we had advantages.

The author describes his own experience. How much have we learnt from our own surroundings and communities? Day-to-day social and religious practices have so much to do with the conservation of heritage and nature. When we were children, we drew water from a *Dhara* (natural spring) at Chilaonedhura, Longview Tea Estate at Pankhabari in Darjeeling. All the villagers were literally prohibited to climb over to the area where the spring water actually originated. We were told that it is "Devithan," an abode of gods and goddesses, so one could not go up at all or do anything that would dirty the area and disturb the plants and bushes. Hence, nobody went there. Not going there actually is a conservation practice that has saved this spring to this day. This is how they ensured clean drinking water. Though Uncle Chips and Coca-Cola have reached the author's village, no government or municipality has reached there to this day. The same "Devithan" today, in the popularly used scientific parlance, is a "watershed." However, invoking gods and goddesses was only a deterrent to inject both fear and respect for the unknown. In hindsight, it was a voluntary and costless deterrence and conservation practice.

So what we call watershed management today has actually been a crucial element of everyday social and religious practices in the mountain region. What a beautiful combination of spiritualism, science and education. "Devithan" was spiritualism, not to disturb the origin of spring water was science and telling the children about such practices and making us abide by these unwritten norms was education. Our communities did it so well without studying botany, physics and geology and without seeing any drinking water development agents. They were so well versed with watershed management and in the understanding of how nature works and what it demands from us to give us back something priceless. This is a traditional wisdom that touched every member of the community and was respected by the entire community.

In many countries, we are serious about implementing the second-generation reforms, whereas the first-generation reforms themselves have not reached or made any inroads in many parts and among several communities. In many cases, the state and the government have started withdrawing from projects and programmes before they have reached the villages and the people.

Climate change and disasters

The issues of global warming and climate change have started affecting us even when there is not much awareness of them at the very local level. The farmers have no control over events at the global level but get struck by the adverse impact so profusely. This is where institutions like universities and other agencies have to play a very critical role. The knowledge base that is available in scientific and other professional institutions needs to be urgently transformed into easily accessible public goods for collective actions.

The author raises some crucial issues here.

Water security is so very critical to any discourse on sustainability. It is the hub in the sustainable development process.

South Asia's water issues possibly have no parallels –the pollution affecting fresh water availability, trans-boundary environmental flows and diversions of rivers, privatization of water and the melting of glaciers, and the destruction of watersheds and the rising water conflicts. The very management is a critical issue. For instance, in many countries in South Asia, water is managed by several ministries at the national level, namely, rural development, urban development, agriculture, power, water resources, food and environment and forest and to a certain extent an eighth ministry – health. The plethora of institutions at the grassroots level do show how poorly these institutions coordinate and harmonize their activities related to drinking water and management of the dwindling water resources of the country.

Four varieties of conflicts over the issues of water resources management are seen: firstly, a conflict within the country, like the Cauvery water controversy among the southern states in India, primarily an internal affair; secondly, a conflict arising out of the discontentment and the discord caused by sharing water resources at the bilateral level, for example, the Indus and the Ganges (If the famous Yarlung Tsangpo in Tibet, i.e. the Brahmaputra River, is diverted, what would be its implications on the lower riparian countries including India and Bangladesh?); thirdly, a conflict that has emerged out of perceptions, like inequitable sharing of benefits in aided projects like the India-funded Kosi and Gandak project of Nepal; and finally, conflict with private investors arising out of privatization.

By 2030, disaster management is going to be a major priority for South Asia. The very nature, frequency, depth and dimensions of disasters are expected to undergo drastic changes. The cross-border environmental injuries emanating from disasters and other calamities are likely to be more serious. For instance, the Kosi flood in Bihar, the Indus flood in Pakistan in 2010, the Kedarnath flood in Utta-rakhand in 2013 and the Srinagar Flood in 2014 devastated and brought huge destruction. The 2010 Indus floods submerged one-fifth of the area of Pakistan with seventeen million acres of water that included most fertile agricultural land. It killed 200,000 livestock and washed away valuable assets of millions. A total of 1.89 million homes were destroyed in eighty-two districts. All these disasters had an intensely visible cross-border character. There is adequate literature on how the Kosi flood from Nepal affected Bihar and Jhelum, the Indus flood affected Pakistan and the Kedarnath deluge affected adjoining areas of Dharchula in Nepal and indi-cated the urgent need for regional management of these disasters.

No country can work alone to mitigate this. All these controversies clearly indi-cate that interdependence is critical in environmental risk assessment. This is more so in the trans-border context as eco-systems do not respect national boundaries. Nations cannot treat economic and ecological interdependence at par. In the for-mer, border controls could manage and regulate the degree and impact of inter-dependence, whereas in the latter case, the fortress option is not available in a situation like that of trans-boundary pollution.

How do we bring all these critical observations and damaging phenomena to the classroom and laboratories? How do we prepare our young minds and com-munities to cope with such steadily ripening and vicious situations? How do we convert this information into knowledge and further transform them into social and state policy actions? In other words, could the media, universities, educational and other institutions be used to connect the villages and urban conglomerates and communities and bring them to the knowledge generation and sharing platforms for sustainable solutions of various public interest problems?

Energy security

Given what we have been trying to undertake in South Asia, a critical area where India and its neighbours are expected to work closely by 2030 is energy security. By now, the deeper advantages emanating from cross-border exchanges of energy are very well established as can be seen in many other regional groupings, like those of several gas and oil pipelines in Europe, Central Asia and North America and electricity exchanges like Nord Pool in Northern Europe, which encompasses Norway, Sweden, Finland and Denmark. The South African Power Pool (SAPP), encompassing South Africa, Lesotho, Mozambique, Namibia, Malawi, Zimbabwe and Zambia is another example.

There are compelling reinforcing factors that are bound to promote energy exchanges in this region. Huge power crises, tremendous public pressure on the respective governments to act to improve the energy supplies, reforms in the energy sector, the building of significant infrastructure in the energy sector and the strong possibility of cross-border exchanges could lead to an altogether newer dynamics of energy security. The SAARC Framework Agreement for Energy Cooperation signed in the eighteenth SAARC summit held in Kathmandu in November 2014 is only an indication. By 2030, at least five arrangements, including bilateral power trade, pool-based exchanges, a wheeling facility, truly local exchanges and inter-regional pipelines and power grids are likely to happen.

What is going to be increasingly focused on by 2030 is human security. The question is what makes human beings secure? Another way around would be to ask why people feel insecure? Ample work has been done at the national and global levels on these issues. Hardin's *The Tragedy of the Commons* (1968), D. H. Meadows and others' *The Limits to Growth* (1972), Brundtland's *Our Common Future* (1988), Homer-Dixon's "Environmental Scarcities and Violent Conflict" and UNEP's *Caring for Nature* (1991) all do indicate that environmental security is key to human security. In our own region, institutions like SDPI, the Indian Social Institute, the Council for Social Development and the Centre for Science and Environment, IIDS in Kathmandu, BUP and BIDS have done pioneering work in these areas.

Many of us regarded technology as the solution to all our ills and laggardness. However, the true colours of the overwhelming sway of technology even over nature blatantly came forth more recently in the nuclear power plants in Fukushima in Japan in the aftermath of the tsunami. The choice apparently is getting narrow between what they call "technological heart" and what we regard as "natural soul." So what kind of technology we want for sustainable development is a far-reaching question. We are sure the young minds gathered here will address this question passionately.

The global world has a lot to learn from us also. Why only localization of the global? So far, it has been mostly only one way. We read them, studied them, listened to them and assimilated and absorbed them from physiocrats, mercantilists and neo-liberalists in economic history and from the French revolution, the dissolution of the Soviet Union and the fall of Gaddafi in political evolutions and from Neil Armstrong to Steve Jobs's iPads in technology transfers. Our children are still taught Morgenthau and Almond and Powell, Huntington and Samuelson and the Rio summit and carbon credit. However, we also have our own stories to tell, a pool of knowledge and wisdom to share. We have our own theoretical framework to put forward in the paradigm of understanding and forecasting, and we have our own dialogues and conversations to blend with the global discourse. Therefore, by 2030, the globalization of the local is likely to happen, and globalization trends will be reversed. This is what the South Asians actually aspire for.

2

CHALLENGES AND OPPORTUNITIES IN SOUTH ASIA

Mahesh Bhatta

Introduction

South Asia, despite having tremendous prospects for development and growth, has the world's largest concentration of poverty. Causes of underdevelopment as well as the ways to regional progress have been well recognized. However, a regional misfortune is that none of the states in the region act and take initiatives for collective growth. Unfortunately, nationalism rules over regionalism in South Asia. The absence of regional unity and identity has brought into question the existence of the regional association SAARC. In the past thirty years, even after the inception of SAARC as a regional body, the region has not been able to lessen its collective problems. Rather, wide-spread poverty, political turmoil, poor connectivity, insurgencies and terrorism, natural disasters, mutual distrust and suspicion have become the identity of South Asia.

While the future of South Asia is full of enormous opportunities, the challenges to convert the potential into promise are equally large/daunting. Lack of trust and poor bilateral relations, particularly between India and other member nations, are perhaps the biggest hurdles of regional growth today. India holds a position as the de-facto guardian and mentor; therefore, it must take the lead to enhance the mutual trust and create a more promising future in the region. In the past eighteen summits, a couple of agreements and conventions have been signed, covering aspects related to trade, development and social welfare. However, when it comes to the implementation, SAARC has remained dismally poor compared to its counterparts like the EU, ASEAN and many more. This question of under-performance lies at the heart of the debate concerning the future of SAARC.

Major challenges in the region

South Asia is possibly one of the most highly challenged regions in the world predominately in terms of economy and politics, despite having tremendous potential and opportunity to develop. In the presence of tremendous opportunities, SAARC has become the subject of high expectations since its very inception. But it has not been able to effectively meet its commitment as was envisioned. SAARC has only been able to frame its future roadmap; it has not been able to follow the path. However, its counterparts, such as ASEAN and the African Union, which came into existence more or less in a similar period, have moved much more ahead in enhancing their economic, social and cultural development. There are various hurdles in the progress of South Asia as a region, however. This article illustrates some of the key hurdles in the process of regional holistic growth.

Lack of political desire and leadership

The deficit of political trust on bilateral/multilateral relations among the member states in South Asia has always been the key concern in the journey of regional growth. The fact remains in South Asia that none of the member states have similar socio-political and economic positions, despite having similar problems. Therefore, it is significantly essential for all the states to realize the ground reality and enhance the political willpower for regional development by keeping all the political disparity aside. Moreover, it is required that one particularly strong country should take the lead for the collective and holistic growth of the entire region. In the present context, India is the only country which holds the capacity to lead the region, and other member states should also trust its leadership and support it simultaneously. South Asian regionalism is unlikely to grow without India's serious support and strong desire. In comparison with other member states in the region, India enjoys an absolute comparative advantage in almost every sphere.

The historical rivalry between India and Pakistan since their independence has always been the primary reason behind the lack of regional consensus and growth. In fact, some of the SAARC summits in the region could not take place in the past because of the wars and never-ending blame game between the two countries. Moreover, lack of trust of and consensus among the other member countries for Indian leadership is based on their fear of India's hegemony, potential expansionism and unsolicited intrusion in their domestic affairs. There is a lack of trust for India's benevolent hegemony in South Asia. Indian failure to build trust in South Asia has considerably slowed the progress of SAARC since its inception. In addition, India, on its part, remained less enthusiastic about SAARC primarily because of two reasons: potential use of the SAARC platform by neighbours to discuss their bilateral conflicts with India and the belief that India is unlikely to accrue substantial economic benefits from any SAARC arrangements.

The Berlin Wall has fallen, but in South Asia old walls remain and new ones are being built. India, being the regional power, has immensely failed to give equal importance to its neighbouring countries. There are very limited meetings and visits among the heads of the states and delegates in the region, unlike in the other regional associations like the EU and ASEAN.[1] For instance, Nepal is one of India's closest neighbours, but it took seventeen years for India's high-level delegation to visit Nepal. This long gap was broken by Narendra Modi when he visited Nepal as his second foreign destination after becoming the prime minister.

Lack of political desire for regional growth, immense mistrust among members and unseen potential leadership has stopped South Asia from achieving its political and economic expansion.

Least connected region

South Asia is one of the most dynamic regions in the world but also one of the least integrated and connected regions, particularly in political, physical and economic terms. Despite geographical proximity and many other similarities and enabling factors, the region is one of the least integrated and worst connected regions. With shared history and culture, the South Asian region has a huge potential for economic integration, but issues of national identity and internal consolidation have caused political tensions and mistrust between the countries, and as a result, intra-regional integration is limited. By building common interests across borders, regional integration could enhance stability in this volatile region, which is home to more than forty per cent of the world's poor.

Even three decades after the formation of SAARC and despite of having multiple plans and policies to be physically connected among the member states and grow its market by regional economic enhancement, the region has negligible achievements. Implementing the outcomes of the past SAARC summit is still a far cry for the region. Six member states in the region have land proximity, and two member states have sea proximity; however, there is no strong railway, waterway or road connectivity among them. Neither is the existing air connectivity among the member states satisfactory. Rather, the past accessible mechanism of connectivity has been shut down in the name of political and security threats. As a result, the region does not have other options to be connected via countries from outside of the region. For instance, to travel from Pakistan or the Maldives to Nepal, it is comparatively easier to travel via the Middle East or from Southeast Asian countries. During the eighteenth SAARC summit, Narendra Modi accepted and described that "today, goods travel from one Punjab to the other Punjab through Delhi, Mumbai, Dubai and Karachi – making the journey 11 times longer and the cost four times more."[2]

People-to-people connectivity is possibly one of the best ways to enhance trust and develop relations between the countries. It is the regional misfortune that there is poor connectivity among the common people. The visa, travel and trade constraints that exist between the countries of South Asia make it the world's least connected region. Visa problems, predominantly for Indians, Pakistanis, Afghans and Bangladeshis, have stopped common people from travelling in each other's countries. It not only closes the possibility of the movement of people but also obstructs the prospect of exploring different cultures and learning from each other's way of life and civilization, which is very unlikely in other regions like Europe and Southeast Asia.

Connectivity is especially very crucial for landlocked provinces/countries, including Afghanistan, Bhutan, Nepal, Bangladesh, northeast India and Northwest Pakistan for cross-border trade. The strong connectivity among the member states does not merely enhance the economic status of the respective countries but eventually strengthens and promotes the regional economy as a whole. However, the reality remains that despite tremendous opportunities, the region has not been able to utilize its available resources and capacity to the maximum and remains as one of the least connected regions.

Trust deficit and blame game

South Asia, a highly significant region for international politics, remains grounds for political trust and mistrust. A trust deficit among the member states of SAARC has been a hurdle in the process of various regional collective growths. Numerous past projects and potential opportunities have not been able to flourish in South Asia because of a dearth of trust among the states. Despite having a regional mechanism called SAARC, countries in the region have not yet been able to trust each other for regional holistic growth and are mostly concentrated on national benefits. It is very crucial to realize that regional development will ultimately help each and every member nation, from smaller to larger, to grow simultaneously.

The enmity between India and Pakistan has been deeply rooted since their independence. Doubting each other in every crisis, particularly military confrontations and terrorist attacks, is their rooted culture. The hostility between these two nations has resulted in the three wars of 1947, 1965, and 1971 and further fuelled the aggression by declarations of nuclear power by both countries. Unfortunately, both countries remain too caught up in their constructed narratives of "the other" as "the enemy" to move forward. After every clash or conflict, the blame game starts. Incidents such as the Mumbai attacks and Samjhota Express are a few of many. A lack of trust has not only fueled previous bilateral issues but also has had implications for regional politics.[3] Both sides interpret the economic and strategic policies of the other with suspicion. Some examples include the increasing Indian role in Afghanistan, Pakistani-Chinese economic cooperation, Pakistani support of the Kashmir movement and Indian-Iranian economic relations. Both states are key players in the region; thus, the hostility between them negatively affects regional stability.

However, the blaming game is not just between and limited to India and Pakistan; it also exists among other member countries: Afghanistan-Pakistan in the name of terrorist attacks and security concerns, Nepal-Bhutan in the name of refugee issues, Bangladesh-India in the name of water disputes, Nepal-India in the name of redundant political interference and many more. Unless all these member states stop being skeptical of each other and develop confidence-building measures, South Asia as a region will still lose its productive time with member states blaming each other in the years to come. South Asia, being a crucial region for international politics, holds a critical global status. Instability not only affects the region but also has implications for global politics. Mistrust is a major reason contributing to instability. Thus by building trust measures at political, military, economic and, most important, social levels, regional stability can be attained on strong grounds.

Outdated SAARC charter

Charters are the basic principles and guidelines that help countries to achieve set goals. In order to fulfill the objectives of the holistic growth of the region and its people, SAARC also developed its charter. However, the charter needs to be reframed with the demands and natures of changing times. Since its inception, SAARC has not revised its charter, and some of it is, in fact, creating obstacles in its plan for executing and implementing processes.

Article 10 of the SAARC charter, under its general provisions, clearly mentions the *unanimous decision* and *exclusion of the provision of bilateral and contentious issues*.[4] SAARC is a regional association which holds the primary purpose of working for regional benefits but not to favour particular nations; therefore, the member states should support and believe beyond their national benefits and work for the region. Unfortunately, because of the existing unanimous decision provision, if any of the member states have hesitations and perceive uncertain challenges for individual countries in the proposed agendas, then it is very likely not to have agreement. The failure of many past proposed agreements has clearly proven this. History has shown that if one or the other country has some strong reservations about the proposed agenda, it will eventually lead to failure in implementation. The variance of connectivity cooperation on the eighteenth SAARC summit because of Pakistan's reservation about coming on board on the connectivity agreements is one of the examples.

SAARC, as a regional association, should also understand and function as a platform to work out bilateral issues if they are not being solved by the two concerned member states and result in a crisis in the region. For instance, the bilateral dispute between India and Pakistan has directly and indirectly caused problems in the process of regional development. In fact, some of the SAARC summits could not take place because of the political and armed conflicts between the two states. The disputes between the two countries have mutual impacts in the region and eventually result in a collective failure. Similarly, there are other disputes on various interconnected issues like water sharing, border problems, terrorism and so on, and these issues should also get space in the regional forum if not solved by the concerned member states. SAARC as a regional organization should be able to solve all these issues by respecting the principle of mutual cooperation, sovereign equality, peace, amity and common benefit. Moreover, the SAARC charter should also allow and promote sub-regional cooperation in a full-fledged manner. There is an urgent need to move SAARC from the declaratory to the implementation phase.

Nationalism rules over regionalism

Member countries in the region are not yet completely ready to accept the ideology behind the notion of regionalism, not being able to acknowledge the philosophy and principles of regionalism. The fact that exists in the region is that all the member countries have been more concentrated on their national benefits and not determined towards the region as a whole in the expected and needed amount. This is one of the reasons why the economic growth of the SAARC region has not gone beyond six percent. India, being the largest country in the region, in every possible way, has given more importance to countries outside the region for its economic benefits and political ties and ignored the intra-regional possibilities. This is followed by the remaining countries as per their capacities. SAARC, as a region, has immensely failed to learn lessons from its counterparts like the EU and ASEAN on how the member countries associated with these regional organizations have been balancing both national and regional interests. Nation might come first; however, to respect the ideology behind creating the regional organization, it is equally important to give priority to the region. Moreover, SAARC was formed with the consent and wish of all of its founder members. It is high time to understand and execute the essence of the Gujral doctrine, and India, being a relatively powerful nation, should take the lead in this process.

South Asia will flourish once all the member countries prioritize the agendas and mechanisms for regional growth along with their own national growth. If SAARC can find ways to give less weight to talk of bilateral disputes than in the past and actively pursue the agenda of common regional interests, then SAARC can also help ease out bilateral stumbling blocks. The history of European nations, who fought with each other for decades in the past, have now demonstrated to the world the most advanced form of regional cooperation. If European states can thrive by overlooking their historical hostilities and collaborate together, SAARC should also be able to do the same and cooperate for its common benefits.

Future challenges ahead

South Asia faces a number of challenges: poverty, terrorism, natural disasters, intra- and inter-state war, political turmoil, leadership crises and so on. Unfortunately, today's SAARC hosts about forty percent of the world's poor population. This chapter illustrates some of the key future challenges in the region.

Security challenges: nuclear terrorism

South Asia is often described as the most dangerous place on earth. Member states in the region have had conflicts either in the form of civil war or internal armed ethnic conflicts. South Asia is well known in the world for its poverty and politically unstable member nations. All the nations in the region have excessive poverty, low GDP, internal conflicts, political unrest, terrorism threats and many other similar problems. However, still, the member states are more focused on strengthening military weapons, particularly the two major nations: India and Pakistan; they are first in this race. The provoking message of religious excuse from Pakistan's foreign chief Zulfikar Ali Bhutto, "There is a Christian bomb, a Jewish bomb and now even a Hindu bomb. It's high time we got a Muslim bomb," is the example of the proliferation of nuclear weapons in the South Asian region. Despite knowing the fact that both the countries have so many other social problems to solve to ultimately establish socio-political stability not merely in their nations but in the entire region, they are giving high priority to military fortification and the race of leading in the "nuclear club."[5] If these countries cut up their annual military expenses and invest that money in domestic infrastructures and social development, then they would be in a position to fulfill the domestic needs and establish sustainable peace in the region.

Nuclear terrorism is yet another problem not just for South Asia but the entire world. However, South Asia is more vulnerable because of the strong presence of terrorism in the region. None of the nations of the South Asian region are free from conflict, either in the form of civil war or internal armed ethnic conflicts. Four nations in the region – Afghanistan, Pakistan, India and Bangladesh – are highly vulnerable to terrorist attacks. The rapidly increasing presence of terrorism (state- and non-state-sponsored) in South Asia has become the primary challenge to the regional and global peace process. Well-known terrorist organizations like Al-Qaeda, the Taliban, LeT (Lashkar-e-Taiba), HIG (Hizib-i-Gullbudin), HuM (Hizb-ul-Mujahiddeen) and so on are rooted in South Asia.[6] The question here is what would happen if the nuclear weapons were being controlled by the terrorists. The examples of the USA attack (11/9/2001), Indian Parliament attack (13/12/2001), Mumbai attack (26/11/2008), Ahmadiyya Mosque Attack in Lahore (28/05/2010), Peshawar School attack in Pakistan (2014) and so on have proved that if the nuclear weapons were controlled by the terrorists, they would create mass destructions. Pakistan and India, which are nuclear powers, may be attacked and threatened by these terrorist organizations. Hence one of the major tasks of these two nations is to develop enough security for nuclear weapons and protect them from terrorists.

The nuclear threat to South Asia is not just from its nuclear members but also from its closest neighbour, China. China has a huge interest and influence in the South Asian region. The paradox, here, is that China has very good relations with one of the nuclear powers of the region, Pakistan, and equally aggressive relations with another nuclear power. Sino-Pakistan relations have a long history of amity, including their nuclear agenda. India borders China and Pakistan and is certainly aware of this partnership. India does not have faith in either. The nuclear exercise in the region will not be limited in itself, but China would be the first interested because of its geographical proximity, security interest and nuclear weapons commonality. Were a conflict to spark off, it would be trilateral and include not only India and Pakistan but China as well. These three nuclear powers, two from inside and one from outside the region, have been a threat to the regional peace of South Asia and further to the global peace. Being the nuclear weapons holders and most arms-developed member nations in the region, they have the primary responsibility of obtaining the principles of the NPT (Nuclear Non-Proliferation Treaty) and giving primary precedence to the task of nuclear disarmament from the region. Nonetheless, remaining member nations of the region also have equal responsibility to apply pressure to these two nuclear powers to establish regional peace in South Asia through nuclear non-proliferation and disarmament.

Climate change

Climate change and global warming have become the key threats to the world, and South Asia as a region cannot remain untouched. The impact of higher temperatures, glacier melting in the Himalayas, variable precipitation, extreme weather events and sea level rise are felt in South Asia and will continue to intensify. Two countries in the region, the Maldives and Bangladesh, are at most risk, and other member countries will also have similar impacts sooner or later. Reports state that climate change, which has increased the risk of floods and droughts, is expected to have a severe impact on South Asian countries, whose economies rely mainly on agriculture, natural resources, forestry and fisheries sectors. In fact, although South Asia has low greenhouse gas emissions, climate change has already deeply affected the economic growth and development of the region. About seventy per cent of South Asians live in rural areas and account for about seventy-five per cent of the poor, who are the most impacted by climate change.[7]

Food security is the primary concern in the region since most of the rural poor depend on agriculture for their livelihood. Densely populated low-lying areas of mega deltas are at risk. Sea-level rise is the most obvious climate-related impact in coastal areas. The impact of sea level rise will be mostly felt by poor rural people in Bangladesh, the Maldives and India. Every year, thousands of people in the region have been killed because of various natural disasters like floods, tsunamis, cyclones and so on. The SAARC as a regional forum should develop new mechanisms for the safety of the people from these disasters. Meanwhile, it should also put forth an effort to strengthen the already existing regional mechanisms particularly by SDMC and make its optimal utilizations when required. Improved understanding of the climate change impacts, vulnerability and the adaptation practices to cope with climate change could help this process.

Natural disasters

South Asia is one of the most disaster-sensitive regions in the world. It faces the wrath of natural disasters with greater frequency and intensity. In recent years, countries in the region have endured a series of catastrophic disasters in various forms. Besides yearly recurring floods and droughts, the region has faced devastating catastrophes such as the 2001 earthquake in Gujarat (India), the December 2004 tsunami, the 2005 earthquake in the Kashmir region of Pakistan, the 2010 flood in Pakistan, the 2013 flood in Uttarakhand (India) and the April 2015 earthquake in Nepal. The region, which is home to more than one-fifth of the global population, is highly exposed to the risk of any disaster, be it natural or man-made in nature. Extreme levels of poverty and the poor response mechanisms to tackle disasters place this region at risk of natural calamities. The region has poor indicators of human development and suffers from high levels of poverty. It is the second poorest region in the world, with 38.6 per cent of the population living below the poverty line. Frequent disasters not only destroy and kill thousands of people in the region but also obstruct the regional potential economic growth every year.

Recurring disasters pose a great developmental challenge to all SAARC countries. Apart from socio-cultural commonness, member countries in the region also share the wrath of disasters. When a disaster hits one particular country in the region, other neighbouring countries are also affected, and eventually it spreads out as a regional disaster. The flood in Nepal and Bangladesh is not merely limited within the national boundaries, but it affects equally or even more so India, and the same is true in the case of earthquakes and other disasters. Therefore, understanding the intensity and effects of the disasters in the regional sphere, to collectively reduce it, regional mechanisms have to become a primary need for South Asia.

SAARC member states experienced a number of major disasters in the last one and a half decades, which took the lives of about half a million people and caused huge economic losses and massive destruction in the countries' economies.[8] Frequent disasters pose a great development challenge for all SAARC countries. In that context, a SAARC Comprehensive Framework on Disaster Management and Disaster Prevention was articulated. SAARC developed a Comprehensive Framework on Disaster Management and Disaster Prevention in 2005 and established a number of SAARC centres in member states. The SAARC Centre for Disaster Management and Preparedness (New Delhi), SAARC Coastal Zone Management Centre (Male) and SAARC Meteorological Research Centre (Dhaka) were established to reduce regional disasters.[9] However, establishment of the SAARC Centre for Disaster Management and Preparedness (SDMC) was the key step. Over the last decade, SDMC has produced regional guidelines, conducted technical trainings and developed a mechanism for collective emergency responses for ratification by states. Despite these and other SAARC efforts, DRM has not been able to achieve its goal.

Frequently occurring disasters in the region and the poor system to tackle them bring into question the South Asian regional mechanisms and ability to deal with the disasters in the region. Though SAARC has developed some methods and mechanisms to deal with the disasters in the region, in practice, it has failed to achieve its goal. The role of SAARC after the massive earthquake in Gujarat in 2001, the Kashmir region of Pakistan in 2005, the Uttarakhand flood in 2013, Nepal's earthquake in 2015 and other major natural calamities in the region has been nothing more than that of a silent observer. Moreover, the negligible role of SAARC in the 2015 earthquake of Nepal, despite the existence of a regional framework on disaster management for almost a decade, proved the organization as a quiet observer. SAARC Food Bank has 253,000 tons of reserved food in its stock and the SAARC Development Fund has approximately $7 million at its disposal. SAARC should make use of its available resources during regional disasters, which will eventually strengthen the presence of SAARC regional mechanisms in disaster risk reduction.

SAARC as a regional organization should learn lessons from other regional organizations and their practices to manage the disasters. Our next-door regional organization, ASEAN, has developed remarkable means and mechanisms to deal with disasters. Despite being one of the most disaster-prone regions of the world which is exposed to all types of natural hazards, ASEAN has developed multiple approaches to lessen the calamities. While SAARC went one step forward and five steps backward, ASEAN has moved ahead by leaps and bounds. They adopted the ASEAN Agreement on Disaster Management and Emergency Response (AAD-MER) in 2005 and completed the process of ratification of the agreement by 2011, which is the first legally binding regional agreement on disaster management.[10] The SDMC, in contrast, was established in 2005, and even after a decade, it has not been ratified by all the member countries.

Achievements and opportunities ahead

From a modest start, the areas of cooperation in SAARC have now enhanced and diversified to encompass areas from poverty alleviation to trade, culture to environment, social development to science and technology, tourism to terrorism. Many agreements have been made in the past for holistic regional growth, including SAFTA, tackling terrorism, the SAARC Food Bank, the SAARC Development Fund, SDMC and so on. In addition, the SAARC Seed Bank, the Multilateral Arrangement on Recognition of Conformity Assessment, the Rapid Response to Natural Disaster and Implementation of Regional Standards were signed during the seventeenth SAARC summit in the Maldives. Similarly, the SAARC Framework Agreement on Energy Cooperation was signed during the eighteenth summit in Kathmandu in 2014. The fresh agendas were also discussed, such as the launching of a regional communication satellite, railway services, the SAARC motor vehicle agreement and so on. The Kathmandu declaration (2014) expresses the commitment of the leaders to enhancing support to the least developed and landlocked member states in their development efforts. The declaration also emphasizes the need for implementing projects and programmes in a prioritised, result oriented and time bound manner.

Strengthening the role of the SAARC Secretariat

It is pleasing to note that South Asian leaders have realized the importance of enhancing the role of the SAARC Secretariat and have expressed their commitment to strengthening its institutional capacity. It is high time the secretary general's status be upgraded to the ministerial level so that s/he can have easy access to the heads of state or government in the SAARC countries for promoting and strengthening the regional organization in pursuing the objectives enshrined in the charter. The ASEAN secretary general enjoys such status immediately after launching the association in 1967.

Opportunities ahead

Geo-strategic location

The presence and composition of eight countries make South Asia a separate regional entity in the world. All the member states of the region have had their own historical essence. It comprises the Sub-Himalayan SAARC countries and adjoining countries to the west and east. Topographically, it is dominated by the Indian plate, which rises above sea level, as Nepal and northern parts of India situated south of the Himalayas and the Hindu Kush. South Asia is bounded on the south by the Indian Ocean and on land by West Asia, Central Asia, East Asia and Southeast Asia.

Geographical location and size matters immensely in international relations. Economy and development might not have a direct relationship with geography, but when it comes to geo-strategic planning and power demonstration, the size and the location of a region shall still have a presence in global politics. During the post-Cold War era, small nations like Switzerland, Singapore and Japan proved that a country's size does not really matter in issues of development and economic prosperity. However in an arms race, economic marketization, geostrategic arrangement, demographic potency and socio-cultural diversity, the geography and physical size of a region matter. In Asia as well as in world politics, South Asia's geographical location and its size put it in the global limelight. South Asia's geography has become a boon for its physical regional connectivity in the continent. South Asia covers about 5.1 million km², which is 11.51% of the Asian continent and 3.4% of the world's land surface area.[11] Moreover, its access to the Indian Ocean to the south, Arabian Sea on the south-west and Bay of Bengal on the south-east have made it an important region from the point of view of maritime security and defence strategy, which attracts global powers to it. Therefore, now SAARC as a regional organization, should be able to understand its significance in global politics and utilize it for regional benefits.

Potential booming economy

Significant economic reforms carried out by India have already transformed the region into one of the fastest-growing economies in the world. Led by robust growth in India, South Asia shows resilience in the face of turbulent international markets and remains the fastest-growing region in the world, with economic growth forecasted to gradually accelerate from 7.1 percent in 2016 to 7.3 percent in 2017, according to a World Bank report.[12] India's economic growth rate is not just highest in the region but also third largest in Asia and tenth largest in the entire world by nominal GDP and the third largest by purchasing power parity (PPP). It is one of the G-20 major economies as well as the nineteenth largest exporter and tenth largest importer in the world. India has been observed as a regional power and potential global power in the near future because of its rapid economic growth, which will eventually have positive impacts on South Asia's collective growth.

In international relations, economy plays a predominant role in making a nation/region dominant. Considering existing global politics, one cannot disagree with the fact that an economically sound region has direct or indirect influence on the countries and regions dependent on it financially, the case of the EU being a suitable example. And South Asia can be no exception to this; therefore, it is crucially important for SAARC to enhance its economy by promoting intra- and inter-regional trade concurrently. Currently, trade between South Asian states remains relatively low when compared to other regional blocks. Moreover, political and economic ties between the states rest on shaky foundations. Divisions among South Asian countries have made regional cooperation difficult and have led states to pursue their economic goals bilaterally. SAARC is still a valuable forum for political dialogue in South Asia, but its economic role in the region has been mitigated by conflict and tension among its member states. Nonetheless, the fact is that this region has tremendous resources both natural and human, which can change its economic structure in the future if utilized properly. Therefore, SAARC should strengthen existing trade fora like SAFTA and look for future prospects to fortify its economic status as a whole.

Demographic dividend

South Asia holds almost one-fifth of the population of the world. Its large population had been seen as a big challenge in the region, particularly because of its poverty and under utilization of available resources to satiate the existing population. Nonetheless, the economic reform of India after 1990 has transformed its large population into a huge market and has strengthened the national economy. To a large extent, the nation has proved that a large population can also be transformed into demographic dividends through economic revolution. The strong possibility of economic acceleration in India because of its population (market) has made it evident that the entirety of South Asia can establish a huge market in the region itself because of its existing population. South Asia's large population has already attracted lots of multinational corporations and international companies to this region. Moreover, the presence of South Asian diaspora all over the world has helped the region to spread its culture globally. However, South Asia still has to utilize its existing population to the maximum and transform it into a global market. The demographic dividend is a unique window of opportunity that South Asian countries must not miss. The region must prepare itself for the irreversible demographic transition that will follow.

Region with young population

One-fifth of the population in South Asia is between the ages of fifteen and twenty-four. India alone has some 200 million young people. This is the largest number of young people ever to transition into adulthood, both in South Asia and in the world as a whole. Needless to mention that the young population is observed as the most productive population. South Asia has the young population, and it is an opportunity for the entire region to utilize its young energy and mind for regional growth. Neglecting the issues young people face today can result in adverse economic, social and political consequences. Therefore, governments and policy makers across the region should focus on the issues of the youth with high priority, mainly education and employment, and their impact on the countries' development.

Today's youth of South Asia are much more vibrant, less rigid and believe in peaceful coexistence. The abhorrence of war and the desire for regional harmony is visible in the youth. If SAARC as a regional forum can bring the youth in the region together through various mechanisms and make them understand the need for regional cooperation, then a glorious time for the entire region is not that far away. And one of those possible mechanisms is through education. To optimize the raw strength of regional youth to the maximum and switch their potential energy into existent energy, it is crucial to provide education to the youth in the region. In order to do so, SAARC should create educational platforms where students from all member countries can study and spend time together. These regional educational institutions should be a hub of academic learning and should also offer opportunities for cultural exchange. At present, South Asian studies is being taught in renowned universities all over the world, but ironically and unfortunately, there are very few universities in South Asia which offer this course. There is only one South Asian University (SAU) which is yet to become fully functional.

If SAARC envisages a peaceful and prosperous South Asia, it should establish educational institutions in all member countries and encourage student/youth exchange. Establishment of regional educational institutions will cultivate the seed of cooperation in due course. Investment in the field of education today will ensure a peaceful and progressive future for South Asia tomorrow. When an Afghan student gets the opportunity to celebrate Durga Puja and Deepawali with a Nepali Hindu in an educational institution in Karachi, and when a Buddhist Bhutanese will be able to learn Pashto and Dari languages from an Afghan student in a Colombo-based educational institution, then the dream of bringing together the youth of the region will come true. This, in the long run, will drive the South Asian youth towards regional cooperation.

Conclusion

South Asia has significant magnitude and value in today's global politics; therefore, there is a scope for this region to grow and prosper. However, the existing challenges in the region have been the bottlenecks in the process of growth. The betterment of regional cooperation under the SAARC platform is a challenging task in view of unresolved political issues and absence of sufficient political will. The strong political commitment for collective growth and the sense of mutual trust between the member states of the SAARC will be a strong force which can accelerate the tremendous regional growth in the near future.

Being located geo-strategically between Central Asia, West Asia, China and Southeast Asia, South Asia functions as a bridge between the four regions and reaps immense economic and strategic benefits. This dream can be transformed into a reality if all the member states act collectively. In fact, the failure of SAARC as a regional association has taught us that we have no options left other than to work together. For SAARC nations, acting cooperatively is a necessity, and the leaders have no other choice except to pave the way for a meaningful cooperation among states and people at different levels.

Notes

1 Sambhu Ram Simkhada, "South Asia: National Transformation through Regional Integration", *Deeper Integration for Peace and Prosperity in South Asia*, 2015.
2 M.P. Lohani, "A Critical Response to 2014 Kathmandu Declaration", *Deeper Integration for Peace and Prosperity in South Asia*, 2015.
3 Mahesh Bhatta, "Carrying On, Regardless", *South Asia*, November 2014, pp. 30–31, see www.southasia.com.pk/Images/archives/2014/sa-nov14.pdf (Accessed on 11 May 2016).
4 SAARC, SAARC Charter, 1985, see www.saarc-sec.org/SAARC-Charter/5/ (Accessed on 16 May 2016).
5 Global Zero Technical Report, Nuclear Weapons Cost Study, June 2011, see www.globalzero.org/files/gz_nuclear_weapons_cost_study.pdf (Accessed on 18 May 2016).
6 Peter R. Lavoy, "The Costs of Nuclear Weapons in South Asia", *USIA – U.S. Foreign Policy Agenda*, September 1999.
7 Mannava V.K. Sivakumar and Robert Stefanski, "Climate Change in South Asia", see file:///C:/Users/user/Downloads/9789048195152-c2%20(1).pdf (Accessed on 20 May 2016).
8 Naseer Memon, *Disasters in South Asia: A Regional Perspective*, Karachi: Pakistan Institute for Labour Education and Research, May 2012.
9 SAARC, SAARC Comprehensive Framework on Disaster Management, 2005, see http://saarc-sdmc.nic.in/pdf/framework.pdf (Accessed on 23 May 2016).
10 Stacey White, *The Role of SAARC in Building the DRM capacities of South Asian Countries*, Washington DC: Brookings Institution, May 2015.
11 See https://en.wikipedia.org/wiki/South_Asia (Accessed on 25 May 2016).
12 "South Asia Remains World's Fastest Growing Region, but Should Be Vigilant to Fading Tailwinds (2016)", *World Bank Report*, see www.worldbank.org/en/news/press-release/2016/04/09/south-asia-fastest-growing-region-world-vigilant-fading-tailwinds (Accessed on 27 May 2016).

3

GEOPOLITICAL CONFLAGRATION IN SOUTH ASIA BIASED TO GEOGRAPHICAL PRIMACY AND HISTORICAL LEGACY

Y. Yagama Reddy

Introduction

The complementary and interdependent relationship of geography and history is signified by fundamentally inseparable common terms, such as *space* and *time, area* and *era* and *places* and *events*.[1] In fact, history is replete with instances of struggle among the states for territory in pursuit of living space and economic resources.[2] Certainly, an inquiry into geographical causation in history would offer an insight into the importance of geographical determinism in the historical momentum; in other words, "the wisdom of geographical determinism," Kaplan further explains, is all about the knowledge of spatial dimension concerning historical events. While interpreting the facts of geography in pursuit of preventing future world conflicts, Mackinder advocated the need for recognizing the geographical realities and the steps to counter their influence by measuring the relative significance of the great features of our globe as tested by the events of history.

The historical geography of South Asia amply explains that the spatio-temporal dimension has always subscribed to the formal relationship between geography and history.[3] Of much relevance to the South Asian context is the vision of Meinig that "geography, like history, is an age-old and essential strategy for thinking about large and complex matters" and that "geography is not just a physical stage for the historical drama."[4] "South Asia is one concept, culturally and geographically, though not politically" was the candid observation of former Indian foreign secretary Nirupama Rao, who was quoted to have recounted "how the shared history and culture of South Asian nations could be the basis for developmental partnership despite the region's political fragmentation." To its advantage, South Asia has shared cultural heritage that can act as a pillar of support for regional integration.[5] However, in South Asia, like in Central Asia, the political systems at work are intimately associated with the historical, geographic, cultural and economic issues. Implicitly, there existed confusion due to the lack of a clear boundary – geographical, geopolitical, socio-cultural, economical or historical – between South Asia and other parts of Asia, especially the Middle East and Southeast Asia.

South Asia has long endured the lack of a coherent definition owing to a lack of academic studies but also a lack interest for such studies.[6] In fact, the common concept of South Asia is largely inherited from the administrative boundaries of the British Raj, which became administrative parts of South Asia.[7] South Asia has emerged with a distinct geographical identity[8] that has distinguished it from other parts of Asia.[9] Even as the historians Sugata Bose and Ayesha Jalal construed the Indian subcontinent as being tantamount to South Asia "in more recent and neutral parlance,"[10] the term "South Asia," according to Indologist Ronald B. Inden, is becoming more widespread. That these two terms are reckoned as synonymous is amply testified by a good number of geographers, for instance, Sir Dudley Stamp, because of the Indian subcontinent's separation from the rest of the Asian landmass by a continuous barrier of mountains in the north. Thanks to geography and historical trends, the entire Indian subcontinent has traditionally been united. Certainly, the Mauryan Empire (322–185 BCE) conforming to the geographical frontiers of South Asia amply demonstrated "*the idea*" of India as a "political entity," which Kaplan ascribed to "the geographic logic over a vast area."[11] "Chanakya's geopolitical understanding of the time," according to Vijesh Jain, who was involved in cross-cultural research, accomplished "the job of uniting a number of independent states on the Indian continent and around."[12] But as the history unfolded, South Asia had begun to be politically fragmented into countless native states of various sizes and power potentials, often manifesting in intra-regional differences and interstate conflicts. Indeed, many ethnic, linguistic and social conflicts within South Asian countries are the legacy of the British colonial role. The colonial administration had largely created the South Asian states by executive orders that paid scant attention to the pursuit of boundary-demarcation among the nation-states that emerged from the British colonial empire. The burden of resolving the unresolved and bitter territorial or border disputes fell on subsequent national elites.

The notable aspect of the historical geography of South Asia has been linked with the chain of mountains and expansive desert. Forming something like a roof over the sub-continent, the chain of mountains has South Asia physically separated from Europe and Asia. Thus, the region, although enduring political fragmentation manifesting in a raft of sub-regions, was itself physically separated from the hinterland of the African continent, Europe and the Asian interior and also insulated from the European influence for over a millennium until the fifteenth century. With the discovery of sea routes to different parts of South and Southeast Asia, Great Britain eventually gained almost an effective control over the sea lanes across the Indian Ocean and established its colonial empire over the entire Indian subcontinent (including Sri Lanka). The concern of the British colonial administration for its Indian empire can be better understood against the backdrop of the geopolitical theories postulated from the beginning of the twentieth century. Mackinder's heartland theory included the Indian Ocean littoral zone as part of the Inner

(Marginal) Crescent and the Insular (Outer) Crescent, while Spykman's rimland theory portended the possibility of an Asiatic littoral zone exercising control over the Eurasian heartland. The political fragmentation consequent upon decolonization manifested in several independent states led to the regional conflicts entailing the Cold War geopolitical nuances. The hasty retreat of British colonial power disrupted the traditional complementarities and cohesion; consequently, the South Asian states failed to get themselves reconciled to the spatial idea of India. The concept of nationhood, materialized in truncated forms by the colonial power, often betrayed territorial, ethnic, religious or cultural traditions and posed challenges to the subsequent independent states.

Of late, modern definitions of South Asia are very consistent in including Afghanistan, India, Pakistan, Bangladesh, Sri Lanka, Nepal, Bhutan and Maldives as the constituent countries. With an area of about 5.1 million km² (1.9 million mi²), South Asia accounts for 11.51 per cent of the Asian continent or 3.4 per cent of the world's land surface area.[13] Accounting for about 39.49 per cent of Asia's population (or over 24 per cent of the world's population), South Asia has a high population density; yet there are intra-regional variations in the distribution of population. South Asia is home to a vast array of peoples, manifesting diversity in its human population with a mixture of indigenous peoples, and hence the region has sustained the acculturation process. South Asia has a long and closely interwoven history noticeable in certain cross-border similarities in traditions, languages and customs based on culture, ethnicity and religion. As a logical corollary, South Asian identity is based on their common values rooted in the historical, cultural, social, ethnic and civilization traditions, which serve as linkages among people across national borders, and such a discernible semblance qualifies the South Asians as being closer to each other than to the peoples of other regions.[14] The composite culture, which was a blend of Buddhism, Hinduism and Islam, provides a common basis for the norms and lifestyles of all segments of civil society,[15] besides turning South Asia into a "single civilizational whole." For all its several decentralized structures and shades of culture, South Asia began to be identified as one political entity, "Bharat Khand." Significantly, South Asia has its own identity that fetched a semblance of unity, offering scope for the cultural, political and economic processes of integration,[16] thanks to the movement of peoples, trade and ideas over space and time. The complex mix of religious, social and cultural influences in South Asia manifests in diversity with no parallels elsewhere in the world. South Asia has emerged as the homeland of ethnic groups encompassing several major religions and hundreds of languages of the Indo-Aryan subgroup of the Indo-European family. Boundaries of nation states in South Asia have fractured the long history of cultural and economic contacts, but, as Pattanaik argues, the bordering states, without compromising the national sovereignty, have evolved a shared cultural ambience so much as to engage the people across the border.[17]

Save the island-nations of Sri Lanka and Maldives, the Indian Ocean forms the boundary of South Asia in the south, of course, favouring India with a preponderantly lengthy coastline. Explicitly, South Asia has its land borders shared with Iran

(West Asia), Turkmenistan, Uzbekistan, Tajikistan (Central Asian republics), China (in the north) and Myanmar (Southeast Asia). If the hill ranges have a decisive impact on the monsoon pattern manifesting in spatio-temporal variations in the rainfall in South Asia, the coastal plains have formed the core of the agricultural economy and the zone of dense population while the islands acquired utmost strategic significance on various accounts. Geography has its impact left on the course of events, to the extent of South Asia getting it identified as an entity within the Asian realm, epitomized by a set of commonalities discernible in geography, geology, climate, economy, history, culture and polity. As well as commonalities, the region is endowed with immeasurable and diversified potentialities manifesting in complementarities which entitled the region to emerge as a "geo-economic unit" becoming conducive to promoting regional cooperation and thereby regional economic integration. Even on the flipside, as things stand today, South Asia has certain distinct common features, as evident from extreme poverty, mega-urbanization, immense disparities between rich and poor and fundamental problems in the areas of infrastructure, energy and the environment, besides high levels of internal conflicts and political instability within the region.[18] Thus, comprehensive understanding of commonalities and complementarities between India and Southeast Asia would be of immense significance in advancing my argument for integrating these two regions in pursuit of regional cooperation. Thus, regional identity, if primarily based on the semblance within a given physical environment, tends to sustain economic linkages and also become relatively homogenous if itis associated more with common concerns than with the compulsions. Cohen, while delimiting the macro-regions, felt that

> few communities are destined to have closer political, cultural and economic ties with some communities than with others; and the macro-regions (so evolved), would get united on account of complementarity in their outlook/ behaviour and would exhibit potentialities for further integrations.[19]

The neighbouring states, especially the riparian states, could become the focal point of regional and sub-regional connectivity. Geographical contiguity of the member countries is the cornerstone for the formation of regional blocs; consequently, people in a region have a sense of nostalgia for their respective regional frameworks. The idea of building cooperation in South Asia had its historical roots. But the attempts made by India to develop regionalism beyond and outside the bipolar framework of the Cold War, however, turned to be futile exercises. The nonchalant attitude towards regionalism was also due to the absence of any perceived common security threat to South Asia, which was fortunately not polarized along East-West lines, save Pakistan's membership in the Southeast Asia Treaty Organization. Lack of either a sincere, collective and grand vision or even a strong political will among its member states pushed the idea to a state of hibernation for a considerable period. The ill-conceived and ill-drawn boundaries undeniably defied the basic principles of boundary-formation, viz., the 4 Ds – definition, delineation, demarcation and defence. South Asia's political dilemma, rather its complexities, as termed by Kaplan in his book on *South Asia's Geography of Conflict*, is a product of the colonial administration that had drawn the imperfect and unacceptable borders with scant regard to the basic tenets of history and geography.[20] The political division of South Asia has thus been at the base of geopolitical tensions among the South Asian nations which are hardly responsive to the spirit of cooperation.

The flow of peoples and ideas shattered South Asia's regional identity and consciousness, perpetuating ethno-religious discord. It is also a great paradox that the overlapping of religious and linguistic groups across national boundaries becomes a trigger for internal conflicts[21] and intra-regional political instability. Unlike the countries in Europe, which are roped in the European Economic Community, South Asian countries do not belong to one civilization. Notwithstanding the argument of the definition of civilization sustained by Samuel Huntington in his book *The Clash of Civilizations*, peoples of South Asia "do not have the feeling of belonging to one region," and they "do not have a common bond of belonging to one particular country," as evident from high levels of internal conflicts and political instability within the region.

Despite sharing certain common civilizational links, the member states cannot agree on a common future, and there is no consensus on fundamental norms or values. The South Asian countries having semblance in a set of similarities appears to be a dubious distinction, in as much as the region is a heterogeneous group in several respects.[22] South Asia's long and convoluted history of illegal migration owes to political upheaval and transformation as much as to the poorly demarcated borders and cultural affinities. These cross-border/trans-national migrations, often referred to as infiltrations, have become a ubiquitous phenomenon that persists thanks to the porous borders among almost all the countries of South Asia. The problem would be further accentuated in that event of coastal plains getting inundated by salt water with the rise of sea levels as a consequence of global warming. Climate-change is making India a centripetal stage for intra-regional migration from all other SAARC countries. This would also set the stage for re-enacting the captive bank politics by the vested political parties, and India would become an arena of geopolitical games often provoking other external powers to interfere in it.[23]

The geographical location of India vis-à-vis its South Asian neighbours is a source of its perpetual worry. The basic apprehension has stemmed from India's geographical size, demographic and economic potential and political weight. Though India for long pursued Mackinder's continental strategic outlook with heavy reliance on the army,[24] New Delhi has of late subscribed to the Curzonian maritime strategy of dominance of the Indian Ocean, and it began maintaining the largest naval force and militarized its outlying islands. In his analysis of South Asia's history and geography, Kaplan highlights India's pivotal role in the region as being capable of determining "the course of geopolitics in Eurasia in the 21st century."[25] The geographical contiguity on account of common land borders among the countries of peninsular South Asia has become of no significance for the development of transit facilities and transport networks. SAARC members have few connections with each other apart from SAARC itself, some historical links with British imperialism and geography. As a corollary, SAARC countries share a degree of common social, cultural and historic roots. They can restore friendly relations and progress together, if they are willing to do so.[26]

India has land or sea borders with every other SAARC country, while the other SAARC states do not have common borders among themselves and thereby direct physical access to other SAARC member-states, except the solitary instance of a common border between Afghanistan and Pakistan. However, these two do not have direct geographical access to the other SAARC members, except through the Indian territory. Similarly, Nepal, Bhutan and Bangladesh are also deprived of direct access among them, on account of their borders being separated from each other by just 22-kilometres of Indian corridor, known as the "Chicken Neck," or "Siliguri corridor." The key impediment to strengthening regional cooperation, as pointed out by the then Secretary-General Sheel Kant Sharma in his speech on the prospects and challenges of South Asian regionalism at the Indian Council for World Affairs, is "lack of physical and soft connectivity in SAARC."[27] It has been widely admitted that trade is impeded because of transport costs and lack of connectivity, including across northeastern India, Nepal, Bhutan and Bangladesh. If the landlocked countries, Bhutan and Nepal, are dependent on India for external trade, goods from Tripura's capital Agartala are required to reach Kolkata port through the Chicken Neck, although the southern border of this northeastern Indian state is closer to Chittagong port in Bangladesh.

In 1947, trade among South Asian countries accounted for around twenty per cent of their total trade, which has fallen to a mere five per cent.[28] But intra-regional trade in South Asia suffers from unevenness in market information, grumbling of defaults on trade-related payments and other risk factors, and hence financial connectivity has become as important as transport connectivity. The low intra-regional trade, representing the dubious distinction of being the highest in the world, points at the high cost of trade that overshadows competitive advantages because of geographical proximity and intra-regional supply-demand complementarities.[29] The infrastructure constraints made South Asia "one of the least connected regions in the world constituting a major structural impediment," and the cost of intra-SAARC trade is the highest in the world.[30] But the underutilization of the infrastructure is not due to lack of it but lack of connectivity of the region's transport links and the outdated attitudes of decision-makers, besides an inadequate degree of complementarity of interests and lack of "region-ness" in South Asia.[31]

Despite recognition of India's help in facilitating faster economic growth, smaller states in South Asia are reluctant to work with the former, fearing that such cooperation will admit Indian dominance in SAARC.[32] For its part, India has its own fears of its neighbours in terms of their possible union to oppose the country's interests. Kaplan, who looked at India as a regional power stuck with neighbours that are volatile and dysfunctional, has further critically observed that

> Without a doubt, while India overwhelmingly dominates the subcontinent, the subcontinent's frontiers are, in a geographical sense, subtle transition

zones that have allowed for other, smaller states to establish themselves. And because these other states, precisely they occupy these transition zones, are often prone to ethnic, sectarian and regional divisions, they are also, in turn, prone to radical and unstable politics.[33]

To Kaplan,

> the subcontinent is a blunt geographical fact, but defining its borders will go on indefinitely. In fact, India and South Asia in general have a dangerously misunderstood geography. Understanding that geography delivers one to the core of South Asia's political dilemma. . . . The very technologies that defeat geography also have the capability of enhancing geography's importance.

Justifiably, Kaplan calls upon the American policy-makers "to grasp with India's age-old highly unstable geopolitics" that they are entwined with South Asia's geography and history. *The Geopolitics of South Asia*, as Graham Chapman succinctly observes, "is a thoroughly readable account of the geography and history of this region."[34] Equally important to bear in mind is that the natural geography of the region, so abruptly abridged by the processes of recent history and the designs of states, reasserted itself with a vengeance.[35]

The Indian sub-continent has, thus, a long history of various phases of transformation – from the glorious chapter of cultural and trade relations on equal-footing (good neighbourhood), through European incursions and exploitations (imperialism), manifesting in intrusion into the indigenous societies, to a zone of power contested by super-powers during the Cold War period, which afflicted South Asia in numerous ways, like fomenting the border disputes, mistrust and tensions. SAARC, as the representative of South Asia, needs to be looked upon as a "single development unit" for accelerating the movement of people, goods and ideas as well as for sharing the capital technology and natural resources.[36] Deserving much appreciation is the People's SAARC Declaration adopted in March 2007:

> We, the people of South Asia, not only share a contiguous geographical space but also a social and cultural history that shapes our life styles, belief systems, cultural particularities, material practices and social relationships. . . . There have been similarities in our histories as a result of our constant interactions for thousands of years. Our belief systems and cultural practices have been influenced by each other and exhibit some distinct similarities.[37]

For all the overt and hidden constraints looming large, the programme of regional cooperation was expected to benefit immensely from the historical and cultural ties connecting people across national borders in South Asia. South Asian countries are expected to gain from, among various other things, geographical proximity, which becomes conducive to accomplishing regional integration.[38] The increased economic cooperation among geographically contiguous countries is the quite obvious feature of the global political economy. India, Pakistan and Bangladesh, which were once part of a single political entity, British India, should utilize their historical links and shared interests in buttressing economic integration, which, in the first instance, calls for a considerable flow of goods and services between them, and their historical links and the shared interests should underpin modern-style economic integration. It is imperative for SAARC members to strengthen SAARC,[39] along with the process of enhancing prospects of cooperation with other regional bodies like BIMSTEC, MGC, ASEAN, EAS and BRICS.

It becomes imperative for the people to identify such common elements that could build up a feeling of South Asianness or South Asian identity among them. In the context of South Asia being perceived as a "geo-strategic, geo-economic unit," what matters most are the relative efforts at cooperation rather than the concrete steps taken towards integration. When globalization has set free both opportunities and challenges, there is a need for the revival of commonality among people of South Asia as has been done in both Europe and Southeast Asia. The fact that South Asia is not merely a geographical expression but also a historical creation portraying "an association of ideas, experiences, interactive cultures and aspirations straddling the past and the future" entails the existence of geopolitical challenges which warrant constructing a South Asia on the flank of cooperation without succumbing to accidents of conflict.

Notes

1   Donald Meinig, *The Shaping of America: A Geographical Perspective on 500 Years of American History*, New Haven: Yale University Press, 1987, p. xv.
2   Robert D. Kaplan, "The Revenge of Geography", *Foreign Policy*, May–June 2009.
3   Malcolm McInerney, "Entwining History and Geography", *Spatialworlds*, 27 April 2011; see http://spatialworlds.blogspot.com/2011/04/entwining-history-and-geography.html (Accessed on 13 January 2015).
4   Meinig, n.1.
5   Rabindra Sen, "India's South Asia Dilemma and Regional Cooperation: Relevance of Cultural Diplomacy", *Strategic Analysis*, vol.38, no.1. 2014, pp. 68–78.
6   Vernon Marston Hewitt, *The International Politics of South Asia*, Manchester: Manchester University Press, 1992, p. xi.
7   Navnita Chadha Behera, *International Relations in South Asia: Search for an Alternative Paradigm*, New Delhi: Sage Publications India, 2008, p. 129.
8   Saul Bernard Cohen, *Geopolitics of the World System*, Lanham, MD: Rowman & Littlefield, 2003, p. 304.
9   Dallen J. Timothy and Gyan P. Nyaupane, *Cultural Heritage and Tourism in the Developing World: A Regional Perspective*, London: Routledge, 2009, p. 124.
10 Sugata Bose and Ayesha Jalal, *Modern South Asia*, London: Routledge, 2004, p. 3.
11 Robert D. Kaplan, *South Asia's Geography of Conflict*, Washington, DC: Center for a New American Security, 2012.
12 Vijesh Jain, *Geopolitical Scientists of Ancient India*, 15 July 2012, see http://vijeshjain.com/2012/07/15/Geopolitical-Scientists-of-ancient-India/ (Accessed on 24 June 2013).
13 Encyclopedia of Modern Asia 2006.
14 Delinic Tomislav, *SAARC – 25 Years of Regional Integration in South Asia*, KAS International Reports 2/2011, p. 11, see www.kas.dewfdockas_21870-544-2-30.pdfl 10209123437 (Accessed on 10 January 2013).

15 Swaran Singh, "India and Regionalism", in Alyson J.K. Bailes, John Gooneratne, Mavara Inayat, Jamshed Ayaz Khan, and Swaran Singh (eds.), *Regionalism in South Asian Diplomacy, SIPRI Policy Paper No. 15*, Bromma, Sweden: Stockholm International Peace Research Institute, February 2007.

16 Mavara Inayat, "The South Asian Association for Regional Cooperation", in Bailes, Gooneratne, Inayat, Khan and Singh, *ibid*.

17 Smruti S. Pattanaik, "Federalising India's Neighbourhood Policy: Making the States Stakeholders", *Strategic Analysis*, vol.38, no.1, 2014, pp. 31–48.

18 Tomislav, n.14.

19 Saul B. Cohen, *Geography and Politics in a Divided World*, 2nd edition, New York: Oxford University Press, 1973, p. 62.

20 Kaplan, n.11.

21 Aditi Paul, "What Impedes Regionalism in South Asia?", *Counter Currents*, 24 March 2012.

22 Binod Khadria, *Migration in South and South-West Asia*, Global Commission on International Migration, 2005, see www.iom.int/jahia/webdav/site/myjahiasite/shared/shared/mainsite/policy_and_research/gcim/rs/RS6.pdf (Accessed on 14 May 2015).

23 Y.Yagama Reddy, "Inexorable Cross-Border Illegal Migrations Entangled in Geopolitical Exigencies in SAARC", *International Journal of South Asian Studies*, vol.5, no.1, January–June 2012, pp. 10–23.

24 Ashley J.Tellis, "South Asia", in Richard J. Ellings and Aaron L. Friedberg (eds.), *Strategic Asia 2001–02 Power and Purpose*, Seattle: National Research Bureau, 2002, pp. 262–263.

25 Kaplan, n.11.

26 Akanksha Khullar, "SAARC Still Marred by Divisions", *East Asia Forum*, 4 November 2015, see www.eastasiaforum.org/?p=48235 (Accessed on 2 January 2016).

27 Secretary General, *Trade Is Key to SAARC's Success*, New Delhi: Indian Council of World Affairs, 14 September 2010, see www.thaindian.com/newsportal/business/trade-is-key-to-saarcs-success-secretary-general_100428441.html (Accessed on 20 July 2015).

28 Pradumna B. Rana, "As SAARC Drags Its Feet, South Asia Should Turn to Sub-Regionalism", *East Asia Forum*, 25 December 2014, see www.eastasiaforum.org/2014/12/25/as-saarc-drags-its-feet-south-asia-should-turn-to-sub-regionalism/ (Accessed on 22 December 2015).

29 Bipul Chatterjee and Joseph George, "We Must Improve Trade Connectivity in South Asia", *East Asia Forum.org*, 26 June 2014, see www.eastasiaforum.org/2014/06/26/we-must-improve-trade-connectivity-in-south-asia/ (Accessed on 28 December 2014).

30 Secretary General, n.27.

31 Nitasha Malhotra, *South Asia-Political and Economic Region*, New Delhi: The Association for Geographical Studies, University of Delhi, n.d.

32 Asima Noreen, "Challenges for SAARC", *Pakistan Times*, 17 February 2011.

33 Kaplan, n.11.

34 Graham P. Chapman, *The Geopolitics of South Asia: From Early Empires to the Nuclear Age*, Aldershot: Ashgate Publishing Limited, 2009, p. 382.

35 Pratap Bhanu Mehta, *SAARC and the Sovereignty Bargain*, November 2005, see http://himalmag.com/component/content/article/1674-SAARC-and-the-sovereignty-bargain.Html (Accessed on 10 January 2013).

36 Anil Kumar Mohapatra, *Small States in South Asia: A Security Perspective of the Himalayan States*, Bhubaneswar: Panchashila, 2008, p. 193.

37 *People's SAARC Declaration: Justice, Peace and Democracy*, Kathmandu, 25 March 2007, see http://peoplesaarc.blogspot.in/ (Accessed on 30 July 2013).

38 Ahmed Sadiq and Ghani Ejaz (eds.), *South Asia: Growth and Regional Integration*, Washington, DC: The International Bank for Reconstruction and Development/the World Bank, 2007, p. 7.

39 Y.Yagama Reddy, "Strengthen BIMSTEC to Revitalize SAARC", in T. Nirmala Devi and A. Subramanyam Raju (eds.), *Envisioning a New South Asia*, New Delhi: Shipra Publications, 2009, pp. 235–244.

4

SAARC NEEDS CHINA OR CHINA NEEDS SAARC?

Praveen Tiwari and Rashmi Mahat

Introduction

The South Asian Association for Regional Cooperation (SAARC), a group of eight South Asian developing countries, has one common motive: bringing economic and social development and peace in the region. The South Asian region has huge market potential as well as cost-effective human resource availability.

China, the world's fastest-growing economy has strongly projected its "forth-coming super power" image in the world. It got observer status in SAARC in 2005. By increasing investments in almost all SAARC member countries and promoting friendly bilateral relations with them, China wants to get involved in South Asian trade. A desire to become a maritime power and reestablishing the Maritime Silk Route for economic as well as security purposes are other reasons behind China's interest in SAARC.

The chapter analyzes the bilateral relations of SAARC member countries with China and focuses on China's strategy behind its huge investment in the South Asian region. It makes an attempt to find out whether China should get permanent status in SAARC or not. India's insecurity with China's closeness to SAARC countries is also explored.

Bilateral relations are given more priority in SAARC, and this is the reason why all the member countries are focusing more on their own benefits. China's huge investments in SAARC countries are not letting them think on the other side of the issue. Giving permanent membership status to China in SAARC will cause other big hurdles for the development of the region, as China's aggressive foreign policy cannot be ignored.

In modern international political and economic arenas, South Asia is a region which is interpreted as full of opportunities for the rest of the major powers of the world. A regional group having more observer states than member states explains the importance of this region. The SAARC came into existence in 1985 with the motive of economic, cultural and social cooperation within the region. After more than two decades, the achievements of this regional group could not reach up to its expectations. Despite having geographical, historical and cultural similarities, several hurdles like mutual distrust, political instability, lack of infrastructure and absence of a strong economy have kept this region still very behind in the world platform.

With irregular summits and several agreements, SAARC has worked for the development of the region, yet a lot of work remains to be done. Several incidences occurred in this region within the time frame of five years. Constitutional deadlock and a natural disaster in Nepal, India–Bangladesh water-sharing issues and political tension in Maldives are some of those issues which revealed the instability in the region. Though several initiatives have been taken by the member countries to sort out the problems and to maintain peace and prosperity in their nations, because of a lack of collectiveness, these problems could not be solved. The region is also struggling with the feeling of single-country domination. Since India is geographically and economically prominent in the region, sometimes other countries feel insecure or dissatisfied with India's decisions and policies.

In the present scenario, China provides an alternative option for some SAARC members. The desire to counter-balance the feeling of India's superiority in the SAARC also motivated some of the members to support Chinese permanent membership in the forum. Probable linkages between the observer status of China in SAARC in the Dhaka summit in 2005 and the membership of Afghanistan in SAARC shows China's growing influence in the regional group.[1]

China, one of the world's fastest-growing economies, has also shown its keen interest in the South Asian region. Growing trade relations between China and South Asian countries explain this fact. China's huge investment in developmental projects of different SAARC countries like Maldives, Nepal, Pakistan and Sri Lanka shows the priority given by China to SAARC. China is India's largest trading partner. Apart from the economic angle, China's growing interest in the Indian Ocean as part of its aggressive foreign policy can also be interpreted as the main motive behind the desire of getting permanent membership in SAARC.

Does SAARC really need China? What are India's concerns over China's closeness with SAARC? Is SAARC experiencing India's dominance as a big brother, and can China act as the balancing power in the SAARC as a permanent member? Will SAARC benefit, or will it lose relevance when China becomes a permanent member of it? These are some of the questions that occur when one looks towards China's presence in South Asia.

SAARC countries' perception of China

China's interest in South Asia can be seen through its growing bilateral relations with SAARC member countries. Some of the SAARC countries have shown their interest in Chinese investment in their domestic projects. China's trade with

SAARC countries has grown from $6.5 billion in 2001 to $73.9 billion in 2012.[2] SAARC countries are still suffering from lack of infrastructure for the development of their economies. In this case, China's growing investment is helping to strengthen the economic potential of SAARC countries. On one side, China is seeking benefits from the huge market opportunity available in South Asia for its export in return for investment in and development of the infrastructure of the region, while on the other side, most of the SAARC countries are also seeking such investment through which they can establish themselves. China's "Go Global" initiative in 2001, which relaxed Chinese control over investment restrictions is one of the examples of its interest in liberal economic activities all around the world, including in SAARC.[3]

China and Bangladesh's diplomatic relations began in 1971. China obtained observer status. In the same year, China's government donated $1 million to Bangladesh for relief and reconstruction of cyclone-hit areas. Because of the high cost of projects, limitations in labour practices and tough competition in Western countries, China has given priority to investing in Bangladesh's developmental projects. Even Bangladesh, which is going through the challenges of unemployment, poverty and lack of infrastructure, has realized the importance of Chinese investment. Bangladesh's Prime Minister Sheikh Hasina's visit to China in 2014 strengthened the relations of the two countries. China exported $4,400 million in 2009 to Bangladesh, which reached $7,800 million in 2011.[4] Bangladesh is the third largest trading partner of China in South Asia. China has invested largely in different developmental projects, like a rail bridge over the Jamuna River and some others railway projects. Even though Bangladesh is facing loan repayment issues with China, overall, it considers China as a big key to unlock its developmental challenges.

The "China-friendly relationship story" is not the same in Bhutan's case. It has such a distinct geographical location that neither India nor China can ignore it. Chumbi Valley, which connects Bhutan, India and China, has a very significant role in the trade and commerce relationships between these countries. Bhutan has a territorial dispute with China, the Jakarlung and Pasamlung Valleys on the Bhutan-Chinese north central border and the Dokalam Plateau in Eastern Bhutan.[5] Tension between China and Bhutan started after Chinese aggression against Tibet, which was an autonomous region. It became worse in 1954 and 1958 because of anti-Chinese revolts in Tibet. During the 1962 Sino-India War, Bhutan remained neutral with both the countries. Though several series of border talks, including the 1998 China-Bhutan bilateral agreement regarding maintaining peace on the border, have been done, unlike other SAARC countries, Bhutan has had bitter experiences with China. The visit of the foreign minister of Bhutan, Rinzin Dorjeto Beijing, in July 2014 has shown some positive indications from both sides to strengthen the relationship. In the present situation, when Bhutan has become more sovereign in terms of deciding its foreign policy, it has shown its inclination more towards India rather than China.

Afghanistan, a key area to access Central Asia and South Asia and full of natural resources, has been very important in terms of geo-strategies. All major powers of the world are ready to invest in Afghanistan as they saw huge economic and trade benefits from the new member of SAARC. China is one of those emerging powers who realized the importance of Afghanistan, and that is a reason why it became the first country to establish official relations with President Hamid Karzai by reopening its embassy in Kabul in February 2002 after the US invaded Afghanistan in 2001.[6] On one side, China is seeking the revival of the ancient silk route through Afghanistan with the motive of gaining economic advantages. On the other, it is also in favour of offering security services as US and NATO forces are slightly withdrawing from Afghanistan. Their own security concern is the main reason behind the Chinese effort to bring stability in Afghanistan. Afghanistan got observer status in the Shanghai Cooperation Organization (SCO) in 2012 at China's request.[7] So at present, Afghanistan does not see any loss in accepting Chinese investment, and it does not have a negative attitude regarding China.

As far as India and China relations are concerned, they have been through so many twists and turns. From the Nehru period to the current prime minister of India, Narendra Modi, India has shifted its policies from liberal to defensive and then again from defensive to liberal. Though territorial disputes and the 1962 Sino-India War brought huge tension between the countries, India later modified its policies by understanding the importance of trade and investment relations with China. India and China trade relations began from 1978, and in 1984, both countries signed the Most Favoured Nations (MFN).[8] India has benefited from China in multiple fields like economics and trade, cultural exchange, education cooperation and science and technology exchanges. Indian Prime Minister Narendra Modi's three-day visit to China on 14–16 May 2016 gave more strength to the relations of the countries. In terms of bilateral relations, India and China are heading towards a friendly neighbour relationship.

Though India has good bilateral trade relations with China, it always remains insecure of Chinese bilateral relations with other SAARC member countries. Both are nuclear powers, and they are trying to get South Asian countries in their favour. As far as India-China bilateral relations are concerned, it is very constructive, but while talking about SAARC, India always tries to move China away from core members of the SAARC group.

Pakistan, being a nuclear power and having a huge population, has its own strong position in SAARC. In agriculture, economy and defense, it has a significant place among other South Asian countries.

Pakistan's relations with China are much stronger than any other South Asian country's. The basis of their strong relationship is not only economic but also political. China and Pakistan have some common interests. Sino-Pakistan ties started strengthening after the 1962 India-China war when the two states agreed to sign a boundary agreement recognizing Chinese control over a portion of the disputed Kashmir territory.[9] Both countries worked for the development of the "China-Pakistan Economic Corridor (CPEC)," a long-term plan which is mainly about three key areas: transport, energy and industrials parks.[10] During Chinese president Xi Jinping's visit to Pakistan in April 2015, there was a total of fifty-one memoranda of understanding (MoUs), including the CPEC agreement, which proved to be a milestone for the better relationship between the countries. China announced around $46 billion in investment in CPEC.[11]

Through two maritime cooperation dialogues held in Beijing (July 2004) and in Islamabad (February 2016) both countries have taken initiatives to solve maritime issues like rescue and relief operations, maritime science and technology cooperation, security of sea lanes and of communications and so on.[12]

Pakistan played a major role in providing observer status to China in SAARC, and in comparison to other SAARC member countries, Pakistan has its own huge interest from China. The all-weather friendship between China and Pakistan gives an indication of China's possible active involvement in SAARC.

Maldives and Sri Lanka are two island states which are also permanent members of SAARC. The Republic of Maldives is situated in a strategically important location in the Indian Ocean. This is the reason why despite being such a small island country, it is one of the centres of attraction for the foreign policy of major countries situated within the Indian Ocean area as well as beyond it. China is known in the world for its strong maritime power, and it has shown its interest in investing in Maldivian developmental projects. In 2013, China-Maldives trade relations significantly improved and reached $89.68 million. Maldives is getting big revenue through Chinese tourists. In 2013, around 302,000 Chinese tourists visited Maldives. Maldives has also established an office for trade and tourism promotion in Kunming, China.[13] Chinese president Jinping's visit to Maldives in September 2014 has indicated growing Chinese interest in this island state. By initiating a maritime silk-route for better trade and economic relations, investment in tourism and telecommunication sectors, ocean research, environmental protections, disaster prevention and so on, Chinese multi-dimensional involvement in Maldives has been increased.

The visit of Maldivian president Abdulla Yameen to China in August 2014, attending the second summer Youth Olympic Games in Nanjing and acceptance of $16 million aid granted from China shows the interest of Maldives towards China. Now multiple Maldivian projects have been given to China, including the construction of the minister of foreign affairs building, the national museum, different housing projects, renewable projects and so on.[14]

However, from the Chinese point of view, all these investments in Maldives are basically being done in order to fulfill certain geopolitical interests. All in all, Maldives has a constructive bilateral relationship with China, while China is seeking Maldives' support to get permanent membership in SAARC. China also wants to make its presence strong in the Indian Ocean. Through a joint statement, the presidents of China and Maldives declared the acceptance of building a 21st-century Maritime Silk Road to enhance cooperation between them.[15] It clearly shows the constructive relations between the two countries in order to fulfill their mutual interests.

Sri Lanka, another island state in SAARC, has quite neutral relations with China as well as India. China has invested in multiple areas, like trade and infrastructures development in Sri Lanka. Several delegates from both sides have visited each other and signed different cooperative agreements in areas like agriculture, trade and commerce and so on for strengthening their relations. In 2013, their bilateral trade had reached $3.621 billion, which is a significant trade amount between these two countries. China also gave $50,000 as assistance to Sri Lanka during the flood in early 2013.[16]

China's growing interest in the Indian Ocean can be understood by the fact that Chinese officials attended the fourth Galle Dialogue Maritime Conference held in Sri Lanka in November in 2013.[17] China has also shown its deep interest in gaining economic benefits through investing in several Sri Lankan developmental projects. Some of the projects are Bandaranaike Memorial International Conference Hall, the Colombo-Katunayake Express, the Hambantota port and the Colombo Port City project.

After a political shift when Sri Lankan president Mahinda Rajapaksa lost power and the Sirisena administration was sworn in, a shift from pro-China policy has been observed. Temporary suspension of the Colombo Port City project, suspension of the execution of the Northern Expressway until investigations are completed, cancellation of different mega projects funded by the government of China and several other strict decisions have been taken by the ruling party.[18]

Despite having such a tough time, China puts its efforts into maintaining smooth relations with Sri Lanka while Sri Lanka also understands India's unease at China's presence in other SAARC countries. It is also aware of India's worry about China's "String of Pearls" strategy and its efforts to functionalize the Maritime Silk Route. Hence, present Sri Lankan foreign policy can be interpreted as neutral towards China as well as India.

Nepal is one of the founding member countries of the SAARC group. It has also chaired the eighteenth SAARC summit held on 26–27 November 2014. Its geographical location makes it very significant for India as well as China to form their security strategy. After the Chinese invasion of Tibet in 1950, Nepal's trade and pilgrimages were also affected by Chinese restriction, and it led to a tense relationship between the countries. Later on, by initiating diplomatic relations, their relationship became stable.[19] By successfully conducting the elections and enacting the new constitution, Nepal has given a signal to the whole world about its stability and willingness to develop fast. Through several official visits between China and Nepal and growing interest in increasing their trade, their relations seem likely to be more constructive in the near future.

China has provided huge financial aid to Nepal during its natural disaster period. Apart from increasing their trade relations, China has also worked to increase people-to-people contact between the countries. During the crisis in drafting the constitution in Nepal, strain between India and Nepal and oil scarcity in Nepal due to the unofficial oil blockade by New Delhi also created an opportunity for China to act as an alternate solution for Nepal, which was highly in need of oil. This incident changed the equation of the Nepal–China relations.

In general, it can be said that at present, almost all SAARC member countries have either neutral or better bilateral relations with China. Relations with China are mainly trade and infrastructure centred since all the SAARC member countries are in a developing stage. These countries are also looking towards China as an alternative major power which can act as a balancing factor in the group. Countries are looking for another source for their development by engaging themselves with China. Some of them are also aware of the aggressive foreign policy of China, but at present, most of them are taking things positively.

There have been several incidences when some SAARC member countries were not happy with India's policy on certain situations, such as India's lesser interest in developmental projects of these countries. This resulted in a kind of mistrust between India and other SAARC states. India-Pakistan relations have always been one of the biggest hurdles in the way of the progress of SAARC. All these factors motivate these countries to go for any other big country so that they can get greater benefit.

India's insecurity with China

Among all the SAARC countries, India is very much in a leading position in terms of area, population, economy, military strength and so on. India is the only country in SAARC which has direct connectivity with each member nation, and the rest of the countries are sharing their borders with India. Almost all SAARC countries have India as their biggest trading partner, and their economy is somehow highly dependent on the latter's economy. Hence, India's geography, economy, demography and military power give it a strong position in SAARC, which helps it to fulfill its national interest. India does not want to lose this comfortable position, and it is the main reason why it looks at China as a threat.

India and Pakistan's strained relations and Pakistan's closeness with China are other reasons behind India's suspicion towards China in SAARC. Since the 1962 war, India has had bitter experiences with China due to which it is not in favour of China's inclusion in SAARC. China's claim on the South China Sea, declaration of ADIZ (Air Defense Identification Zone), huge investment in Gwadar port and interest in the Iranian Chabahar port are some of the examples which are being observed by whole world very keenly, and they were interpreted as part of China's dominating strategy. China's stress on a maritime silk route and its growing maritime power along with its strong economy are forcing India to look beyond the scene and predict the future consequences of China's presence in South Asia.

China's intention in South Asia

China, with the world's largest population and second largest land area, is one of the fastest-growing economies, which may even surpass other major powers after a certain number of years. With its strong economy and cost-effective manufacturing, China has become the world's largest trading partner.

China's interest in South Asia and its willingness to be a permanent member of the SAARC group shows China's foreign policy towards South Asia. China is maintaining a friendly relationship with SAARC member countries so that it can get permanent membership in the group. China's growing investment in developmental projects of South Asian countries like Sri Lanka, Maldives, Pakistan and so on has shown its interest in the region. If China's interest in South Asia is analyzed, it can be understood that mainly economic and strategic interests are the core of China's policy.

The economic crisis of 2008 has weakened the economies of Western countries. Even Asian countries had to suffer a lot, but after this crisis, the growing vast market for trading in Asia and especially in South Asia has been noticed. China also wants to benefit from this region rather than depending only on European and other Western countries.

Another possible interest behind China's inclination towards SAARC is its geopolitical strategy and aggressive foreign policy. By proposing a maritime silk route, China not only wants to benefit through maritime trade; it also wants to get access to the Indian Ocean, which will help it to become the strongest maritime power.

Is China healthy for SAARC?

The importance of any regional group occurs with its members' needs. In the case of SAARC, almost all members have an optimistic opinion regarding China's involvement in South Asia except some countries like India. At the same time, since most of the countries are facing developmental challenges, their whole focus is on getting technical and financial support, and they do not want to look towards the probable scenario that China will get veto power in SAARC.

If China had only economic interest in SAARC, then it would need not to ask for a permanent membership in this group because it can easily practice its economic relations with other countries. Hence it can also be said that China has some political interest in this region, and it is just using its technology and economy as a tool to get more involved in SAARC and to get permanent membership. Involvement of China as a permanent member will also weaken the regional cooperation spirit because it will generate the sub-regional grouping among the member states, and again, it will lead to a lack of unity in taking decisions in the regional group.

The SAARC charter promotes the sovereignty of a nation and non-interference in its internal matters. China has projected the image of an aggressive and dominating country, especially in case of territorial issues like in Tibet, the South China Sea and the Senkaku Islands. Hence, it will not be a good idea to expect China to practice and promote the SAARC charter.

Increasing the members in a regional group in order to solve certain problems may lead to some other problems. SAARC is already facing certain challenges, and including China with the motive that it could be a better solution for the problems may create other unfavourable issues. And those issues may prove to be more problematic than the current one.

Another point of view is that if China gets full membership, then there might be a healthy competition between India and China to get a significant place in the group, and while doing so, more development will be seen all around the region. It may also lead to a powerful Asia in whole world, which can mean even more leverage in the world platform.

Conclusion

While analyzing the expectations of SAARC and China for each other, it can be said that both are in need of each other. Instead of thinking of giving permanent membership to China and expecting peace and smooth functioning in SAARC, it is better to wait and watch to see whether China has the spirit of cooperation in the region. China's aggressive foreign policy cannot be ignored. Better economic relations can't be the only factor for permanent membership of any country in a regional group. China needs SAARC more than SAARC needs it. Hence, China should stay as an observer member and prove to the region that apart from helping a nation financially, it can promote principles like non-interference, sovereignty recognition and mutual cooperation. Instead of focusing on the future relations of an individual country with China, the future of the whole region should also be an area of focus. Since a regional group demands more stress on a multilateral relationship rather than a bilateral one, SAARC member countries should make their vision much broader and view the SAARC's future if China enters the group. Because, ultimately, it is member countries who have to face the consequences of any wrong decision.

Notes

1 Anu Krishana, "SAARC 'with' China: An Opportunity with a Multitude of Possibilities", *Science Technology and Security Forum,* see http://stsfor.org/content/saarc-china-opportunity-multitude-possibilities(Accessed on 7 January 2019).
2 Liu Zongyi, "China's Economic Relations With SAARC: Prospects and Hurdles", *China Institute of International Studies,* 1 December 2014, see www.ciis.org.cn/english/2014-12/01/content_7409453.htm (Accessed on 10 January 2019).
3 *Ibid.*
4 Emily Brunjes, Nicholas Levine, Miriam Palmer and Addison Smith, "China's Increased Trade and Investment in South Asia (Spoiler Alert: It's The Economy)", Presented a Paper in a Workshop in International Public Affairs, Robert M. La Follette School of Public Affairs, University of Wisconsin-Madison, Spring 2013.
5 Brian Benedictus, "Bhutan and the Great Power Tussle", *The Diplomat,* 2 August 2014, see http://thediplomat.com/2014/08/bhutan-and-the-great-power-tussle/(Accessed on 8 January 2019).
6 Tiffany P. Ng, "China's Role in Shaping the Future of Afghanistan", *Carnegie Endowment for International Peace,* 1 September 2010, see http://carnegieendowment.org/files/china_role_afghanistan.pdf (Accessed on 2 January 2019).
7 Angela Stanzel, "China Moves into Afghanistan", *European Council on Foreign Relations,* 26 November 2014, see www.ecfr.eu/article/commentary_china_moves_into_afghanistan634(Accessed on 2 February 2019).

8 Joginder Singh, "A Comparative Study of India-China Bilateral Trade", *IRACST – International Journal of Commerce, Business and Management* (IJCBM), vol.3, no.2, April 2014, pp. 269–279.

9 Harsh V. Pant, *The Rise of China: Implications for China*, New Delhi: Foundation Books, June 2012, p. 234.

10 "China and Pakistan", *Ministry of Foreign Affairs of Republic of China*, see www.fmprc.gov. cn/mfa_eng/wjb_663304/zzjg_663340/yzs_663350/gjlb_663354/2757_663518(Accessed on 28 January 2019).

11 Gulam Ali, "Mutual Interest Underlie a Strong China-Pakistan Relationship", *East Asia Forum*, www.eastasiaforum.org/2015/06/04/mutual-interests-underlie-a-strong-china-pakistan-relationship/(Accessed on 24 January 2019).

12 Yen-Chiang Chang and Mehran Idris Khan, "China – Pakistan Economic Corridor and Maritime Security Collaboration: A Growing Bilateral Interests", *Maritime Business Review*, 2019, https://doi.org/10.1108/MABR-01-2019-0004.

13 "China and Maldives", *Ministry of Foreign Affairs of the People's Republic of China*, www. fmprc.gov.cn/mfa_eng/wjb_663304/zzjg_663340/yzs_663350/gjlb_663354/2737_663478/(Accessed on 2 February 2019).

14 Srikanth Kondapali, "Maritime Silk Road: Increasing Chinese Inroads into the Maldives", *Institute of Peace and Conflict Studies*,13 November 2014, see www.ipcs.org/comm_select. php?articleNo=4735 (Accessed on 15 May 2019).

15 *Ibid.*

16 See "China and Maldives", n.13.

17 *Ibid.*

18 Peshan Gunaratne and J. Berkshire Miller, "Sri Lanka: Balancing Ties Between China and the West", *The Diplomat*, 26 May 2015, see http://thediplomat.com/2015/05/sri-lanka-balancing-ties-between-china-and-the-west/(Accessed on 20 January 2019).

19 Arun Kumar Sahu, "Future of India – Nepal Relations: Is China a Factor?" *Strategic Analysis*, vol.39, no.2, 2015, pp. 197–204.

5

BILATERALISM IN SOUTH ASIA

Future scenario

Adluri Subramanyam Raju

Introduction

Regionalism has been increasing in different parts of the world. Isolation can no longer be an option for any state in the changing power dynamics as well as in the globalized world. Further, several issues and problems are transnational[1] in nature and could be addressed through cooperation between the states. And the economic growth or trade-off any country can be enhanced through cooperation with other countries.

The success of regionalism depends on strong bilateralism among the countries in the specific geographical entity. Following are the basic characteristics of grouping countries as an entity: geographical close proximity, interaction among states, economic and diplomatic linkages of states, common security concerns and socio-cultural homogeneity. Further, a change at one point affects other parts of the system or regional grouping.

Further, regional security has been discussed by Barry Buzan. He states, "security is a relational phenomenon. Because security is relational, one cannot understand the national security of any given state without understanding the international pattern of security interdependence in which it is embedded."[2] He argues that the strategic factor holds importance in the making of a region. He defines a security complex as "a group of states whose primary security concerns link together sufficiently closely that their national securities cannot realistically be considered apart from one another."[3] He says that

> The "national" security problem turns out to be a systemic security problem in which individuals, states and the system all play a part, and in which economic, societal and environmental factors are as important as political and military ones. From this integrative perspective, the levels and sectors appear

more useful as viewing platforms from which one can observe the problem from different angles, than as self-contained areas for policy or analysis.[4]

Though geographical continuity remains the greatest asset for SAARC, this potential is yet to be harnessed because boundaries have become the manifestation of national identity in the region. Moreover, most of the countries in South Asia are geographically closer to India, and unlike the latter, no country in the region has geographical proximity with more than two countries. The population and landmass of India are three times greater than the combined of all other South Asian countries. Military and economic developments are dominant and make the region Indo-centric.

Scenario building

One can look at whether South Asia is a region. South Asia has been a region without regionalism.[5] The following factors can be viewed further as obstacles to regional cooperation: suspicion and trust deficiencies between India and its neighbours; partitioning of the subcontinent by a colonial power; the perception that bilateral relations mainly between India and its neighbours are dominated by India; rivalry between two major countries (India and Pakistan); meager regional trade; the inability to resolve border issues; and prevention of illegal migration. Conflicts and disputes converted the region backward. No common external threat was perceived by the region's states. Absence of collective identity and lack of sense of belonging do still exist in the region.

In view of this, it would be difficult to look at regional cooperation in South Asia. However, the author believes that bilateralism between India and its neighbours in South Asia would enhance cooperation at the regional level. The chapter focuses on how bilateralism would be strengthened between India and its neighbours in South Asia in the future by building different scenarios.

The following are some of the future projections. Though it is difficult to predict the future, this chapter aims at constructing/building future scenarios of South Asia.

Scenario 1: Bilateral relations between India and its neighbours will be strengthened

India is a larger country in terms of population, landmass, defence and resources and is also emerging as a major economic powerhouse. There are reports that India will emerge as the third largest economy in the world by 2030. If this is going to be a reality, then neighbouring countries would certainly benefit by associating with India through cooperation.

At the regional level, India has disputes with Pakistan on Kashmir, Siachen, Sir Creek and the maritime boundary in the Arabian Sea and with Bangladesh on water and migration, whereas the dispute between India and Nepal involves Kalapani. Since the boundaries are the manifestations of national identity in the region, the states are rigid in their stand, and disputes continue between India and its neighbours. The political differences and disputes have stalled the prospects of economic cooperation in the region. Since India is the larger country in the region, the neighbours feel that the former dominates the region and poses a threat to their security. However, they have never collectively expressed their apprehensions against India. In other words, neighbouring countries do not want to antagonize India.

Most of the countries in South Asia show little interest in regional cooperation. They may feel that when they go for cooperation at the regional level, they could lose their national identity and bargaining power. In any negotiation, a country will have more advantages while bargaining at the bilateral than at the regional level. And hence, they may prefer bilateral cooperation with India because they get more benefits and concessions. However, India should improve its bilateral relations with its neighbours. At the foreign policy level, there have been efforts to expand India's outreach beyond South Asia. India is seeking to build strategic, political and economic alliances at the bilateral, regional and global level. It has also been trying to enhance its capabilities and capacities to ensure its strategic autonomy, which will in turn help it achieve greater power status. It realizes the fact that unless it improves its relations with its neighbours, it is difficult for New Delhi to transcend its role beyond the region. Its global presence has been steadily visible, and its role in the world makes it difficult for South Asian neighbours to ignore it.

Scenario 2: Geographical proximity has become one of the factors for either India or for neighbours to come closer

Geography plays a significant role in determining relations between the neighbouring countries. India shares a border with almost all South Asian countries; hence, its geographical proximity with its neighbours can become instrumental in bringing countries together and strengthening regional cooperation. This dimension is not without its challenges. For example, India has been trying to get Iranian gas via Pakistan for nearly a decade now. Apart from the challenges of cooperation between India and Pakistan, experts like Ariel Cohen, Lisa Curtis and Owen Graham[6] have been vocal about the challenges to regional security. It could be inferred that apprehensions such as these stem from the fact that both India and Pakistan are nuclear powers, and Pakistan has never committed itself to the "No First Strike" policy. At best, Pakistan's nuclear doctrine has remained ambiguous,[7] giving rise to apprehensions among experts. While the proximity with Pakistan is laden with these challenges, India's relations with other neighbours have also encountered pitfalls. A discussion on these would, however, divert this article from its objective. It would therefore suffice to infer that in order to convert geographical proximity to building bilateral relations, countries in the region have to step aside from their suspicions and look at the prospect of maximizing their proximity factor to their individual and mutual advantage.

Scenario 3: Neighbours will depend on India to address most of the issues/problems which tend to be transnational in nature

The region is affected by many non-traditional security threats,[8] which have trans-national dimensions, and no individual country would be able to tackle them. Now it becomes a challenge for every country to address threats; hence, cooperation among the countries in the region is required. An example for this level of bilateral arrangements was seen in 2003 when Bhutan and India jointly flushed out Bodo, ULFA and KLO militants and their camps in Bhutan.[9] India has more advantage in tackling (non) traditional security challenges in South Asia, particularly in the domain of human security viz., poverty alleviation, health and safety, human resources development and higher education. Scholars like Zahid Ahmad find "that greater cooperation in common human security areas has a potential to pave the way for a cooperation on issues of a 'contentious' nature, particularly terrorism."[10] Hence, this can be treated as a source of stimulation for cooperation. The neighbours will seek help from India; otherwise, it would be difficult for them to address the challenges.

While India has developed tremendous potential and is capable of assisting its neighbours in areas related to human security, it must also safeguard from patronizing the neighbours since perception of such an attitude on the part of India could offset the goodwill that it can obtain through human security assistance.

Scenario 4: Pakistan fails to remain as a major power in South Asia

During the Cold War period, bipolarity provided stability, determined both by the US and the USSR. In the post-Cold War period, scholars debated whether bipolarity would transform to uni-polarity or multi-polarity or any country could emerge as a major power to replace the USSR and compete with the US. It seems to be that multi-polarity would emerge in international politics.

At the regional level, India and Pakistan emerged as major countries in South Asia and were more capable than other countries to change the environment in the region. In other words, India and Pakistan became more capable in maintaining bipolarity in the region. However, in recent times, Pakistan seems to have failed to emerge as a strong country to continue to maintain bipolarity in the region. Pakistan could not attain parity with India (which was one of the goals of Pakistan) to compete with the latter. Pakistan's nuclear stance is to be understood in this regard, for it has been carefully built around the perceived necessity to checkmate India. However, with ISI, the Pakistani Army and many militant groups being in the power-sharing matrix in Pakistan, the control and safety of its nuclear arsenal[11] being firmly in the hands of responsible democratic leadership is doubtful.[12] An assessment made by the Association of American Scientists in early 2018 actually indicated that the Pakistani tactical nuclear arsenal could be accessible to terrorist groups.[13] Unless Pakistan addresses the concerns of the international community in this regard, it is unlikely to find bilateral acceptance with India or any other South Asian neighbour.

Improving bilateral relations between India and Pakistan will not only benefit these two countries but also enhance regional cooperation. Cordial relations between them will lead to regional stability, progress and peace in South Asia. However, it does not seem that cordial relations between the two countries are possible in the foreseeable future.

Scenario 5: Unipolar South Asia: India's Dominance

India was uncomfortable with the bipolarity system at the global level during the Cold War period. Since the disintegration of the Soviet Union, India has been advocating for a multipolar world at the international level, whereas at the regional level (South Asia), it seems to be in favour of uni-polarity.

India is growing rapidly in both military and economic terms, unlike other countries in South Asia, which would depend on it for their development. Hence, India has become the dominant country in the region and will continue to remain as such in the years to come. Though there would be challenges from China, India would emerge as a dominant country in the subcontinent. India's regional preponderance is inevitable, and neighbours have to accept the reality. Geographical advantage, rising literate population levels, economic progress and technological supremacy stand to India's advantage. These, combined with the cultural identity across borders, could be to India's advantage at the regional level.

Scenario 6: India and China relations

China and India are neighbours, maritime powers and nuclear states and are emerging as major economies in the world. Trade between them is growing. There is a convergence of interests between them and shared interests, such as safeguarding free navigation, a focus on development and energy security, eradication of poverty, and dealing with social unrest; climate change; environmental, demographic and resources constraints; corruption; political unrest; non-state actors' roles; and so on. They have increased their collaboration with regional groupings such as BRICS, BCIM and trade and investment.

India and China are trying to improve relations to enhance their economic development rather than countering each other. Both the countries want to rise peacefully.

However, some of the issues which are irritants between them are border disputes, the Tibet issue, China's relations with Pakistan, India's relations with the US, expansion of their presence in the Indian Ocean region and competition over access to resources. If China is plagued with potential threats from its eastern coast and internal challenges, then Beijing may not show interest in countering India. China understands that India and the US are likely to be closer than either one will be to China.[14] It realizes the importance of India and the US to its economic development. It is not clear whether China would gain by expanding its presence in South Asia and containing India.[15] Though India and China do not trust each other, they have to work together for their development. Trade has become one of the motivations for both the countries to depend on each other. If these two countries improve their relations, China may have less concern for India's neighbours. Hence, India's neighbours (including Pakistan) would have to improve their relations with New Delhi. Even if this scenario is not possible, India will be recognized as an important player by its neighbours.

India and China should search for areas of cooperation by keeping aside their differences. If the two countries have cordial relations, the following advantages would be available to both:

1 India's involvement in Tibet will not cease, granting China full suzerainty over Tibet.
2 India's alliance with the US, Japan and other littoral countries in the Indian Ocean would be limited.
3 China would support India to be part of the Nuclear Suppliers Group.
4 China will minimize its relations with Pakistan, and in return, Pakistan will minimize its adversarial activities against India.
5 The majority of their (India and China) trade, which sails through the Indian Ocean, would be secured.
6 Both can peacefully rise as major economies.

The growth of the world economy in the next decade, it is expected, will be powered by Asia. China, Japan and India are important actors in Asia. It is a challenge for the major countries of Asia to collectively work to make Asia an important continent and address their differences among themselves, because the continent lacks strong regional institutions to resolve their problems. Asia's future will be determined by the relations between these two countries and other major countries in Asia, including Japan. Hence, both countries, as responsible actors in the global arena, would opt more for cooperation than confrontation. They can address various issues through cooperation, and they can create a better future for Asia.

Scenario 7: India's role beyond South Asia

India's foreign policy choices were earlier constrained by the Cold War politics that defined its political, economic and security relations with other states. The post-Cold War global politics are witnessing changes in power equations, and India is no longer constrained to South Asia by the Cold War rubric. India's nuclear tests in 1998 and its steady economic performance have changed not only its perception of itself but the world's perception of New Delhi. On the economic front, India's performance in infrastructure and growth in the IT and manufacturing sectors have changed its economy to a major extent. India's legal structure, corporate governance, banking system, financial sector, skilled manpower and young workforce have become the new engines of economic growth and icons of major power status.

India's economic growth is largely driven by domestic factors, such as rising consumption and domestic investment, favourable demography, growing affluence and long-term encouraging growth prospects. It, despite the low per capita GDP, is a major market. On a purchasing power parity basis, India is the fourth largest economy in the world, and it is the second fastest growing economy. India's imports have grown rapidly, both in value and share. Thus, India is increasingly being seen as an engine of economic growth in Asia. India, to project itself as a dynamic country, has to play a greater role in ensuring stability, security and peace beyond South Asia.

India is trying to transform itself into a competitive, developed and prosperous country. Its foreign policy looks beyond the immediate neighbourhood to secure its economic interests – especially to have access to raw materials and energy supplies. In recent times, India has been seeking to expand its presence and influence by enhancing bilateral cooperation with the US, European countries, China and Russia, as well as by engaging and participating in regional arrangements and international organizations. It is also seeking to create a new multilateralism with a proactive role in IBSA (India, Brazil and South Africa), BIMSTEC (Bay of Bengal Initiative for Multi-Sectoral Technical and Economic Cooperation), MGC (Mekong Ganga Cooperation), BRICS (Brazil, Russia, India, China and South Africa), India-ASEAN Cooperation, EAS (East Asian Summit) and so on. India's search for a nuclear power status and a permanent seat on the UN Security Council raises a number of questions at regional and global levels. Thus, in the emerging scenario, on one hand, India is reorienting its policy towards its neighbours, and on the other hand, it is transcending its role/presence from the region to the rest of the world. India's neighbours in South Asia have acknowledged India's role beyond South Asia, and they would certainly realize the importance of improving relations with India.

Scenario 8: India's credibility

India's policy of non-aggression, its cultural and philosophical virtues and its relation with its neighbouring states through ethnic and religious ties strengthened its relation with other countries. Its policy towards non-alignment, universal disarmament and panchsheel and its moral superiority further provided legitimacy to its role in different parts of the world. India emerged itself as a responsible state by assisting in the supply of goods, such as humanitarian relief and disaster assistance, search and rescue (particularly during 2004–2005 tsunami relief operation), relief efforts following cyclone Nargis in 2008, and so on. India is seen as a security provider and thus enjoys an elevated profile. For instance, in its maritime strategy, India explicitly states that it will strive to ensure the safety of the ocean's sea lanes of communications:

> Our strategy recognizes that the sea lanes of communication passing through our region are critical for our economic growth and to the global community.

Smaller nations in our neighbourhood as well as nations that depend on the waters of the Indian Ocean for their trade and energy supplies have come to expect that the Indian Navy will ensure a measure of stability and tranquility in the waters around our shores.[16]

In view of its credibility, the neighbouring countries in South Asia should not ignore improving their relations with India.

The way forward

While the author has attempted to construct different scenarios, it must be understood that no single scenario can be said to be the most probable one. A combination of factors, political and economic primarily, would dictate how much of any of these scenarios will play out. Apart from the constraints already present in the environment, key aspects critical to achieving regional cooperation through bilateralism are the clarity of vision in political leadership and the ability to sustain momentum. Unless mature leadership emerges (and is sustained), bilateral arrangements could plummet to new levels of decay. A classic example would be the initiatives taken by late Indian Prime Minister Vajpayee towards building bridges with Pakistan. Those initiatives did not survive the momentum during the successive regimes both in India and Pakistan.

It is also presumptuous to hold political intent and continuity as the most important factors to forge healthy bilateral and regional relations. South Asia has one asset that is not exploited fully in this dimension – the cultural and emotional bonds of the populace across borders. The historical links are to be nurtured to develop a bond that can permeate political divisions. When we look at Europe, for example, recognition of such links eventually resulted in the integration of East and West Germany, and a unified Germany has mended fences with France with which it had calamitous wars in the beginning of the twentieth century.

Conclusion

If India emerges as one of the major economies in the world, its neighbours would certainly benefit by associating with the former through cooperation.

Though India was reluctant to join the SAARC initially, it has played and continues to play a significant role in the SAARC. Seventy-five per cent of regional trade is contributed by India. It was reported by ADB that if infrastructure and trade facilities improved, trade would be increased from five to twenty-four per cent. This can be possible with India's active involvement. Though the SAARC charter does not permit bilateral issues to be discussed at the regional level, bilateral relations between India and its neighbouring countries will play a major role in bringing stability, peace and security in South Asia. The author predicts that bilateral relations between India and its neighbours will enhance regional cooperation in South Asia.

Notes

1 There are hardly any pairs of states in South Asia that are not affected by trans-border spilling of ethno-nationalist, communal and militant activity.
2 Barry Buzan, *People, States and Fear: An Agenda for International Security Studies in the Post-Cold War Era*, Hertfordshire: Harvester Wheatsheaf, 2008, p. 187.
3 *Ibid*, p. 190.
4 *Ibid*, p. 368.
5 See Shibashis Chatterjee and Sulagna Maitra, "Space and Regional Cooperation: The SAARC Story", in T. Nirmala Devi and Adluri Subramanyam Raju (eds.), *Envisioning a New South Asia*, New Delhi: Shipra Publications, 2009, pp. 25–46; C.K. Lal, "Imagining South Asian An Unipolar World", in Adluri Subramanyam Raju (ed.), *Reconstructing South Asia: An Agenda*, New Delhi: Gyan Publishing House, 2007, pp. 263–272.
6 Ariel Cohen, Lisa Curtis and Owen Graham, *The Proposed Iran – Pakistan – India Gas Pipeline: An Unacceptable Risk to Regional Security*, The Heritage Foundation Report No.2139, 30 May 2008. See www.heritage.org/asia/report/the-proposed-iran-pakistan-india-gas-pipeline-unacceptable-risk-regional-security (Accessed on 14 April 2019).
7 Smruti S. Pattanaik, "Pakistan's Nuclear Strategy", *Strategic Analysis*, vol.27, no.1, 2003, pp. 94–114.
8 See V.R. Raghavan, "Non-Traditional Threats to South Asian Security", in Raju (ed.), *Reconstructing South Asia*, no.5, pp. 129–135.
9 Tashi Choden, "Indo-Bhutan Relations Recent Trends", Regional Conference on *Comprehensive Security in South Asia*, Kathmandu: Institute of Foreign Affairs, 2004, pp. 112–121.
10 Z. Ahmed, *Regionalism and Regional Security in South Asia*, London: Routledge, 2013.
11 The Trump administration assessment in 2018 was "We are particularly concerned by the development of tactical nuclear weapons that are designed for use in battlefield. We believe that these systems are more susceptible to terrorist theft and increase the likelihood of nuclear exchange in the region."
12 "US Worried Pakistan's Nuclear-Weapons Could Land Up in Terrorists' Hands: Official", *Economic Times*, 25 August 2017, https://economictimes.indiatimes.com/news/defence/us-worried-pakistans-nuclear-weapons-could-land-up-in-terrorists-hands-official/articleshow/60220358.cms(Accessed on 14 April 2019).
13 Hans M. Kristensen, Robert S. Norris, and Julia Diamond, "Pakistani Nuclear Forces", *Bulletin of the Atomic Scientists*, vol.74, no.5, 2018.
14 Aaron L. Friedberg, "The Geopolitics of Asia in 2030: An American Perspective", in Ajey Lele and Namrata Goswami (eds.), *Imagining Asia in 2030: Trends, Scenario and Alternatives*, New Delhi: Academic Foundation, 2011, p. 472.
15 *Ibid*, p. 475.
16 India Navy, *Freedom to Use the Seas: India's Maritime Military Strategy*, New Delhi: Integrated Headquarters Ministry of Defence, Navy, 2007, p. iv.

PART 2

Democracy in South Asia

6

SOUTH ASIA IN FUTURE

Democratization and the politics of transformation

Shibashis Chatterjee

Introduction

If the past is any indicator, the way South Asia might shape up fifteen years from now is not very difficult to predict. Since the retreat of colonial powers and the advent of modern nation-states in this rather old region, South Asia has been marked by a bitter conflict between India and Pakistan that has stifled efforts to transform it into an economically integrated, prosperous and peaceful place. While the dispute between India and Pakistan is the primary geopolitical problem of the region, India has varied problems with all its South Asian neighbours. However, the region, being Indo-centric, the social, political, economic and cultural divides cut across the sub-continent rather than run along territorial lines. Moreover, South Asia remains a contested space, where divergent notions of politics, cultural imaginations and fundamental economic divisions convulse all states from time to time.

Can South Asia come out of this gloomy scenario in thirty years' time? Can effective economic, political and security integration be achieved here under conditions of plurality and diversity? Most scholars have, in their own ways, proposed that to make sense of where the region might go three decades from now, three broad questions must be answered. First, one needs to grapple with the elusive issue of how regions are configured and transformed. Second, one needs to historicize the sub-continent, by focusing on two political processes of modernity that introduced a new kind of space-making, namely, nationalism and state formation.[1] Third, the future of the region is inextricably intertwined with the fate of democracy. Democracy has indeed become stronger across South Asia in the last decade. The future of democracy remains open-ended, as politics of exclusivity and denial mark the region. While electoral democracy has progressed quite admirably in the last ten years, institutionalization and mass empowerment remain weak.

While one cannot prognosticate the actual shape the region will assume in 2030, upon a careful historical and political reading of available trends, it can be argued that the future depends on what happens to the contradictions that define the region. In this chapter, we look into democratization in South Asia as a way to prognosticate its future. The argument is that what will happen in South Asia in three decades or so hinges primarily on how the democratic experiment unfolds. The other two arguments, namely, the spatial imagination of the sub-continent and the contestations over national identities, have not been pursued here for the reason that no major transformations are likely to happen to them in this period. Spatial imaginations take time to change. They are contingent upon the nature of elites who dominate the political system. National identities are malleable but require a much longer time horizon for meaningful transformation. Again, the primary agency here is the ruling elite whose political career is essentially governed by the democratic experiments at work. In a sense, it can be said that the first two piggyback on the third cause.

The chapter evolves in three sections. The first section deals with the broader issues of democracy and democratization, particularly in the context of India. The second part articulates the challenges involved. The third section tries to make predictions for trends to show up around 2030 by reading the contemporary trends closely. The article does not offer concrete predictions; rather, it sets a framework for the democratization process to yield certain broad trends. The article discusses the democratization processes of India, Pakistan, Bangladesh and Sri Lanka. While the Himalayan kingdoms of Nepal and Bhutan are integral to the South Asian narrative, their cases are not discussed in this article.

Democracy, democratization and the Indian experiment

The kind of democratization that is supposed to be a prerequisite for peace is missing in South Asia as of now. This does not, of course, mean that such a desirable form of democratization and liberalization cannot grow in South Asia. However, one needs to admit that this is not going to be easy. Democracy and market institutions do not grow in a vacuum. The social and economic interests of the elites in many South Asian states militate against strong democratization and welfare liberalism. A part of the problem is structural; they inhere in the given socio–economic mosaic of South Asia through which democracy and market institutions assume concrete form. The other part of the problem resides in South Asia's links with the outside world or the international system. In brief, there is no compelling evidence of dominant international forces pushing the democratic agenda in South Asia, on the one hand, and supporting the cause of welfare liberalism (as opposed to speculative capitalism/liberalism), on the other. The democratization and economic prosperity of South Asia, therefore, will depend, first, on how a culture of popular legitimacy grows independent of social forces that are inherently authoritarian; and second, how market forces can cause the expansion of people's choices and capabilities rather than creating enormous economic differences between the rich and the poor.

Although ruled either directly or indirectly by the British, the oldest parliamentary democracy in Europe, the South Asian states do not have an enviable record in democratization. India, the largest South Asian state, of course, is an exception among Third World countries to have sustained open, democratic rule despite enormous social diversity, poverty and mass illiteracy. Being the core of the British imperial order in South Asia, India inherited the advantage of an established state structure, being the recognized legatee of the colonial power. Pakistan and Bangladesh, born out of two partitions, had to create state structures virtually from scratch and through their own efforts by collating the fragments of state authority within their borders. Nepal and Sri Lanka also inherited established core structures but faced greater problems in their efforts to adjust these structures to their new, post-independence situations. Nepal remained a monarchy, and the struggle towards democratization created deep fissures within the Nepalese polity, ultimately leading to massive polarization and radical subversive tendencies. Sri Lanka became and successfully maintained a parliamentary democracy but suffered from intense ethnicization of its polity that created problems of vertical and horizontal sovereignty and enforced legitimacy along ethnic lines.[2] Lacking the consolidation of democratic values and institutionalization of democratic structures, Pakistan and Bangladesh frequently ran into spells of military authoritarianism. Bhutan remained a theoretical monarchy without provoking a strong pro-democracy movement against itself.

As one may expect, scholars differ about the democratic prospects of the subcontinent. While Ayesha Jalal seems to underplay the distinction between democratic and authoritarian political systems in South Asia, most scholars take the divide between the vitality of the Indian democracy and the democratic deficit and weaknesses of other South Asian states as real.[3] A good illustration of the point is the work of Stanley Kochanek, who finds the secret of India's democratic resilience in the high level of popular participation in local elections, noisy interest group activities, the release of private space following the gradual withdrawal of an interventionist state and the demonstrated autonomy of the media, which manages to counter the perils of political instability, low growth and increasing regionalism within the polity.[4]

Another interesting contrast consists of the works by Larry Diamond and Maya Chadda.[5] Diamond issues the following pessimistic thesis: given the overriding problems of instability, violence, corruption and poverty, the quality of democracy in Asia in general, and South Asia in particular, is rather low. He, unfortunately, errs by exaggerating the shortcomings and deviations, particularly when it comes to his analysis of the Indian case. In sharp contrast, Chadda strikes a note of bold optimism by insisting on the historical, political and sociological distinctiveness of the South Asian democratic experiment. She views democracy as a dynamic, ever-expanding process rather than judging it by institutional indicators. In essence, she advances a communitarian reading of South Asian democracy against the more numerous right-based ones. She finds democratic promise in the efforts of the state to find consensus on developmental goals and policy issues together with a complex process of nation-state consolidation in each South Asian state.[6]

Although the South Asian states began their journey with distinctive national projects, their unity lay in their commitment to becoming strong states with consolidated national identities. This commitment, however, had to be worked out through complex social structures that inevitably became intertwined with the political dynamic itself. All South Asian states had three goals in common – to achieve rapid economic development, create a strong national identity, and preserve territorial integration in the face of myriad challenges to state authority, including threats of secession.[7] The nature of social elites who came to dominate these South Asian states decided the character of political rule. As Ayesha Jalal's comparative analysis of three South Asian states – India, Pakistan, and Bangladesh – has shown, democracy and authoritarianism were never clearly differentiated ideas in the subcontinent, and therefore, their pairing (rather than exclusive treatments) allows a more incisive historical analysis of the structures of dominance and resistance in this part of the world.[8]

History is important here for two reasons. First, it helps us understand the opportunities and betrayals of democratic projects across South Asian states, in terms of ideology and class. Second, history is significant for indicating the malleability and flux of South Asian societies, their transformation(s) and challenges and the inevitability of continuity and change. Trends suggest that democratization has become strong in South Asia as a whole, although problem(s) of democratization have multiplied. Three factors are crucial here. First, states of South Asia face a remarkably similar political challenge: how to respond to the growing pressure of the demand of the underprivileged, the marginal and the weaker sections to enter the political arena and be heard.[9] In brief, all South Asian political systems face a challenge of representation and need to respond to the accusation of serious representation(al) deficit.[10] This provides a great opportunity for democratization since no other political system exists that can accommodate the marginalized, the dissidents and the hungry yet politicized masses.

Second, the South Asian states also face a crisis of centralized authority and tight federal models.[11] Centralization no longer seems to work. Coalitions of regional formations are increasingly becoming vocal, and in some cases dominant, and authoritarian devices of displacing their demands show decreasing efficiency. The aspirations of the outlying regions have acquired greater strength because of globalization and the weakening of the direct economic capacity of the state. As regions can now directly articulate networks of capital by escaping central vigilance and control in various degrees, their bargaining capacity vis-à-vis the centre has increased substantively. Although regionalism by itself is no guarantee of democratization, as the example of Pakistan shows, it mobilizes the political system more feverishly. High mobilization within a polity tends to give rise to a democratic framework. As regions become more and more important, the impetus for democratization is likely to increase steadily.

Third, with globalization, the information revolution, a new consciousness for human rights (however repressed it might be for such South Asian states), the expansion of the middle class and the rapid spread of consumerism, the profile of civil society is bound to change in the South Asian sub-continent.[12] An autonomous civil society might not develop in the short or medium run in South Asia; the civil society might not also escape its domestication by the territorial nation-state qua a deadly and recursive logic of national security.[13] It forces renegotiation of identities by the state or impels their politicization. As identities acquire strength and are politicized, they cannot be left outside the political power game. In this sense, identity politics, despite its many hazards and shortcomings, trump authoritarian practices and accentuate the tendency towards democratization.

For India, there are two contrasting explanations. The first argues that despite many problems and serious misgivings, "the federal reconciliation of regional identity with autonomy" has been democratically achieved.[14] The second interpretation denies the liberal character of the Indian state. As the state was forced to define communities as relations of power vis-à-vis the nation, it evolved a strategy to negotiate with them that sought to harmonize, universalize and totalize rather than liberate, particularize and empower the communities as subjects of rights. The need to reproduce the reason of the nation in the life-worlds of the diverse communities turned the former into a perverse other of the latter, thereby consigning Indian democracy to a complex competition for spoils amongst shifting coalitions of groups, defined along communal lines.[15] No South Asian state is free from this danger, although the manifestation of the same has tended to vary considerably among them. This is a theme that requires a more detailed exposition.

All South Asian states feel they are safe when their core values can be preserved without recourse to war and if they can maintain these values even during conflicts. Thus, communalism is widely accepted as a threat to internal security because it violates the logic of secular nationalism understood as the core value of any multicultural, postcolonial, noisy democracy. This makes it evident that the nature of the threat posed by communalism can only be fathomed in relation to two other related "issues" – nationalism and secularism. Communalism, in the sub-continent, is imbued with negative connotations, unlike in the West, where it is often used in a positive sense meaning community-based action.[16] Secularism also assumes a new meaning specific to South Asia.

Political secularism, in the Western context, involves strict separation of the affairs of religion from the business of the state, requiring mutual respect for the boundary between religion and politics. The South Asian understanding of secularism, however, does not require an exclusionary insulation of state and religion from each other. Rather, it demands an equal respect of the state for all faiths. Such an understanding of secularism complicates matters for the state because it knows not whether to subscribe to the principle of equidistance from all religions, to practice a policy of equal proximity and equal proactive encouragement to all faiths or to stand aloof with unflinching impartiality. This ambiguity makes the state vulnerable to critique from all sides, particularly when secularism fails to provide the basis for a consolidated nation to a state troubled with genuine anxiety over territorial integrity and national unity since its birth. In the Indian context, the political leadership, particularly those in power, have to harp continuously on India's secular credentials to retain its claim as a safe home to both the Hindus and the Muslims, which is in contrast to the state of affairs in its neighbouring states.

However, the continued emphasis on the need for a strong state to preserve secularism itself stands in the way of realizing the end of turning India into a peaceful haven for minority communities because their very status as perpetually endangered is the only causal explanation of the need to enforce secularism by a strong state. This is a secularism which, like the decisive ideology of communalism, calls attention to divisions which justify its necessity in the life of the state. Nationalism, though it unequivocally condemns communalism as a "threat," particularly in a multi-religious context, has an equally problematic relationship with it. Once denied the crucible of anti-imperialistic struggle, which was necessary to nurture the rudiments of a fragile national identity, the modernist project of nationalism has to employ the pre-modern categories to evoke a sense of belonging to a shared memory, imagination, history and culture. It is here that the plural heterogeneous states of South Asia face a complex problem. The incongruence of cultural and political frontiers disallow an appeal to shared history because it will only make the real fissures in it more apparent, and revival of shared memory is also more likely to revive bitterness than to inspire harmony.

The challenges before the contemporary Indian democratic experiment are many. Of these, two are particularly germane. First, with the rise of the Bharatiya Janata Party (BJP), India now has a mainstream faith-based outfit, a trend that complicates virtually all the pillars of the Congress-dominated political order. Particularly, it threatens to throw out the erstwhile tenuous consensus of a weak, secular-liberal and non-interventionist state and embrace an increasingly Hindu-ized and masculine version stripped of the many equivocations and moral chasms of the past. If this Hindu state ultimately takes root, it will not only change India for good but would have enormous consequences for the democratization projects throughout South Asia. While the multiple cleavages and fragmentations of the Indian polity may ultimately frustrate the drive towards the Hindu state, the increasing tendencies of intolerance across the world and the growing crisis of political liberalism in the post-colonial world does indeed open up the possibility of an eventual hard right-wing swing in Indian politics.

Second, identity politics is on the rise in India, and both caste-based and ethnic parties have increasingly become popular. The politics of recognition and redistribution in India, despite its myriad limitations and shortcomings, have mobilized new social forces, gave them a voice to articulate their case and made some difference to their lives. The empowerment of the under-classes and Dalits in India has proceeded qua an outright political process that rivets on to the patronage-dispensing capacity of the state. The situation is complex, given the unmistakable shrinkage of the welfare state in India following the neo-liberal ascendancy both internationally and at home. However, the politics of recognition and dignity have become possibly the most potent axis of Indian politics that stands in confrontation with the confessional politics of cultural nationalism parleyed by the BJP and other Hindu political outfits. The Congress has been caught off-guard in this virulent polarization, and its older version of secular liberal nationalism seems increasingly arcane to the relatively newly mobilized political forces that find little patience or prospect in its painstaking logrolling of interests.

How Indian democracy may look in 2030 is difficult to tell. India's political institutions are resilient, and its social forces have, by and large, adjusted well to the democratic game. The forces that have, over the years, shunned democratic institutions have not fared well in India. The Maoist challenge is the latest case in point. The Indian state and the ultra-leftists are badly stalemated. The Maoists still occasionally inflict violence on state personnel, and the state violently retaliates. The underlying economic and social context of the Maoist challenge has remained largely unaddressed. This remains perhaps the biggest challenge for India's democracy. Unless the plight of the dispossessed tribal population is negotiated politically and justice delivered, the democratic experiment will remain incomplete. Secondly, the Indian state remains contested in Kashmir and parts of the northeast, and unless it faces up to the challenge of legitimacy, the problem will only be aggravated in the future. Indian democracy, like many other democracies, is not bereft of violence. Its reliance on force may or may not grow depending on how it measures up to some of the democratic blind spots. On balance, the present trend is more likely to continue, and fundamental challenges like those of radical redistribution (Maoist violence), legitimacy (Kashmir, Manipur and Nagaland) and recognition (Dalit politics) are likely to linger on.

The promise

Democratization in South Asia has undeniably become stronger in the last decade. The pressure for political legitimation of regime performance is steadily growing in the sub-continent. Democratic forces in the recent past have almost unexpectedly won some spectacular battles. The uncertainty remains over whether the democratic forces in each of the South Asian countries can consolidate their gains despite challenges like steering the economy through global economic recession, curbing the extremist forces in the fringes of the country, integrating alienated communities within the national mainstream and not compromising, at least in popular perception, the nation's sovereignty or territory in the face of external or internal aggression. Another worrying trend is that the installation of democratic governments has not remedied and in some cases has even increased human rights violations and the level of violence. This has raised questions about the efficacy of the elected governments. These issues are relevant for each and every country in South Asia, especially those who have recently adopted democratically elected governments, like Nepal, Bangladesh, Pakistan and Bhutan.

Bangladesh has considerably consolidated its democratic institutions and culture. The army has not only gone back to the barrack but has shown no inclination to reenter the political game.[17] The record of the democrats in responding to Bangladesh's enormously difficult economic crisis is far better than authoritarian solutions in many other comparable cases. The ferment of popular discontent against the traditional elites and an acute paucity of vital resources promise the consolidation of the multi-party political system, despite a veritable shortage of political institutionalization.[18] This reinforces the thesis that democrats can manage their economies at least as efficiently as their authoritarian counterparts, if not better. What is more, there is considerable evidence of empowerment of marginal groups, particularly women, and improvement in many crucial human development indicators of the state. In the perception of the average Bangladeshi citizen, democracy can solve major socio-economic problems, establish people's rights, provide legitimation opportunities and generate trust. In Sri Lanka, despite a formal end to the ethnic conflict, democracy in the country is still overtly ethnicized, though there is little danger of its structural undoing. As mentioned before, the challenge before Sri Lanka is the renegotiation of the national project by drawing a fresh social contract between the two communities. Political attitudes suggest that people have understood they have a better chance of working out a new deal through democratic means than by any other alternative route. Pakistan has finally bowed to systemic pressures for legitimation of rule, created a rather robust civil society and taken to economic development amid many challenges. The question is whether the consolidation of democratic norms and structures in Pakistan will lessen the intensity of the Indo–Pak conflict in the future. In other words, the central question is will democratization in any way impact upon the security dilemma of the state?

The pitfalls of democratization in South Asia

Whatever form(s) democratization might assume in South Asia, two general limitations are sure to persist. First, South Asian democracies will continue to display a strong elite-bias, and second, they will not be free from corruption and other popular misuses of power. The charge of corruption is nothing peculiar to South Asian political systems. Throughout the world, all political systems show a variable capacity to tolerate, accommodate, fight and extirpate corruption. Democrats, again, are neither more nor less corrupt than their authoritarian counterparts. Therefore, corruption may distort the nature of democracy, but it won't perhaps seriously affect the capacity of democratic states to build peace.

While democracy is the road to a productive and qualitative transformation of South Asia, where people can ultimately come to exercise meaningful political choices, there are several shortcomings of the democratic experiment in South Asia that induce a degree of much-needed caution. There is a fairly dominant point of view that considers democracy the best available option for a plural society and holds communalism as a direct outcome of decline in democratic politics and participation and ineffective citizen action. The argument here is that communalization of politics must be seen as a necessary concomitant of the decline of democratic infrastructure resulting in its distortion into majoritarianism and mere concern with an electoral game of numbers. The suggested remedy is rejuvenated citizen initiatives forcing the state to concede minorities' demands.[19] However, in functional terms, democracy entails principled acceptance of majority decisions, and a settled consensus in a democracy has no obligation to yield space to minority voices. Though language, religion and culture are also vital ingredients in the formation of an identity in the multi-ethnic democratic contexts of South Asia, electoral compulsions have made use of primordial identities as a rule rather than an exception.

A second general danger concerns the politics of the disproportionate allocation of resources amidst a general condition of relative scarcity. The conventional dialectics of class exploitation account for a part but not the whole of this puzzle. Castes and other social groups, powerful cartels of interests in complex decisional settings and parasitic rentier interests of diverse kinds, among others explain the intense competition for resources in South Asia. However, what is crucial here is to note the unmistakable mobilization of democratic forces and hitherto marginal groups who are seen to challenge the existing patterns of state allocation of resources in all the South Asian states. While this is an encouraging trend, neither is this tendency irreversible in the context of fraught politics of the sub-continent nor is it possible to say with any degree of accuracy the specific forms this might assume over the long term. Given the powerful ascription-based identities in South Asia, politics of identity is a double-edged sword. On the one hand, it is needed to empower the historically marginalized identities. On the other, once politicized and mobilized into action, these may become self-entrenched categories that may often assume zero-sum postures vis-à-vis other such groups and weaken the general capacity of the state to dispense patronage among them.

Pakistan

At a more micro level, two dangers are particularly alarming. First, the dominance of conservative elements can gather greater potency if the state faces a security dilemma of an exceptional kind. Pakistan's inability to sustain brief democratic interludes is not entirely explained by the dominance of the military-bureaucracy-ulema combine or the weakness of political parties and pressure groups. Given the seriousness of the problem and the military takeover of power in Pakistan, analysts have expressed their reservations about the survival of the fledgling democracy in the country. Thus, Stephen Cohen writes,

> When the civilian government did return to Pakistan after Zia's death . . . it was called democracy but was really one struggling regime followed by another, with the army again looking over the shoulders of its leaders . . . There were elections in 1988, 1990, 1993, 1997, and 2002, but the actual turnout in each succeeding election declined from 50 percent in 1988 to a government-declared 35 percent (but probably closer to 26 percent) in 1997, and 25–30 percent in 2002.[20]

The enormous geopolitical significance of Pakistan, coupled with its anti-Indian revisionism, inflates the power and social prestige of the military above all other groups. The perpetuation of the geo-political challenges coming from both sides of the border prevents de-politicization of the armed forces, since such threats are defined as requiring the professional expertise of the army for appropriate responses. Rampant corruption, lack of public faith in the efficiency of political parties and strong fundamentalist tendencies provide further opportunities for military rule. The military, in turn, has utilized its powers to consolidate its position by altering the organic law of the country. Mohammad Zia-ul-Haq in 1985 amended the Constitution of Pakistan to allow the president to dismiss elected governments. Subsequently, the military has cited corruption and abuse of power to dismiss elected governments in 1988, 1990, 1993 and 1996. In the words of Anuradha Mitra Chenoy: "While the process of Islamization and increased militarism occurred primarily during the military dictatorship of Zia ul-Haq, the civilian regimes of Benazir Bhutto and Nawaz Sharif did little to halt this process or rein in the army."[21]

The lack of genuine international concern for reestablishment and consolidation of democratic rule in Pakistan encourages the military to perpetuate its dominance. Sumit Ganguly, in his book *Deadly Impasse*, says that India's lack of territorial ambitions vis-à-vis Pakistan apart from claims on the Siachen Glacier makes New Delhi a status quo power. However, the security establishment within the Pakistani state continues to define, shape and implement the country's national security. Altering the status quo in Kashmir and later establishing a foothold in Afghanistan has been its twin objectives. Ganguly opines that the Pakistani state, regardless of what regime assumes office, whether democratic or authoritarian, has not abandoned its fundamental goal of wresting Kashmir from India. This intransigence suggests that Pakistan is not a security actor; rather, its behaviour is distinctly predatory. He concludes that the Indo-Pakistani relationship cannot be construed as a security dilemma by providing evidence.[22] In a comparable account, T.V. Paul describes Pakistan as a warrior state, whose militaristic elite provide overwhelming priority to military security that conveniently sidelines the much-needed considerations of sustained socio-economic development. This undermines the role and significance of the affluent, forward-looking and educated sections at the altar of the predatory needs of a security-obsessed state.[23]

The West in general, and the United States in particular, have unscrupulously condoned such authoritarianism in the past. Given the threat of global Islamic terrorism and the fear that Pakistan's nuclear arsenal might fall into the hands of Islamic fundamentalist forces and Islamic terrorist groups, it looked for some time as though the military regime, in fact, had become the *de facto* condition of security of Western interests in the entirety of West and South Asia. Eventually, however, the military rule bowed out to popular internal dissent after losing the power struggle with the Pakistani judiciary. Significantly, the political parties, primarily the Pakistan People's Party (PPP) and the Pakistan Muslim League (PML-N) temporarily joined hands to topple the military dictatorship and also amend the constitution to strip the president of his powers to dismiss the democratically elected government. Thus, in March 2008, Pakistan returned yet again to democracy after more than a decade of military dictatorship.[24] While the Western world welcomed the installation of a democratic government in Pakistan and provided massive developmental aid to the country, the repeated NATO attacks in the SWAT region apparently to flush out the terrorists have, in popular perception, raised doubts about the present government's ability to retain its sovereignty.[25]

Since 2008, Pakistan has shown considerable promise in democratic consolidation. It has met the basic criteria of holding free and fair elections and kept the non-elected institutions from formal decision making. In the words of Niaz Murtaza, "It also possesses a rights-based Constitution despite dictator-era distortions, independent courts, a pesky media, a thriving civil society, plurality of power among political parties across provinces and increasing devolution, which all ensure basic accountability."[26] The conclusion seems to be that the alternatives have failed. The military has not delivered on the promises, and technocratic alternatives are not supposed to perform any better. However, there is also the realization that democracy is a necessary but not sufficient condition for the transformation of Pakistan. In the words of Touqir Hussain,

> The liberal/secularist segment, especially the more vocal or activist elements of it, which is Western educated or oriented, is most passionate about the Western liberal model focusing on freedom of choice, free speech, civil liberties, an independent judiciary, and of course elections. This segment is relatively better off economically, and well-connected socially and is not engaged in a struggle for survival. That is why even though it may write eloquently about social ills, poverty and injustices it does not quite empathize with the depth of feelings of the poor and their expectations of democracy.[27]

There are two clear dangers here. First, democracy would invariably pit classes against each other, and the resilience of a political system will be put to its severest test since the class cleavages may not be democratically negotiable. More critically, the future of democracy also hinges on making society amenable to its norms. Democracy is not merely an assortment of institutions and practices for finding a stable equilibrium among competitive political groups. It is more about the ethos or culture of society; particularly about societal commitments to a plurality of ideas, gender equality, minority rights, human rights, and faith in the rule of law. Therefore, democracy remains a struggle in Pakistan, not merely at the level of fending off non-democratic forces but also in connecting meaningfully to the aspirations of the teeming millions trying to achieve upward mobility through protracted mobilization. What happens to democracy thus hinges critically upon its success both within and outside the "political arena."

Projecting trends over fifteen years is a risky business, particularly in a state like Pakistan that has succumbed to dictatorial interventions in the past. However, one needs to consider some factors here. First, Pakistan's geostrategic significance makes its military and bureaucratic elites peculiarly powerful and resilient. While they may find the cost of direct intervention outweighs the benefits, the levers of control of national security and foreign policy issues are likely to remain in their hands. While Nawaz Sharif has shown occasional enterprise to initiate new security and foreign policy initiatives, the overwhelming significance of national security against India has effectively tied his hands. There is, as yet, little promise that democratic practices are having a powerful impact on how Pakistan thinks about India, and whatever evidence is available is far from encouraging. Second, Pakistan has become a social cauldron, with religious extremism becoming a pervasive ideology that happily coexists with democratic institutions. Religious zealots and radical preachers dot the social mosaic of the state and a large section of the population finds emotive succor in confessional politics that protects them from allegedly Western and, therefore, inauthentic, adulterated and impure ideas of life. The antipathy to a liberal way of life is not limited to the largely impoverished and socially backward sections of the population alone. The highly educated and the affluent youth have also found solace in the form of violent religiosity that offers a certain kind of elixir to their frustrations and despair over the state's inability to gain sufficient respect before the world. This is certainly more a failure of liberalism than democratic politics; however, it prepares the ground for forms of illiberal mass-based plebiscitary politics that strengthens the case for an obsessively national-security-oriented polity. Third, Pakistan has also become a hotbed of terrorist and extremist violence that has proved lethal to its political stability and encouraged militant forms of sectarian politics that democracy can hardly contain. Political democracy can encourage different kinds of constituencies, as democracy involves strategies of mobilization and is not limited to seeking out norm-governed political spaces. The fate of Pakistan's democracy hinges on how these challenges are negotiated. Unless the abnormal dilation of national security gives away to a more sober orientation, the fundamental change will be difficult in Pakistan. Democracy can churn the political system and thus articulate the various inflections more potently, but Pakistan's political fate ultimately hinges upon its social narratives that, as of now, remain fraught and potentially explosive.

Sri Lanka

Protracted ethnic conflicts might undermine the case for democracy, as in Sri Lanka. Sri Lanka's blood bath over the decades, in the form of the recently concluded civil war between the majority Sinhalese community and the LTTE-led ethnic Tamils has not destroyed the democratic structure of the state. However, it has stimulated a large number of authoritarian practices, substantially eroding the democratic principles of sharing, trust, reciprocity and peaceful conflict resolution. Sri Lanka's parliamentary democracy has virtually become a consociational polity, where ethnicity controls democratic outcomes and patterns of political legitimation rather than a democratic disciplining of ethnicity. The statist imagination took form in Sinhalese national cultural terms, excluding the rival cultural underpinning of the homeland by the ethnic Tamils. Virtually left out of the state-building process, the Tamil retaliatory posture had come to focus its hope on the achievement of the *Eelam* – a Tamil state in the northeastern part of the island.[28] While a massive military exercise brought the insurgency to an end and elections were held in the region, the alienation of the ethnic Tamils and Muslims from the state has not decreased.[29] Scholars opine that substantial democratization and decentralization will be the basic pre-requisites for integrating these communities with the mainstream Sinhalese population.

The way the Sri Lankan civil war ended is crucial to the point. Sri Lanka could not end the civil distress through democratic means. The LTTE was opposed to any talks unless the state gave up on military operations, while the Sri Lankan state ruled out the prospects of negotiated settlement, despite intermittent offerings of the olive branch to the Tamil Tigers, in the absence of demilitarization by the LTTE cadres. The long and acrimonious political history of the civil conflict is testimony to the many structural distortions of an apparently democratic polity. Sri Lanka, despite all the violence that it suffered from, performed commendably well on both growth and human development indicators compared to other South Asian states and achieved a certain level of governance that can hardly be described as deficient. Nevertheless, violence spoiled its beautiful landscape, and inter-community trust almost decayed over the years. The Mahinda Rajapaksa-led government ultimately crushed the LTTE militarily, partly because of the internal decay of the LTTE, which had degenerated into a dictatorial and mindlessly violent entity, becoming oppressive upon the very members of the community that guaranteed its sustenance. However, the sheer brutality of the exercise revealed the capacity of an apparently democratic state to inflict violence upon a section of its people with an unprecedented viciousness that took away their basic rights.

However, as it often happens in the messy politics of the sub-continent, the defeat and destruction of the LTTE and the concomitant emasculation of Tamil rights failed to guarantee unlimited political dividends to Rajapaksa. In January 2015, Maithripala Sirisena succeeded in defeating the strongman and in the parliamentary elections that followed, the Sri Lanka Freedom Party (SLFP) and the United National Party (UNP), the country's two major Sinhala-Buddhist parties, were victorious and put up a coalition government. The new government pursued a reformist agenda in economics, politics and administration and sought to correct some of the excesses and wrongdoings of the previous regime. Fighting corruption and bringing powerful but corrupt politicians to justice was also one of its leading goals, as was mending frayed ties with India. The promise and performance of that enterprise do not concern us. The most important task before the state remained in creating better inter-ethnic ties by investing liberally in social capital and political trust to restore justice within the political process. In September 2015, the Sirisena announced the four basic pillars of its transitional justice process: a judicial mechanism, a truth commission, offices to deal with disappearances and remuneration.[30]

However, these promises have hardly materialized in the future. The regime has succumbed to hesitations and equivocations and, instead of going against the war criminals, has begun to accommodate them to bolster the government's acceptability among the Sinhala Buddhist population. The same old pattern thus seems to reappear tragically on the island. The Tamils continue to be relegated further, causing bitterness and more alienation and encouraging the radical youth to revive the politics of the gun. Democracy in Sri Lanka, therefore, has failed in creating an inclusive project of aligning the Sinhala and the Tamil people into a shared political contract whereby they can live together with fairness, equality, liberty and dignity. The Sri Lankan case is an unfortunate one. It reveals the limits of democratic politics in clear terms. It shows that moderate levels of economic success and good capacity for governance may not translate into inter-community justice and peace, and violence may come to dominate the terms of political discourse despite the continuity of formal democratic institutions. Can Sri Lanka democratically renegotiate the terms of its ethnic divergence? If the past is any indicator, the reasons for optimism seem limited.

Bangladesh

Despite a history of junta takeover, democracy in Bangladesh has tended to become stronger over time and matured considerably. Since the fall of the military regime of Ershad, the state has sustained a democratic political order, though the polity remains polarized along party lines. Bangladesh, however, faces a new crisis in its democratic career, as the ruling Awami League, led by Prime Minister Shaikh Hasina, refuses to share any worthwhile political space with its opponents, particularly the more conservative Bangladesh Nationalist Party (BNP) led by Begum Khaleda Zia. The tacit political alliance between the Jamat, an Islamist political party, and BNP has substantially contributed to this rift. Critics allege that the Awami League lacks the political will and, more broadly, is pushing the nation towards the eventual collapse of its secular, post-independence democratic tradition by marginalizing the main opposition party, the BNP, and stifling the national political discourse.[31]

The matter cuts much deeper. Bangladesh has witnessed virtually a trial over its political identity as the rift between the secular cum liberal brand of nationalism and the Islamist forces have widened as never before. Many Awami Leaguers maintain that sharing political space with their opponents would mean vindicating a national identity that is dangerously false and is contrary to the goals of the party. The hysteria over the issue of criminal justice against Jamati leaders accused of having committed war crimes during the 1971 liberation war is a case in point. While the government succeeded in hanging some of these men, the action was often portrayed negatively by others who accused Prime Minister Sheikh Hasina of seeking a personal vendetta rather than unleashing a principled war against forces of religious extremism. In fact, the Shahbagh protests in 2013 rocked Bangladesh, which not only highlighted the traditional divide between secularists and Islamists but also revealed the complex relations among secular groups and the Awami League.[32] As the movement evolved, on the historic martyr's day of 21 February 2013, the organizers raised a six-point demand that called for a blanket banning and trial of religious political parties. Though the Shahbag movement started as a popular mass movement with the sole demand of justice for the convicted war criminals, it gradually evolved into a larger political discourse that pitted different groups against each other.

Post-Shahbagh, Bangladeshi politics suffered some setbacks as the Awami League refused to concede to demands by other political parties to hand over power to a caretaker government to facilitate fair elections. As a result, the BNP stayed away from the elections, and the Awami League won most seats unilaterally. While critics read authoritarianism and wanton corruption as the chief causes of this intransigence on the part of the ruling party, they also mentioned the league's proximity to India and New Delhi's unconditional support of Hasina as a major factor that encouraged the league to go ahead with its plans. Democratic norms have thus been weakened considerably in Bangladesh, and the state remains politically divided over the dual base of its national identity.

More critically, Bangladesh is suffering from religious extremism and violence that has led to a spate of brutal killings of secular and atheist bloggers and academics at the hands of unknown religious extremists. These extremists often claim allegiance to the politics of the Islamic State of Iraq and the Levant, also known as the Islamic State of Iraq and Syria (ISIS). The Bangladeshi government, however, claimed that many of these cases were the makings of the local terror outfits. According to a BBC report, over twenty people – including secular writers and bloggers, professors, members of religious minorities and two foreigners – have lost their lives in attacks allegedly carried out by Islamist militants since 2013.[33] The fact is that the Awami League government has done precious little to curb this extremism. As Sumit Ganguly perceptibly points out,

> Worse still, the present regime, in denial about religious extremism, finds this trend to be politically expedient. The ostensible need for sweeping powers to curb such religious violence enables the regime to aggrandize its political power further. If extremist movements are not curbed, Bangladesh could well become an epicenter for Islamic radicalism.[34]

For most commentators, Bangladesh's strange paralysis in coping with this rising challenge of religious extremism is largely due to a fractured political space that has made honest criticism of the establishment virtually illegitimate. For the state, attempts to go against the religious forces must be dealt with using extreme caution so that extremists do not win public sympathy.[35] The fact of the matter is despite laudable achievements on many fronts, political polarization is growing in Bangladesh, and there is little evidence to show that democracy would ipso facto be a panacea for the nation's growing problems.

Conclusion

This chapter has argued that the future of South Asia in the coming decade and a half hinges on what happens to democracy and democratization. The fact that democratization has gathered traction in the sub-continent is a palpable fact. It has brought people more directly into politics, and the ruling elites can no longer ignore their expectations and demands. However, the prospects of democracy remain mixed in South Asia. There are not only major structural constraints that limit the consolidation of democratic norms but more critically, most South Asian societies have not pledged themselves to the democratic determination. In other words, democratic politics and illiberal societies have gone hand in hand in South Asia, thereby putting major challenges in their way.

Primarily, this overview finds that the primordial attachments have adapted themselves well to the imperatives of political democracy and thus categories like caste, religion and ethnic identity have impinged heavily upon the democratization process. Democracy is found to be weak in meeting the aspirations of the newly empowered classes, though on balance, its record is not worse than those of other forms of government that the sub-continent has witnessed. Democratic institutions have largely remained weak in South Asia and have not kept pace with the mobility of classes and social groups.

The article also finds that while most South Asian states have enjoyed a rich democratic dividend since 2005, this has not necessarily transformed their fundamental social and political challenges. Democratization has not changed Pakistan's abnormal security dilemma or reduced ethnic domination in Sri Lanka or repaired political fractures in Bangladesh. Moreover, this chapter has also shown that democratization and violence are not antithetical entities in South Asia. The state has, therefore, often acted with a heavy hand, and detractors have also taken up arms to realize their aims. Religious extremism in Pakistan, India, and Bangladesh and ethnic intolerance in Sri Lanka have weakened the democracy in these states. More significantly, democratic politics has neither propelled peace nor promoted regionalism in the sub-continent.

While such trends appear to depict democracy in rather negative terms, the gains have also been formidable. Most critically, democracy has ushered in a new politics of mobilization in South Asia that has seriously questioned the ability of the traditional elites to dictate the political future of their constituencies, unilaterally. It is this churning, more than anything else, that holds the promise of a new politics of transformation in South Asia. However, 2030 may not be the appropriate timeline for this to happen. The democratization of the sub-continent has ensured the arrival of the subaltern. Moreover, it is the subaltern that will decide the political course we eventually take. Whether they change the spatial identity of the sub-continent or reinforce the old patterns remains to be seen.

Notes

1 We need to delve into the complex issues of identities and connections and come to terms with the process that saw the fluid and non-enumerative spaces being gradually replaced by fixed boundaries of the modern state. Modernity and nationalism transformed the collective identities of the past, and the advent of the post-colonial states valorized territoriality as an absolute value. Yet, territorial identities remain historically and sociologically vulnerable in the sub-continent, and though its political power remains

uncontested, the challenges to its legitimacy have been endemic. It is this peculiar ferment of the old and the new, the cognitive apparatus of the modern state raked against the strange longevity of pre-modern categories, and the claims of exclusivist sovereignty opposed by increasingly evident shared vulnerabilities that produces the dialectics of South Asia as a region. So far, the power-speak of territorial nationalism has trumped both the claims of pre-modern, fluid social identities and the growing insecurities of an irreversible modernity that cannot be contained within the cartographic certainties of a territorialized order.

2 Amita Shastri, "The Post-Colonial States of South Asia: Democracy, Identity, Development and Security", in Amita Shastri and A. Jayaratanam Wilson (eds.), *The Post-Colonial States of South Asia: Democracy, Identity, Development and Security*, Surrey: Curzon Press, 2001.

3 For details, see Ayesha Jalal, *Contemporary South Asia: Democracy and Authoritarianism in South Asia*, Cambridge: Cambridge University Press, 1995. For an opposite view, see Maya Chadda, *Building Democracy in South Asia: India, Nepal, Pakistan*, New Delhi:Vistaar Publications, 2000.

4 For details, see Stanley A. Kochanek and Robert L. Hardgrave, *India: Government and Politics in a Developing Nation*, Boston, MA:Wadsworth Publishing Co., 2006.

5 Maya Chadda distinguishes between democracy and democratization. In her own words, "Democratization is interpreted as democratic integration of a nation's diverse parts into a single political community through free and regular political contests." See Chadda, n.3, p. 18. She insists that the tasks of democratization vary according to the stage of the process. For transitional democracies like Pakistan and Nepal – incidentally, neither are democracies any longer – the task is to protect the original bargain while gradually expanding its support base. For consolidated democracies like India, the need is to perfect conflict-diffusing bargains vis-à-vis their ascriptive constituencies.

6 Sucheta Ghosh, Prothoma Rai Choudhury and Anindyo J. Majumdar, "South Asia: Recent Trends in Research", in A.J. Majumdar and Shibashis Chatterjee (eds.), *Understanding Global Politics: Issues and Trends*, New Delhi: Lancer's Books, 2004, pp. 508–509.

7 Shastri and Wilson, n.2, p. 2.

8 Jalal, n.3, p. 3.

9 Shastri and Wilson, n.2, p. 3.

10 The claims of representation need not be satisfied by an authoritarian regime. However, to the extent such claims remain unaddressed, the danger against the stability/continuity of the system accumulates. If stability is accorded a higher value, then the issue of representation cannot be ignored in the long run. Therefore, a protracted representational deficit creates an indirect opportunity for democratization.

11 Jalal, n.3, p. 3.

12 Shastri and Wilson, n.2, p. 3.

13 Mustapha Kamal Pasha, "Security as Hegemony", *Alternatives*, vol.21, no.3 July–September 1996, pp. 283–302.

14 Harihar Bhattacharya, "Internal Threats to Security: Indian Federalism and the Accommodation of Ethno-Religious Identity in India", in Purusottam Bhattacharya, Tridib Chakraborti and Shibashis Chatterjee (eds.), *Anatomy of Fear: Essays on India's Security*, New Delhi: Lancer's Books, 2004, p. 95.

15 Ranabir Samaddar, *A Biography of the Indian Nation, 1947–1997*, New Delhi: Sage, 2001, p. 138.

16 For the most comprehensive treatment of the subject, see Rajeev Bhargava, *Secularism and Its Critics* (Themes in Politics Series), New Delhi: Oxford University Press, 2005.

17 Swarna Rajagopalan, *State and Nation in South Asia*, Colorado: Lynne Rienner, Boulder, 2001, p. 17.

18 For details, see D. Hugh Evans, "Bangladesh: Unsteady Democracy", in Shastri and Wilson, n.2, pp. 69–87.

19 Rajni Kothari, *Politics and the People: In Search of a Humane India*, New Delhi: New Horizons Press, 1989, p. 37.

20 Stephen Philip Cohen, *The Idea of Pakistan*, New Delhi: Oxford University Press, 2004, p. 86.
21 Anuradha Mitra Chenoy, *Militarism and Women in South Asia*, New Delhi: Kali for Women, 2002, p. 83.
22 For a detailed discussion, see Sumit Ganguly, *The Deadly Impasse: Indo-Pakistani Relations at the Dawn of a New Century*, Cambridge: Cambridge University Press, 2016, pp. 105–120.
23 T.V. Paul, *The Warrior State: Pakistan in the Contemporary World*, New Delhi: Random House India, 2014.
24 CSDS, SDSA Team, "Institutions and People", in *State of Democracy in South Asia*, New Delhi: Oxford University Press, 2008, p. 60.
25 *Ibid*, p. 61.
26 Niaz Murtaza, "Is This Democracy?" *Dawn*, 11 October 2015, see www.dawn.com/news/1212281(Accessed on 8 August 2018).
27 Touqir Hussain, "Understanding Democracy in Pakistan", *Criterion Quarterly*, 25 January 2014, see www.criterion-quarterly.com/understanding-democracy-in-pakistan/ (Accessed on 14 August 2018).
28 See, Jayadeva Uyangoda, "Ethnic Conflict and the Civil War in Sri Lanka", in Paul R. Brass (ed.), *Routledge Handbook of South Asian Politics: India, Pakistan, Bangladesh, Sri Lanka, and Nepal*, London: Routledge, 2010, pp. 291–302. See also, Sumantra Bose, "Tamil Self-Determination in Sri Lanka", *Economic and Political Weekly*, vol.23, no.39,1994, pp. 2537–2539.
29 Sandra Destradi, "India and the Civil War in Sri Lanka: On the Failures of Regional Conflict Management in South Asia", GIGA Research Programme:Violence and Security, no. 154, December 2010, see www.giga-hamburg.de/en/system/files/publications/wp154_destradi.pdf(Accessed on 8 July 2018).
30 Dibbert Taylor, "Sri Lanka, Lost in Transition: Its Uneven Progress Towards Democracy", *Foreign Affairs*, 21 April 2016, see www.foreignaffairs.com/articles/sri-lanka/2016-04-21/sri-lanka-lost-transition(Accessed on 6 September 2018).
31 Simon Tisdall, "Bangladesh's Pluralism Is at Risk If Sheikh Hasina Does Not Stop Extremists", *The Guardian*, 26 April 2016, see www.theguardian.com/world/2016/apr/26/bangladesh-democracy-risk-sheikh-hasina-stop-extremists-gay-rights-lgbt-murders (Accessed on 22 August 2018).
32 On the Shahbagh protests, see Nadine S. Murshid, "Bangladesh: The Shahbag Uprising-War Crimes and Forgiveness", *Economic and Political Weekly*, vol.48, no.10, 2013, pp. 13–15.
33 "Who Is Behind the Bangladesh Killings?", see www.bbc.com/news/world-asia-34517434 (Accessed on 21 August 2018).
34 Sumit Ganguly, "Bangladesh Accommodates Extremism: Spelling Danger for the Region", *Yale Global Review*, 17 May 2016, see www.fpri.org/article/2016/05/bangladeshs-accommodation-extremism-spells-danger-region/ (Accessed on 11 May 2019).
35 Tisdall, n.31.

7

GLOBALIZATION, RADICALIZATION AND SOUTH ASIA

Bringing people in

Amena Mohsin

Introduction

Globalization and radicalization, the two key words used in this chapter, are perhaps the most widely and commonly used terms in contemporary politics. At the practical level, they touch the everydayness of people's lives. They touch, because they have a totality about them, a totality with bearings on people's lives and living; though the bearings as well as the totality have quite different and distinct characteristics. Globalization is linked to a widening and thickening of relations and connectivity, a process of transforming the world into a global village, supposedly based on liberal ideas of free market, democracy and development. This transformation at one level, despite its totality, is reductionist. It does not adequately factor in the differential levels of economies or the complexities of cultures, religions and identities; more precisely, the totalizing is from above or the developed world. Radicalization, however, may be defined as

> a process in which a person gets indoctrinated by others or self-motivation into a rigid ideology, religious or otherwise, equipped with a set of goals and plans that may eventually lead to extremism, militancy and terrorism aiming at national and international systemic change for governance and regulating human lives.[1]

The systemic change is a common major denominator in both globalization and radicalization; in other words, a contest between two forces, each claiming superiority over the other, may be observed here. However, since in contemporary politics, radicalization is increasingly being associated with organized religion, the terms of contest too are being defined through categories like "rational," "irrational," "secular," and "fundamental." A major caveat, however, remains (i.e., the thrust towards homogenization and hegemonization within the two processes). A major contention of this chapter is that there is a nexus between globalization and the present-day radicalization. Globalization, though professing to be a global force, has a truncated mission and vision; the systemic weaknesses and lapses within the system and those aspired and espoused by the forces of globalization, more precisely "democracy" and "development," give vent to radicalization. This, however, is not to suggest that democracy and development are inappropriate, but the point of contention is the failure of the thrust of globalization to seed in and often address the discontents that these categories are producing through the manner they are being practiced, which, it is argued, is a major contributory factor towards radicalization. Ironically enough, this oversight is in-built within the globalization process, which by its very logic is a homogenizing and hegemonizing force. Taking Bangladesh as a case in point, the chapter examines these processes.

Democracy

The end of the Cold War is often regarded as the point when the Western ideas of liberalism, political and economic, supposedly became the trigger points for the onset of a globalized world. Democracy is one of the parameters whereby a state is viewed as a "modern" state. Democracy, while being the best model of governance to date, despite its limitations, has created several divides and fissures in the post-colonial states. In the context of Bangladesh, like most of the South Asian states, both nationalism and religion are intimately linked to democracy; this linkage has created deep ruptures and divides, providing the space for radicalization to evolve and firm itself, exploiting the sentiments of the aggrieved, vulnerable, excluded and marginalized. Radicalization also breeds itself through creating a distorted narrative or using religion for political ends. Let us examine the nexus between religion and nationalism first.

Religion and nationalism

The modern state predicates itself on the idea of nationalism, which is supposedly a secular and progressive force, but nationalism as it evolved in the post-colonial states closely intertwined itself with religion. Religious symbols have been used most generously to advocate a "secular" ideology of nationalism. The Indian nationalist movement that led to the partition of India is a good instance of this. The Bangladesh nationalist movement, however, was secular in its orientation; it took its seeds from Bengali language and culture. This was a reaction to the overt use of religion by the state of Pakistan in its nation- and state-building process. The present state of Bangladesh then constituted a part of Pakistan known as East Pakistan. Seeds of Bengali nationalism were sown in 1948 in the then East Pakistan, when Mohammad Ali Jinnah, the father of the nation, declared in Dhaka that Urdu shall be the state language of Pakistan. Religion was brought in as an alibi for this construction.

It was alleged that Hinduism influenced Bengali language and culture. Thus, in 1949, the Central Minister for Education openly proposed the introduction of Arabic script for Bengali. It was argued,

> Not only Bengali literature, even the Bengali alphabet is full of idolatry. Each Bengali letter is associated with this or that god or goddess of Hindu pantheon . . . Pakistan and Devanagari script cannot co-exist. It looks like defending the frontier of Pakistan with Bharati soldiers! . . . To ensure a bright and great future for the Bengali language it must be linked up with the Holy Quran . . . Hence the necessity and importance of Arabic script.[2]

The East Bengalis perceived this use of religion as a tool of domination, and to counterpoise this "Islamic" nationalism, a secular nationalism emerged in East Bengal that was militant in its emphasis on the Bengali language and culture. The language movement that continued from 1948 to 1952 acquired an emotional and politicized content for the Bengalis on 21 February 1952 when the Pakistan authorities opened fire on students in Dhaka as they were protesting the imposition of Urdu as the state language, resulting in the deaths of four. By the mid-1960s, the Bengalis had moved on to the demands for economic and political autonomy, as discrimination and domination of the West Pakistani ruling elite over the Bengalis were evident in all spheres of life.[3]

The new state indeed based itself on a secular plank. The constitution of Bangladesh, which was adopted by the Bangladesh parliament on 4 November 1972, in its preamble para 2, accepted "nationalism," "socialism," "democracy" and "secularism" as state principles. In the context of Bangladesh, Sheikh Mujibur Rahman, the father of the nation, defined it in the following way:

> Secularism does not mean the absence of religion. Hindus will observe their religion; Muslims will observe their own; Christians and Buddhists will observe their religions. No one will be allowed to interfere in Other's religions, the people of Bengal do not want any interference in religious matters. Religion cannot be used for political ends.[4]

In order to implement the preceding, Article 12 of the constitution stated,

> The principle of secularism shall be realized by the elimination of: Communalism in all forms; The granting by the state of political status in favor of any religion; The abuse of religion for political purposes; Any discrimination against, or persecution of persons practicing a particular religion.[5]

Article 38 para 2 of the constitution further stated,

> No person shall have the right to form or be a member or otherwise take part in the activities of, any communal or other association or union, which

in the name or on the basis of any religion has for its object, or pursues a political purpose.[6]

As suggested earlier in the construction of nationhood in Pakistan, religion had been used as the main tool of domination of the Bengalis by the Pakistani regime. Again in 1971, the Pakistani regime had employed the rhetoric of religion in carrying out one of the worst genocides of history. Secularism was, therefore, a logical outcome of the Bengali nationalist movement. It would thus appear that the new state was set for a secular start. However, the new state being a modern or nation-state has within its very construction the quest for homogenization, which propels it towards majoritarianism. Nationalism's inherent bias towards the majority community compelled Mujib to compromise on the question of religious secularism. It is indeed true that Bengali nationalism as it emerged in East Bengal was secular in its content, but that was the logical outcome of a situation where the Bengalis were being oppressed in the name of religion. Culture and language at that moment appeared as the symbol of unity among the Bengali population of East Bengal, and it also differentiated them from "Muslim" West Pakistanis. But once the hegemony of West Pakistanis was removed with the creation of Bangladesh, the Muslim identity of Bengalis again came to the fore. India's role during the liberation war of Bangladesh and the Awami League's overt association with India had revived fears of Hindu domination among the general people. Besides, according to a political scientist of Bangladesh, "secularism in Bangladesh did not reflect its societal spirit."[7] Even in 1971, during the course of the war, the people in general sought the intervention of the divine to succeed. The Awami League had won the elections of 1970 on the basis of its six-point formula, which was a programme for the political and economic emancipation of Bengalis. In 1969, the Awami League had pledged that the constitution for Pakistan would be based on the teachings of the Quran and Sunnah.

In most of the post-colonial states, mass media and education (being state controlled) are two important sectors manipulated and used by the state for constructing its brand of nationalism. In Bangladesh, the state-controlled radio and television discontinued the practice of Pakistan days of opening the programmes with recitations from the Holy Quran and substituted it with a programme of "Speaking the Truth" based on secular ethics. Sheikh Mujib discontinued this religious neutrality of the mass media. He adopted the policy of equal opportunity for all religions and ordered citations from the Holy books of Islam, Hinduism, Buddhism and Christianity at the start of the broadcasts by the state radio and television. But the citations from the Hindu holy book and coverage of Hindu religious festivals created a backlash among the Muslims.[8]

In the education sector too, the policy of secularism backfired. During the Pakistan period in the primary and middle stage of education (Class VI to VIII), Islamiat or religious education was made a compulsory subject. After independence, the Education Ministry continued with the same policy. The Mujib government, however, set up an Education Commission in 1972, which submitted its interim report in May 1973. The commission recommended the separation of religion from education. The report, however, was submitted before public opinion on the issue had been elicited through the distribution of questionnaires. The answer to the questionnaires showed that secular education was acceptable to about 21 percent of the most educated society of the people of Bangladesh. And 74.69 percent opined that religious education should be an integral part of general education. This revealed the gap between Bangladesh society and Sheikh Mujib's secular polity.[9] A perceptible shift emerged in Bangladesh politics. On 28 March 1975, Mujib revived the Islamic Academy (banned in 1972) and elevated it to a foundation. The Mujib regime was brought to an abrupt end through his gruesome murder by a group of army officers on the night of 15 August 1975.

With the change of regime, nationalism in Bangladesh also took an explicit turn towards religion. The coup leaders used Islam to secure and to a certain extent legitimize their position. It is, therefore, not surprising that the coup of August 1975 was declared in the name of the "Islamic Republic of Bangladesh." But Khondokar Mushtaque Ahmed (a cabinet member of the Mujib regime), who was appointed as the president by the coup leaders tried to balance the situation. His first public address on 15 August was made in the name of the People's Republic of Bangladesh. The speech, however, was punctuated with Islamic expressions, and it evidenced the course that the Bangladesh polity was about to take. Bangladesh, thus, shook off its garb of secularism; the country was to move on towards Islamization.

Following a number of coups, Major-General Zia ur Rahman (Zia) emerged as the strong man in the government. Zia again used religion to legitimize his rule. He opted for a different model of nationhood for the Bengalis. In this new construction, he chose to emphasize that element of nationalism that would have appealed most to the majority/dominant community at that moment. The element turned out to be religion, and the new model of nationhood came to be known as Bangladeshi nationalism. It needs to be stressed here that this shift was primarily made by Zia to secure as well as consolidate his own position. Moreover, through the adoption of Bangladeshi nationalism, Zia could distinctly disassociate his regime from the Awami League.

The manifesto of the political party floated by Zia, the BNP, defines Bangladeshi nationalism as follows:

> Religious belief and love for religion are a great and imperishable characteristic of the Bangladeshi nation . . . the vast majority of our people are followers of Islam. The fact is well reflected and manifest in our stable and liberal national life.[10]

Proponents of Bangladeshi nationalism point out that Bangladeshi nationalism is territorial; it draws a line between the Bengalis of Bangladesh and Bengalis of West Bengal of India. This gives it a totality, which is precisely lacking in Bengali nationalism. This, however, is a mere exercise in semantics, for Bengali nationalism explicitly had a territorial dimension. Bangladeshi nationalism as it evolved in 1975 was in essence a reassertion of the Muslim identity of the Bengalis in Bangladesh. Accordingly, changes were brought about in the mass media, education sector and the constitution to expedite and legalize the process of this new construction.

The change was apparent first in the mass media. The simultaneous recitals from the holy books of the different religions continued as before. But the time allotted to the reading from the Holy Quran (the holy book of the Muslims) increased from five minutes to fifteen minutes. While no religious citation was made at the closing of the programmes during the Mujib regime, the programmes now closed with recitations from the Quran only. Moreover, quotations from the Quran and Hadith (the Prophetic tradition) were now frequently broadcast between programmes.[11] Education too acquired an Islamic orientation. Islamiat was introduced class I to VIII as a compulsory paper for Muslim students and from class IX to X as an elective subject.

Islamic ideals were incorporated into the constitution. By the proclamation of Order no.1 of 1977, "Bismillah-ar-Rahman-ar-Rahim" (In the name of Allah, the Beneficient, the Merciful) was inserted in the beginning of the constitution above the preamble. Through the same proclamation, Article 8, Clause 1 was substituted by

> the principles of absolute trust and faith in the Almighty Allah, nationalism, democracy and socialism meaning economic and social justice, together with the principles derived from them . . . shall constitute the fundamental principles of state policy.[12]

Thus, the principle of secularism as set forth in Article 8 as one of the state principles was dropped from the constitution. Article 12 through which communal political parties were banned in Bangladesh was also dropped from the constitution. Article 9, which stressed the lingual and cultural unity of Bengali nationalism, was likewise dropped. In place of Bengalis, the citizens of Bangladesh, through Article 6 Clause 2 were now to be known as Bangladeshis. These changes were given effect through the fifth amendment to the constitution on 5 April 1977.

Changes were apparent in administrative policies as well. The second parliament of Bangladesh met on 21 May 1979. It started its session with recitation from the Quran only, whereas previously citations were made from the holy books of all the religions. Zia also encouraged the use of certain non-Bengali words and slogans. The Bengali slogan "Joy Bangla," which was akin to the Indian slogan "Jai Hind," was replaced by "Bangladesh Zindabad" (*Zindabad* is an Urdu word which means "long live"), which is closer to "Pakistan Zindabad." Friday, a holy day for the Muslims, was declared a half holiday. These measures helped Zia to consolidate his power base, for Mujib had been accused of being too close to India. The pro-Islamic leanings were interpreted as a distancing of the country, which has a predominantly Muslim population from "Hindu India." The policies, therefore, were taken to please the majority community in Bangladesh. This entrenched the hegemony of Bengali Muslims, for under the new brand of nationalism of the Bengalis, along with Islam, the Bengali cultural heritage too was patronized. Zia had based his Bangladeshi nationalism on the following elements: race, the war of independence, the Bengali language, culture, religion, land (geographical area) and economy.

Zia was assassinated in May 1981 by a group of army officers. The death of Zia brought another change in the contours of state nationalism; from the "liberal Islamic nationalism" of Zia, it moved towards "Islamic nationalism" under General H.M. Ershad (Ershad), who assumed power through a bloodless coup in March 1982 by overthrowing the elected BNP government of Justice Abdus Sattar.

Ershad accepted the Bangladeshi model of nationhood but made it more rigid and totalitarian by giving it a totally Islamic orientation. This move was ostensibly taken to secure and legitimize his own power base, for unlike Zia, he was not a freedom fighter; more important, he was in general considered to be a usurper to power. He de-emphasized the "Bengaliness" (unlike Zia) of the Bangladeshi nationalism and instead attempted to consolidate the Islamic contours of this model of nationalism. The very epitome of secular Bengali nationalism was given an Islamic twist by him on 21 February. In early 1983, he declared that the drawing of "Alpana" (painted designs) at the premises of the Shaheed Minar was an un-Islamic practice and should be substituted with recitations from the Holy Quran. Referring to the significance of the day, he declared, "this time the movement is for the establishment of an Islamic state."[13] This stand negated the very spirit of the day, as it symbolized the struggle of Bengalis to fight the hegemony of West Pakistanis in the name of Islam. The policy could not be implemented because of strong opposition from the entire Bengali community, which cherished its Bengali heritage as much as it cherished its religious beliefs. But it did suggest the course that the polity was about to take. Ershad based his policy of Islamization on two planks: (a) mosque-centred society and (b) Islam as the state religion.

(a) Mosque-centred society: In 1986, Ershad raised the slogan of building a mosque-centred society in Bangladesh. The government officially encouraged the grant of funds to mosques. The government also encouraged foreign assistance for the development of mosques. He made it a regular practice to address the Friday congregations at different mosques. He regularly visited different Pirs (Muslim religious leaders).

(b) Islam as a state religion: Through the eighth amendment to the constitution of Bangladesh on 7 June 1988, Islam was declared as the state religion of Bangladesh (Article 2, Clause A) with the provision that other religions may be practiced in peace and harmony in the Republic.[14] Islam thus was adopted as a cardinal feature of Bengali's nationalism. Ershad was using Islam to consolidate his position·

Ershad also attempted to bring about changes in the education sector. In 1983, he announced that along with Islamiat, Arabic (the language of the Quran) too would be studied as a compulsory subject. This again could not be implemented because of opposition from the students and political parties. He, however, encouraged

Madrasah (Islamic schools) education and put it on par with the corresponding level of general education. The government also introduced an imam (Muslim religious teacher) training programme in 1979. Its objective was to encourage imams to engage themselves in national development efforts.

Ershad was ousted from office in December 1990 through a popular uprising against him in which all the political parties of the country participated. This opposition, however, was not based on any ideological contention. The issues involved were his usurpation of power from a civilian regime and widespread corruption at all levels. The political parties had agitated for his ouster from power and restoration of democracy in the country. This, however, was a contest among the Bengali elites for securing as well as consolidating their own power. It became evident in the election of 1991, when all the major political parties made a liberal use of religious symbols. The Awami League, long considered to be the champion of secular Bengali nationalism, also resorted to the manipulation of religious symbols. Even the Communist Party held religious gatherings in its office premises. These moves attest to the bias of these parties towards the majority/dominant community.

It also created the "minority" question; not only the Bengali Hindus but also the Ahmediyas and Qadiyanis are under attack today largely because of these constitutional changes. One, however, needs to keep in mind the context that the Awami League, during its first tenure in office following the constitutional change, could not revert back to a secular constitution mainly because of electoral politics. However, what is interesting and a paradox is that the Awami League has annulled the fifth amendment to the constitution, which had changed the secular character of the state; it has reverted back to the constitution of 1972 with secularism as one of the fundamental state principles, yet it has retained Islam as the state religion and Bismillah ir Rahmanir Rahim in the beginning of the preamble of the constitution. Retaining Islam as the state religion and yet declaring the state to be secular is a fundamental contradiction. Such is the arithmetic of state politics or majoritarian democracy, which is in favour of majority. This becomes problematic for the minority communities, since no constitutional safeguards have been provided for them, and there is no provision of proportional representation; nor are there reserved seats for them.

The rise of Jamaat in the political arena is often regarded as a contributory factor towards the politics of polarization. One would recall here that the Awami League had formed an alliance with the Jamaat in 1994–96 to oust the then BNP regime. True, it had not made them a ruling alliance partner, like the BNP regime, but the significance of an alliance to oust a regime cannot be understated. One, therefore, seriously needs to ponder at the dividing lines, is secularism versus fundamentalism the issue, or is it merely a matter of the use of religion for political expediency and contestations over power.

Religion and politics

Bangladesh politics have come to a defining moment. The politicization within politics, the use of religion in the name of "secular" politics and the politics of ownership of people's issues like the liberation war of Bangladesh and the trial of the war criminals of 1971 for crimes against humanity by political parties for their parochial interests have finally brought the country to a moment of serious soul searching and reckoning. On 5 February 2013, the country witnessed the rise of people's power in the heart of the capital city Dhaka in the Shahbagh area. This later came to be popularly known as the Shahbagh Square. This began as the protest of a group of youth later joined by a large section of people to protest the verdict given to an alleged war criminal, Qader Mollah, by the International War Crimes Tribunal (ICT). The protestors alleged that the regime in power, the Awami League had made compromises with the Jamaat e Islam, Bangladesh. The alleged criminal, according to the protestors, was given a much-too-lenient punishment in proportion to his alleged crimes, since he was a top leader of the Jamaat; the latter, the following discussion would show, has occupied an important role in Bangladesh's electoral politics. The demands of the movement expanded to calls for banning of the Jamaat and its student wing, Shibir, to the banning of all religious-based political parties. The movement's most popular slogan was *Fashi chara rae nai* (no verdict other than death by hanging). The critical dividing line emerged as the ruling party gave its support to the protestors, and the government machinery was orchestrated to protect the movement. Amendments were brought about in the ICT laws with retrospective effect, which gave the right to appeal the verdict to the state as well, which was the complainant. This right was previously non-existent in the tribunal procedures. There were allegations and dissatisfaction within various sections of the civil society about the procedural strengths of the ICT. The major opposition party, the BNP, had consistently questioned the neutrality and procedural mechanisms of the tribunal, which the government labeled as opposition to the trial of the war crimes. This labeling extended to the organizations and civil society members as well who questioned the procedural weaknesses or critiqued the government on any issue ranging from corruption to misgovernance. This "ownership" of a people's issue by the party in power is indeed unfortunate and, this chapter argues, is a major tool for electoral purposes. The major opposition, the BNP, initially gave its support but found itself in a dilemma, since Jamaat is a major alliance partner of the BNP. This strategic alliance, as argued by the BNP for electoral purposes, sharpened the polarizations existing in Bangladesh politics.

The Shahabagh Square had projected itself as a secular force, branding those who did not join it or questioned its neutrality as communal and anti-liberation forces. This politics of labeling and drawing lines between pro-liberation and anti-liberation wrecked the country and polarized the media and the civil society. The fundamentalism and intolerance inherent within secularism was quite open. To complicate the issue of religion versus secularism, a group of activists on social media, popularly known as bloggers, allegedly resorted to writings in the blogs defaming Prophet Mohammad (pbuh), the prophet of Islam. Bangladesh is a predominantly Muslim country with more than eighty per cent of the population being Muslim. An organization which called itself a social movement, Hefazate Islam (protectors of Islam), which had earlier emerged in 2010 in the wake of the government policy on women, was propelled into the forefront with demands for the death by hanging of the bloggers, labeling them as "nastik" or atheists. It put forward a thirteen-point demand, which included, among other things, the demand for turning the state of Bangladesh into an Islamic state and implementation of the Islamic laws. Women's movement and rights were to be restricted and defined by them according to what they perceived to be Islamic. Religious fanaticism flared up.

The major opposition BNP gave its support to the movement despite being an electoral political party and fully cognizant of the fact that the demands of the movement were unrealizable and undemocratic, to say the least. This is demonstrative of the politics for power, bereft of any idealism or vision. The government initially tried to make compromises with the Hefazat. It allowed the Hefazat to hold two meetings in Motijheel, the commercial heart of the capital, Dhaka. The first meeting, held on 5 April 2013, was relatively peaceful, and they put forward their thirteen-point demand and gave a month-long ultimatum to the government to fulfill those demands. The second programme, on 5 May, exactly a month later, was supposed to be a blockade of Dhaka city, but quite surprisingly, it turned into a mammoth meeting, again in the same venue. It was crushed with high-handedness in the early hours of 6 April, through the deployment of security forces, like the RAB (Rapid Action Battalion), the BGB (Bangladesh Border Guards). The government alleged that the organizers had planned to topple the regime in connivance with the opposition, the BNP-Jamaat. It may be noted that the leader of the opposition, Khaleda Zia, had openly given her support to the Hefazat and had asked her party to stand by the Hefazat people.

Controversy exists on the death total, with the government putting the figure at fourteen and the opposition at 2,500. The truth perhaps will remain unearthed or again a matter of the politics of numbers. However, the major casualty apart from those who lost their lives is the institutionalization of democracy. The Shahbagh and Hefazat also projected an important class dimension. The Hefazat crowd was constituted mostly of young madrassah students, many of whom came from economically depressed classes and had come to Dhaka perhaps for the first time with the impression that Islam was in danger and needed to be protected as the name *HefazateIslam* (i.e., protection of Islam) suggests. The Shahbagh crowd, in contrast, was constituted mostly of middle-class people.

It is an irony that a country that was born out of a movement based on cultural autonomy today finds itself boxed into boxes, which are increasingly becoming militant and violent. The question that emerges is when do politics resort to these shadowy channels? Bangladesh today is caught in a quagmire of rising radicalization, where not only are bloggers being labeled as atheists and targeted for killing but also people publishing materials with dissenting views on religion are being hacked to death. Religious preachers with Sufi orientation, minorities and people with different sexual orientations are being hacked to death. The regime in power has resorted to the trope of secular versus fundamentalist, pro-liberation versus anti-liberation and nationalism. It is critical to note here the contradiction: while, on the one hand, the opposition is being blamed for the rising radicalization and killings, on the other hand, the regime has explicitly stated that it is not going to stand by people who write against religion.

The government has consistently blamed the opposition BNP-Jamaat and has also accused it of conspiracy theories to damage the image of the country, which is fast developing into a middle-income county. The opposition too blames the party in power for the situation. After each killing, ISIS or some other terrorist outfit like al Qaeda takes responsibility. A debate today is raging in Bangladesh on the presence of terrorist outfits in Bangladesh, with the government claiming that there are no external terrorist outfits in Bangladesh and these killings are being committed by "home-grown terrorists," linking them to the BNP-Jamaat, the opposition. The irony is that in a politically stable environment, the issue should not revolve around the existence of external terrorists; rather, it should focus on the existence of terrorists and a concerted and united effort to counter and nab them. But sadly, in this politics of denial, blame and counter-blame, the radical forces are being empowered. It needs to be emphasized that terrorism is a global phenomenon today; it is an ideological battle which seeks to battle out what it regards as "impure" or "polluted" and impose its own version of Islam and world order that it considers to be "pure" and "authentic." This is a global battle, a tool of homogenization and hegemonization; it endeavours to be a globalizing force, so the argument that the acts are committed by homegrown terrorists does not hold much ground, since the ideology is a transnational one. The polarizations and divides of "secular" politics give vent to radicalization in Bangladesh. This has impacted very negatively on the spaces for debates, discussions and dissent, which are fundamental for democracy to sustain itself. The alternative that has emerged is "elected" authoritarianism. With elections being increasingly manipulated and the open use of muscle and money, the phrase *free and fair elections* has turned into a myth. The global powers, in their declared war on terror, on the one hand, call for inclusive democracy and, on the other, continue to work with "elected" but non-democratic regimes for their own economic and strategic interests. These policies are self-defeating. The rising death tolls in the hands of the radical forces bear this out.

Globalization and development

Globalization has impacted upon the developing countries in more fundamental and crucial ways than is apparently discernible. At a very critical level, it has put the state under tremendous stress. On the one hand, through the opening up of markets, information, ideas and technology, it has appropriated much sovereignty from the state; on the other hand, being a pro-rich and pro-technology force, it has raised fundamental questions: If the developing world can meet the challenges and flow with the flows of globalization, what does it entail for the common people? Is it opening up or shrinking spaces for them? And then, how does it impact upon the capabilities of the state? In the context of Bangladesh, one can suggest that it has impacted upon the poor, the women and the indigenous people negatively.

The structural adjustment policies have shrunk the spaces for them, induced forced migration and taken them away from their traditional means of livelihood. It has also increased violence against women, mainly for two reasons: First, loss of livelihood impacts upon women more severely, since they have to take care of the family, and it has been observed that in such situations, men become more violent and take out their frustration on women. Second, when women go out in search of work under such circumstances, often, they are physically and sexually assaulted, and they also become the victims of fatwa (religious decrees). Women working in the garments sector provide a good instance of the latter.

Scarcity of livelihood and aspirations, as well opportunities for a better livelihood, have led to the outmigration of a significant portion and section, mostly the underprivileged, to the oil-rich Middle East countries for their livelihood. This connectivity not only brings in economic changes; the cultural milieu of the migrant is also affected. One of the major consequences has been the import of Wahabism, or orthodox Islam. They also contribute financially to Quomi Madrassahs, where education is provided free of cost to mainly poor children. The curriculum is based on the orthodox teachings of scriptures with no reference to the context. This education does not prepare them for the job market. It is no surprise then that the education they have received gives them a worldview which is quite different from the mainstream hegemonic group's. The sense of marginalization and alienation often takes the form of identity politics, which often are sought in religion. What the West regards as "fundamentalism" is, according to them, their authentic identity, and to establish this identity, which is not only about this world but largely involves the afterworld as well, they are radicalized into fighting battles cloaked in the Islamic terminology, jihad, to attain their objective of setting up a pure and authentic system free from the present corrupt system. According to them, if they succeed, they will set up Allah's rule, and if they die, then they will go to heaven. Financially, these groups are very strong. They have global networks of business and financing, which are part of the present global economic transactions. The families of the deceased are taken care of by the terrorist organizations. This financial support, along with the belief of fighting for a just cause and the promise of heaven, creates among the groups who are disgruntled either economically, politically or even ideologically an imagined community of the pure and authentic people. This time, it is religion or a particular narrative of religion that provides fodder to them.

In 2015, the world was shocked by the discovery of mass graves along the border of Thailand; it also witnessed thousands of boat people floating in the Indian Ocean. Most of them were Rohingya refugees from Myanmar and people from Bangladesh seeking jobs in Malaysia and Thailand. The developed countries, like Australia, closed their doors to this floating population of not only men but also women and children. It is notable that little was said about the human rights of these people. A big racket was involved in this exploitative business, which involved top-level military and political officials from Myanmar, Thailand and Bangladesh. But what is most distressing is that again the issue was being debated around the "image problem" of the country like the terrorism issue and also the networks; little was being said or debated around what propelled or forced the people to take these risks. It was not jihad or promise of a heavenly afterworld; it was their survival in this world, a very secular issue of livelihood. The plight of the Bangladeshi migrant workers in Malaysia is frequently reported in newspapers. They are often required to do the dirty and dangerous jobs on plantations that the locals will not do. What the developed world has forgotten is the simple truth that their development is based on the exploitation and labour of the marginalized and the poor. While the Rohingya refugees are being dubbed as terrorists, there is little questioning of the state-sponsored terrorism in Myanmar which is denying citizenship to the Rohingyas. Myanmar is increasingly being integrated into the global system because of its economic and strategic resources. It is "development" devoid of humaneness, which is uprooting people; to root themselves, the uprooted often find a niche and freedom in religion. It also provides them with an identity and a sense of belonging in a community. The idea of Islamic brotherhood provides them with a sense of equality and dignity that the modern competitive development paradigms deny them. The inequalities created by these paradigms and models provide breeding materials for radicalization. Bangladeshi workers in Singapore have been deported for allegedly planning terrorist activities.[15] Bangladesh is regarded as an emerging tiger in Asia, fast growing into a middle-income country; yet it is a country which is producing "boat people" and radicals. Political and development pundits need to pause and ponder the myth of the statistics and factor in the human element within this development paradigm.

Globalization and digitalization

Globalization has resulted in the death of distance. A major component of it is the fast-track development of technology, which has brought information to the very door of many people. Technology has made an enormous contribution to the economic development and contributed positively to rights and social movements. Social media has created a new space where one might argue people's power is projected quite effectively. A local issue, within minutes, turns into a global phenomenon. The Arab Spring bears this out. The Shahbagh Square is also a testimony to this rising power of technology. However, it is notable that the present generation of terrorists is also making extensive use of social media to propagate their vision and mission. Through blogs and literature, they are trying to project a worldview which is "pure" and "authentic." ISIS, largely because of the economic resources under its control, is able to provide economic incentives to the people who join the group. In a politically authoritarian and corrupt system where mass of the people are starved for their daily livelihood, ISIS often appears like an oasis. To the European youth who have joined it, it provides them with a sense of mission and adventurism. ISIS projects pictures of veiled women receiving gun training; these images carry a different message to many of the vulnerable and often alienated or aggrieved women and youth in Europe, where Islam has often been labeled as a backward medieval religion. As argued earlier, radicalization is a process. It is a process of immersion and emersion, of internalization of values and of commitment. Digitalization has provided an important tool for the process.

Bringing people in

The emergence of radicalized terrorist groups under the garb of Islam in Bangladesh politics is indeed alarming. Bangladesh has been experiencing a wave of terrorist activities. These acts, carried out in the name of Islamic revivalism and puritanism, have literally besieged the state and the people. But then why and how did we reach this point? Pundits and scholars have given various explanations. Madrasah and madrasah education is blamed for this. While there is some truth to it in view of the parochial nature of the curriculum of the Quomi madrasah, one needs to be mindful that it is not only madrasah education but secular education too that is highly fundamentalist and intolerant. The security discourses that the latter produces are trapped within the statist realist paradigm. The state controls the public education system, which is highly nationalistic and, in the context of Bangladesh, given its history of polarization, is regime-centric as well. The political culture of intolerance only heightens the level of intolerance.

Poverty and deprivation are often cited as factors for this rise, but one must not forget that affluence is also associated with it. The funders and sponsors of these activities belong to the affluent class; the sheer organization planning and the need for arms to carry these out require a handsome amount of money. Globalization is another contributory factor. It is a hegemonic and homogenizing force. To counter these forces, religion often is used as a counter-hegemonic force. The worldwide Islam bashing following 9/11 is an important element giving rise to religious militancy. The Wahhabi connection, or a puritan version of Islamism, is also said to be reproducing militancy in the name of religion. Proliferation of small arms adds and gives newer dimensions to terror activities.[16] What is most ironic and mind-boggling in the Bangladesh context in the backdrop of such widespread violence is the continuous lack of understanding between the two major political parties on the need for a consensus and unity; this only creates the space for and strengthens the terrorists and their activities. At this point, the author argues that to reimagine South Asia, we need to reimagine the nation-state, which perhaps has not been adequately imagined. This reimagination will require citizens' spaces as active citizens, not merely as a political denominator.

Citizens' spaces

Modernity is apparently a rational liberal force, but it can be oppressive and conservative as well. The latter is well reflected in the case of post-colonial societies, which have not resolved the tension between primordial and civil ties, and the political actors manipulate and at times exacerbate these for their political interests –in the Bangladesh case, the move away from a secular ideology to a so-called religious ideology. The ideologies of nationalism and democracy were used by the political elite to further their parochial interests, and the state moved towards structures and institutions which increasingly intruded on the private and public spheres of individuals' lives. This overarching state shrank the spaces for democratic dissent in a peaceful and democratic manner. Social justice, equity and citizen's rights became the greatest casualties.

But the autocracy of the state, it is argued, is under challenge today both from within and without through citizens' initiatives. Rights groups have transcended boundaries, and demands for a cohesive, participatory, democratic and just system are being voiced. This, it is argued, is expected to give way to new structures, though the journey towards it might seem arduous at the moment. The point to be noted here is that it is the excluded and the vulnerable that challenge structures. A major emphasis of the movements is the demand of the people for their rights as citizens of the state. The idea of citizenship, the accountability and responsibility of the state towards them, is being flagged very strongly. The notion of justice is inextricably linked to the rights concept. In other words, the various rights movements are demanding a just and inclusive system. Pluralism, multiculturalism, the interconnectivity between the local and the global have given a different culture and voice to the people's movements in post-colonial states. One may even argue that nationalism has lived its day, and it is time to carve out a post-national citizens' state.

Citizenship, however, is a relatively neutral concept and does not evoke emotions like the nation, which is often seen as primordial. Citizenship is a civic concept. Rights and duties are integral to it. It, however, needs to be emphasized here that though state constitutions give equal rights to citizens, the real situation is quite different. In Bangladesh, women's rights have been curtailed through the exercise of personal laws, which privileges men. In the case of ethnic minorities, the non-recognition of their customary laws relegates them to a secondary status, and many of their rights, especially those pertaining to economic rights (i.e., the right to livelihood) have been violated through the exercise of the equal rights of citizens, once again privileging the dominant community. A citizen state, it is suggested here, while conferring equal rights and uniform laws for its entire citizenry, must respect the diversities within and the special needs of its various communities.

The exclusions and violence associated with majoritarian democracy are well reflected in Bangladesh. This strongly suggests the need for the democratization of political parties and the electoral process. Apart from making the registration of political parties mandatory; nomination to minority communities and women should also be made mandatory. Like reserved seats for women, there should be reserved seats for the minorities, but the reservations both of women and minorities should not follow party lines. Rather, they should be nominated on the basis of their services to the community, through consensus between the major political parties and civil society members. One may argue that through these reservations, the majority-minority divide would only be accentuated. While there is logic to this argument, there is no denying the fact that absence of reservations have resulted in the absence of representation and total disregard for the rights of minorities.

Human rights and citizens groups should conduct audits of the performance of the political parties, and these should be made public through the media.

Displacements and refugeehood are creations of political and economic policies pursued by the state. This is indicative of the lack of appreciation for the marginalized, their specific needs and rights, and lack of tolerance for dissent. In a truly democratic polity, this should not have happened. This calls for devolution of power and creation of strong local governance bodies, with minimal government interference. Corruption of government officials and politicians is well known in the South Asian context. While reforms in the public sector are urgently needed; there is also a need for a realistic assessment of the cost of living and salaries of the public servants. The enormous gap between the public and private sectors needs to be bridged. This calls for strong state intervention, which does not necessarily mean investing more powers in the state but alternately building a just and equitable state by involving rights groups in these interventions. In other words, what is being proposed is a strong citizen rights–based state, with the active participation of the different segments of society and involvement of the stakeholders in matters relating to them. The state has to decentre itself from the capital and reach out to the local bodies and local audiences.

The nation-state, a creation of people's movement and people's power, has in actuality disempowered the people. While a strong campaign for creating a corruption-free political and economic system is going on, we the people seriously need to ponder at the processes, not the actions that led to this situation. While actions are important, they are the outcomes of processes. If the latter are not changed, the author feels that Bangladesh's woes and trials with democracy will continue. It is through the creation of a secular multicultural citizen state that Bangladesh and, for that matter, South Asia can move towards a state system where the citizens find themselves empowered.

Cooperation between and among states at the regional level is a prerequisite for fighting radicalization. As argued in this article, radicalized terrorist groups are transnational; their objectives and aims are also transnational. The states of South Asia ought to cooperate not only at the military level but also with soft powers to foster greater cooperation and understanding among themselves. Article 10 of SAARC, which disallows the bilateral discussion of contentious issues, has largely become obsolete given the transnational and global character of threats. SAARC has the potential to transform the region through the use of its functional logic, which can largely act as a remedy to counter radicalization. It is only through debates, dialogues and discussions and arguments that a people's South Asia with pluralities and multiplicities can be dreamt of and experienced.

Notes

1 Cited from a presentation made by Mohammad Humayun Kabir on "Countering Radicalization in Bangladesh", at a Bangladesh-India Security Dialogue held in New Delhi on 3 April 2014, Dhaka: Bangladesh Enterprise Institute, August 2015, p. 9.
2 Anisuzzaman, *Creativity, Reality and Identity*, Dhaka: International Center for Bengal Studies, 1993, p. 107.

3 For details see Rounaq Jahan, *Pakistan: Failure in National Integration*, Dhaka: University Press Ltd., 1972.

4 *Parliament Debates*, 12 October 1972, Dhaka: Government of Bangladesh, 1972, p. 20.

5 *The Constitution of the People's Republic of Bangladesh*, Dhaka: Government of Bangladesh, 1972, p. 5.

6 *Ibid*, p. 13.

7 Talukdar Maniruzzaman, "Bangladesh Politics: Secular and Islamic Trends", in Rafiuddin Ahmed (ed.), *Religion, Nationalism and Politics in Bangladesh*, New Delhi: South Asia Publishers, 1990, p. 69.

8 *Ibid*, p. 70.

9 *Ibid*, pp. 71–73.

10 *Ghoshonapatra* (manifesto), Dhaka: Bangladesh Nationalist Party, 1978.

11 Maniruzzaman, n.7, p. 74.

12 *The Constitution of the People's Republic of Bangladesh*, Dhaka: Government of Bangladesh, 1991, p. 9.

13 Partha Ghosh, *Cooperation and Conflict in South Asia*, Dhaka: University Press Ltd., 1989, p. 71.

14 *The Constitution*, n.12, p. 5.

15 *The Daily Star*, 4 May 2016.

16 See Imtiaz Ahmed, "On the Brink of Precipice: Contemporary Terrorism and the Limits of the State", Paper Presented at the Institute of Diploma Engineers, Dhaka, Organised by the Bangladesh Foundation for Development Research, Dhaka, 30 November 2005.

8

CHALLENGES TO THE DEMOCRATIZATION PROCESS IN SOUTH ASIA

Looking at the future

Smruti S. Pattanaik

Introduction

Democracy and democratization involve a long process of institution building that forms the backbone of any democratic transition. Most of the countries, except Nepal, Bhutan and Maldives, inherited colonial institutions and laws, and their process of democratization has strong roots in British colonial legacy. Yet, these countries are in different stages of democratization, and in some, this process was interrupted. Many of the South Asian countries have seen long periods of autocratic, military and monarchical rule, which have resulted in weak institutionalization of the democratic process through which countries that are transiting to democracy can nurture the institutional framework that is fundamental for consolidating democracy. Democracy in many of the countries is in a nascent stage, and that has meant a mechanical transition from one regime to the other through elections, many times marred by political violence. Yet, this is the only way democracy is understood in the subcontinent, and the power of vote to change the government is immensely valued by the common masses. The yearning for democracy remains strong and has remained a fundamental factor in inspiring democratic movements in South Asia. From representative governments, the people of South Asia have fought for equal rights, equal access to education, gender equality and representation of marginalized people in political structures by institutionalizing these rights. There is also an aspiration to achieve the ideal version of democracy that is conjoined with freedom and the power to change a regime. Therefore, there exists a preference for a flawed and messy democracy that may fail to fulfil their aspirations over a coherent dictatorial regime that may produce better socio-economic indicators but stifles freedom and individual rights and where the national security paradigm is used to undermine liberty.

The post-colonial states of South Asia inherited the British colonial state structure that is symbolized by bureaucratic control. Some analysts, like Hamza Alavi, argue that the problem has much to do with the post-colonial states inheriting overdeveloped states while their society remained extremely underdeveloped and failing to cope with the democratic transition. Scholars like Ayesha Jalal argue that the successful integration of princely states and adoption of a constitution that was federal in form and unitary in spirit allowed India to concentrate on cementing its institutional structure by working out successful centre-state relations and thereby addressing the political aspiration of diverse ethno-linguistic groups successfully.[1] She also identifies the seminal role of the Congress party post-partition in consolidating democracy by drafting a constitution and holding its first election in 1952 in comparison to the declining role of the Muslim League in Pakistan, which resulted in bureaucratic control, political instability and a power struggle between the institutions of the governor general and prime minister's offices. Each of the states followed their own trajectory of state, institution and nation building, which significantly influenced the trajectory of democracy in different countries of South Asia.

While India has been a democracy since its independence, except for the three years of democratic interlude from 1975 to 1977, it faces challenges from ethno-nationalist groups fighting for autonomy and at times demanding independence. Bangladesh transited to a democracy in 1990 after a long period of military rule. Nepal is struggling to have an inclusive democracy after prolonged Maoist violence, while Bhutan is slowly transiting from a monarchical government to a representative government under a constitutional monarchy. Sri Lanka continues to struggle with post-war reconciliation, where the political rights of the Tamil minority will remain central to the consolidation of democracy. Similarly, the process of democracy has been fragile in both Maldives and Afghanistan – the new converts to democracy in South Asia. Pakistan, for the first time in its history, saw a transition of power from one civilian regime to the other. But the civilian regime has to constantly struggle to retain the political space that is often encroached upon by the army, which wields significant power.

This chapter examines the trajectory of democratization in South Asia, taking into account the internal factors that have shaped the process of democratization to analyze what the future holds for the countries of the region. It needs to be mentioned here that many international institutes that evaluated democracy have several criteria which not only include the level of participation, minority rights and the judiciary, which are considered as primary indicators of electoral politics, but also the functioning of the market, a level playing field for private players, the rights of workers, the function of public and private sector banks, expenditure on education, the percentage of enrolment in primary school, and so on. For instance, the Transformation Index produced by Bertelsmann Stiftung in 2016 argues that there was a move towards democracy from seventy-two democratic states and fifty-seven authoritarian states in 2014 to seventy-six democratic states and fifty-five authoritarian states in 2016, though the health of democracy in each of them can be debated.[2] According to their 2018 report, "the share of the world population that enjoys democratic governance has fallen from 59.3 per cent to 56.5 per cent.

For the first time ever, more than three billion people in the world are subject to autocratic governance."[3]

Political transition and institutional continuity

Political transition from one regime to the other through the process of election has become the biggest challenge in South Asia. For instance, the institution that is crucial in any such transition is the election commission. The election commissions in various countries have evolved over a period of time, and in some countries, given the deep political fissure and mistrust among the contenders, the authority to hold elections has taken the form of interim or caretaker governments. Unlike India and Sri Lanka and now Nepal and Bhutan, the role of government or the institutional process of overseeing the election has remained controversial in Pakistan and Bangladesh. Bangladesh's own unique experience with the caretaker government as an important institution came to the fore after the interim caretaker government was successful in steering the political transition in 1990 after the fall to General H.M. Ershad's military regime. In a country where both the political parties remain extremely suspicious of the role of the election institution and have often questioned the election results, the caretaker system remained a panacea. However, Bangladesh formally introduced a system of caretaker government only in 1996 as a part of the constitution to institutionalize the election regime. However, the decision of the Bangladesh National Party (BNP) government in 2006 to increase the retirement age of the Supreme Court Chief Justice to ensure that the then Chief Justice Hasan retired before the elections and as per the constitution took over as the chief adviser of the caretaker government, maker of the Care Take Government (CTG) system, which was supposed to be neutral, was a controversial one. The controversy over the election scheduled for 2007 saw the army-backed caretaker regime assuming power in what is known as an extra-constitutional intervention. Finally, the CTG was abolished through the fifteenth amendment act of the constitution, although the Bangladesh Supreme Court, in its verdict, suggested the next two elections could be held under CTG. The government constituted the election commission, but politicization of this institution with political appointees has made the election commission extremely controversial. The 2014 election in which the main opposition party decided not to participate because CTG was not restored. Similarly, the 2018 election in which the opposition candidates were denied a level playing field, their supporters were arrested and in seventeen constituencies their nomination was cancelled points to the larger malaise that is afflicting the democratic transition. The institutional weakness is inherent in the fact that the tenth parliament lacked opposition and the policies were one-sided without the input of the opposition. With only seven opposition members in the parliament, the eleventh National Assembly will see a repetition of ruling party domination as was witnessed in the tenth National Assembly. Since the elected lawmakers from the BNP have decided not to take the oath rejecting the result of the 30 December election, Bangladesh's democratic transition will entrench one-party rule. Organizations like the police and military in the past ten years have developed deep stakes in the continuation of the Awami League, which is going to rule for the third term. The undermining of electoral institutions like the Election Commission, which is crucial for the survival of democracy and institutionalization of the political transition does not augur well for Bangladesh's experiment on democracy.

Though Bangladesh abolished the caretaker government, interestingly, many in Pakistan argued for the establishment of a "Bangladesh model"[4] in Pakistan to oversee the election in 2013, creating the fear of a soft coup.[5] Finally, Pakistan constituted an election commission through consensus for overseeing the election process. Pakistan also instituted an interim caretaker government under which the EC held the election. However, the 2018 election was not free from controversy. The electoral process was managed by the deep state. The decision of the Supreme Court to jail Nawaz Sharif and his daughter Mariam Sharif was seen as a politically motivated decision to decimate the morale of the Pakistan Muslim League (N), which was popular.[6] The Panama investigation, conducted by a committee of which two officers from intelligence were members, was seen as a larger conspiracy to indict Nawaz Sharif so that PML-N is weakened. While the Pakistan Tehreek-e-Insaf, headed by Imran Khan, was propped up as an alternative, the media was used to demolish the image of Nawaz Sharif as a corrupt politician, and Imran was projected as the non-corrupt alternative.[7] The Pakistan case also makes it evident that in spite of a caretaker government and election commission, the institutionalization of democracy can suffer through a carefully crafted narrative and politically motivated judiciary that colluded with the military establishment to manage the electoral outcome.

Afghanistan has the weakest institutions, and the last election was marred by the accusation of massive rigging, forcing the UN to intervene in the electoral system, which led to the recounting of votes. However, peace was negotiated between the two political oppositional factions through a compromise where Abdul Ghani became the president and his main contender Abdullah Abdullah became the chief executive – a compromise that was beyond the ballot box.

The problem of a weak institutional framework continues to threaten the nascent democracy. The process of election remains hostage to electoral malpractice, characterized by money and muscle power and a collaborating bureaucracy that is eager to please its political master in return for political favour. The security establishment has emerged as the biggest challenger to democracy. In this context, the role of the police force has been extremely controversial. For any election to be held in a free and fair manner, the role of these auxiliary organizations is as important as the role of the election commission. Increasingly, the judiciary is seen as legitimizing controversial elections. As was seen in Sri Lanka, some governments have taken the ambiguous provision to sack an elected government. While institutionalization of the electoral process is significant, it is not sufficient. The challenges to democracy remain many. A fragile democracy inevitably allows unelected authorities to exert power as is happening in Pakistan; a politically subservient election commission is also likely to deliver contrived results to suit the regime's interest. The process of holding elections remains extremely controversial in South Asia. Over a period of time, India has evolved its independent election commission, which is a constitutional body. It has a robust election system, and the results of the elections conducted by the election commission are never questioned by the political parties. However, the institution of the election commission is not as robust in other countries of South Asia.

Electoral politics and the structure of electioneering

The method of electoral politics can be debated in terms of how the election is conducted, whether adequate time has been given to various political parties to campaign and the level of popular participation in terms of voter turnout. The method of election has always been a matter of contest among various stakeholders. Nevertheless, South Asia has seen its own variety of democracy. From basic democracy, initiated by Ayub, to Musharraf's "sustainable democracy" of 2001 or Nepal's recent transition from a constitutional monarchy to a republican state in 2008, Afghanistan continues to struggle to have a foothold in democracy, challenges from the Taliban, which rejects Western democracy, notwithstanding. Sri Lanka witnessed a political transition in 2015, where a historical election unseated an extremely powerful sitting government. Bhutan also saw a peaceful transition in which a new party has assumed power, and the election in Maldives reflected how an institutionally entrenched despot can be defeated by the people, giving hope for a democratic future.

Electoral policy in South Asia is extremely significant, as the region, in the past, witnessed a bloody coup and counter-coup in Bangladesh. The movement for democracy is ingrained in the birth of Bangladesh, where the majority of the population were denied political rights. Bangladesh has seen its moment of flawed transition, when a unilateral election without the participation of the main opposition party was held in 1996[8] and 2014.[9] And the 2018 election has been extremely controversial. Interestingly, Pakistan witnessed the first democratic transition in its political history in 2013 when the power was transferred from one civilian government to the other.

The election process is seen as the only way power can change hands without bloodshed, especially in the context of South Asia's bloody political history. However, this transition to electoral politics has not been an easy one, if one looks at the evolution of the state. Nepal went for bouts of democracy in the 1950s until the monarchy decided to take over power by instituting the Panchayat regime. In 1961, political parties were banned in Nepal when the king instituted the "National Guidance" system, and then he created a four-tier Panchayat system in 1962. A party-less indirect election was held in 1963. The government managed to co-opt some of the workers of political parties while bureaucracy and the army provided complete support to the monarchy. The co-opting of the bureaucrats and the army to strengthen their own regime was also a factor in Bangladesh's post-1975 military coup and also in Pakistan where the military took over power in 1958.

The authoritarian regimes consider political parties illegal. In Bhutan, until very recently, movement for democracy was considered as an act of treason. In the 1990 crisis, some people who demonstrated in southern Bhutan against the monarchy were expelled from the kingdom, as Bhutan did not allow "freedom of speech and expression." Nepal saw the initiation of multiparty democracy in 1990 in which the monarchy remained an important pillar of power.

The political party system in each country was conditioned by the space available for democratic politics. For instance, India saw the emergence of authoritarian political leadership emerging under Prime Minister Indira Gandhi, which resulted in the imposition of emergency in 1975. Apart from a brief interlude between 1975 and 1977, the Congress party was back in power. The 1990s saw the evolution of coalition politics and the rise of regional dynamics that set in motion the local issues finding larger space in the national agenda. The process of India's democratic evolution witnessed a phenomena in which the national parties faced severe challenges from the regional political parties. The process of political mobilization and role of political parties in Pakistan's democratic transition remains limited given the role of the army in Pakistan. Nevertheless, the recent transition is significant in terms of cooperation between the political parties to prevent the army from playing a dominant role. The PML-N, which at one point of time was a protégé of the army, has emerged as one of the major challengers to the army. The army continues to find its alibi in the political circle that wants to entrench the army's domineering role by referring to the issue of national security.

The role of dark money and the influence of business houses in the process of election remains a major factor in South Asia. Though there is an audit of party expenditure in an election, the money spent goes beyond the budget provided by the political parties, giving rise to serious concerns regarding the influence of business houses. Bhutan has state funding of elections, and there is audit of election expenditure.[10] In India, "While candidate expenditure is capped at seventy lakh in most parliamentary constituencies, party expenditure remains unconstrained."[11] In the 2013 election in Pakistan, the election commission stipulated

> no transaction towards the election expenses shall be made through an account other than the account opened for the purpose . . . All transactions relating to the election expenses shall be entered into with GST registered firms/persons, wherever it is possible.[12]

However, this was observed more in violation.

Most of the political parties in South Asia have a dynastic leadership and exercise iron-fist control over the party. Since money plays an important role, the grassroots leaders are dependent on the party leadership. In post-colonial states of South Asia, the role of particular leaders in the party are emphasized and mobilization of voters is done by emphasizing their contribution to the freedom struggle. The leadership continues to articulate the role for their family members in politics while seeking votes. In many cases, the election of the party chairperson remains a mere farce, as they remain a family-oriented party. This is true in the case of the Indian National Congress, the Samajwadi Party and most of the regional political parties in India (except for the Bhartiya Janata Party and the Communist Party in India); AL, BNP, JP in Bangladesh, the PML-N and PPP in Pakistan. The SLFP in Sri Lanka, for a long time, was controlled by the Bandaranaike family and is now controlled by the Rajapakse family. The Nepali Congress was controlled by the Koirala family, and in Maldives, the Progressive Party of Maldives (PPM) is headed by Abdullah Yameen, who is a half-brother of the former autocratic president of Maldives Mohammad Abdul Gayoom. Dynastic leaderships invariably hamper inner-party democracy.

Majoritarian politics

The challenge in South Asia that affects the process of democratization is the majoritarian politics that survive on the basis of the winner-takes-all approach. It is also important to note that homogenization attempts by various countries severely imperil the rights of other minorities. This process is not confined to one country. The homogenization attempt in Nepal,[13] the cultural homogenization attempt in Bhutan in 1988, Bangladesh's construction of a Bengali identity on the basis of language or on the basis of territorially defined Bangladeshi identity with a reemphasis on religion, the 1956 "Sinhala only" policy and later providing primacy to Buddhism in Sri Lanka's constitution and the building of a homogenizing Islamic identity in Pakistan at the cost of diverse ethno-linguistic identities, undermining their political aspiration on the basis of a monolithic Muslim identity have deeply impacted the process of democratization. Majoritarian construction undermines citizenship rights. In South Asia, British colonialism encouraged migration within its colony, creating pockets of minority ethnic communities who moved as indentured labourers to work on plantations. These people, who shared a cross-border ethno-linguistic affinity, became minority citizens of the newly emerged countries as in the context of Sri Lanka[14] and Myanmar.[15] The subsequent partition of British India impacted the process of nation building and defined the relationship between various ethno-national and religious groups; it impacted the plural societal structure in each of the countries as the states, in their bid to build exclusive identities, refused to constitutionally recognize the diversity. Democracy functions on the premise of equal rights and recognition of diversity and the rights of each group living in the nation-state. This majoritarian construction[16] also encourages political mobilization of the majority community as if the "majority" acts as a bloc. As a result, adequate attention is not given to the rights of the minorities. Though diversity is recognized, there is lack of political space for representing diverse political views, as well as diversity of culture, language and religion, as the countries remain majoritarian in their outlook.

In the majoritarian democracy, the minorities have emerged as vote banks for the political parties. Because of the nature of politics in many countries, the minorities support some political parties whom they perceive to protect their interest. For instance, in India, the Muslims tended to vote for the Congress party but have now shifted their votes to the Samajwadi party led by Mulayam Singh Yadav and the Bahujan Samaj Party of Mayawati. Apart from that, in Hyderabad, they have voted for Majlis-e-Ittehadul Muslimeen (MIM), led by Assauddin Owasi, and the All India United Democratic Front (AIUDF), led by Baddrudin Ajmal, in Assam. But these parties' support is much more local, and they do not have a pan-Indian appeal. Ethnic parties also tend to appeal to specific ethno-linguistic groups.

In Afghanistan, the ethnic division has polarized the politics between the majority Pashtuns and the minorities – Tajiks, Uzbeks, Hazaras and other smaller ethnic groups. In the last election in Afghanistan, held in 2014, this ethnic fear was crystallized in the presidential election. Ethnic bargains drove the electoral politics. The majority Pashtuns were fearful of ethnic minorities gaining power in Afghanistan. The Pashtuns have been the majority community in Afghanistan.

Pakistan, for a long time, had the provision of a separate electorate for the minorities, keeping them out of the electoral narratives that defined the agenda of major political parties. However, even after the abolition of a separate electorate by General Musharraf in 2002, issues concerning the minorities are not major political planks, as they constitute less than five per cent of the population and are dispersed across the country. The politics of religion have dominated Pakistan's political landscape for a long time. After declaring Ahmediya as non-Muslim, some Sunni rightist groups demand Pakistan be declared as a Sunni country. Pakistan's tilt towards Sunni Islam was accomplished during the tenure of General Zia ul Haq, who introduced Sunni Islamic provisions of punishment.[17] In the process, it resulted in the marginalization of Shias, who are nearly twenty per cent of Pakistan's population.

In Bangladesh, the minorities constitute nearly eight per cent of the population and are considered part of the Awami League's (AL) vote bank – a party that fought the liberation war and is supportive of secularism, which remains a major appeal for the minority communities. Considering the fact that more than ninety percent of the population are Muslims, the AL plays the majoritarian politics of adopting Islamic symbolism, as illustrated in the fifteenth constitutional amendment which retains Islam as the state religion while restoring Article 12 of the 1972 constitution, which deals with secularism. This has not only marginalized the minorities but also the secularist Muslims, who are now vote banks of the party. Some of the secularists and the minorities do not have much political option in the available political spectrum in Bangladesh to protect their interests. The majoritarian politics, like appealing to the religious identity of the people, undermines the cause of secularism that the party projects as its core value. The undermining of minority identity is accompanied by institutional discrimination and societal insecurity caused by forcible conversion and the grabbing of their property.[18]

In Nepal, the process of political transition has suffered a setback because of the politics of those who consider themselves as the sons of the soil and those who are considered as "migrants" – the Pahari (hill people) vs. the Madhesis (plain people). The Madhesis have close familial and marital relationships with the people across the border in India. They are not considered as true-blood Nepali, as they speak various dialectics that are spoken in India. The new constitution promulgated in

Nepal in 2015 institutionally discriminates the Madhesis. Article 11 (5) and (7) made their children ineligible to contest for president or prime minister if one of their parents is a foreigner. It also discriminated against the Janajatis in terms of their political representation. These issues were addressed in the 2016 constitutional amendment, but the provincial boundary was purportedly drawn Madhesis as minority, except for province no 2, as ethnic-based federalism was rejected. Thus, democracy and democratic representation continue to be an issue for Nepal. It also needs to be mentioned that in the past, the monarchy of Nepal wanted to impose a unifying Brahmanical Hindu culture in its bid to promote a Nepali nationalism that confronted the domineering Madhesis in the Terai Belt.[19] The Janajatis, who mostly practice animism, continue to struggle not only to preserve their identity but also to find representation in the "new Nepal." Their smaller numbers reduce their electoral value in a state where majoritarianism is forged to perpetuate an identity that denies them the democratic dividend of equality.

In Bhutan, the majoritarian politics saw the introduction of a cultural edict called "Driglam Namzha" in 1988. As part of a homogenization effort, Driglam Namzha introduced one dress, one language and one culture, undermining the diversity in the country. Inter-ethnic marriage was encouraged with monetary means as a means of integration. Apart from the Drukpas, the other major ethnic groups are Sarchop and Lhotsampas (people of Nepalese origin). The Lhotsampas, who are concentrated in the southern part of Bhutan adjoining India, were seen as the ethnic "other," given their cross border ethno-linguistic and marital ties, whose loyalty to the state remained a success.[20] The Lhotsampas who protested against these policies and demanded democracy were expelled from the country and labelled as illegal migrants. Many of them who stayed in various camps in eastern Nepal are now settled in western countries that volunteered to settle them in their country as a part of resettlement. Bhutan transited to a constitutional democracy in 2008. The process is nascent, and it has remained a top-down approach. The power continues to remain in the hands of its miniscule minority, the Drukpas.

Sri Lanka is the only country that suffered from protracted ethnic conflict, inflicting them with a thirty-year civil war, which came to an end in 2009. The majoritarian hegemonic policy, which started with the Sinhala-only policy in 1956 to marginalize the Tamils, who were dominant in bureaucracy, went ahead with policies that could handicap the Tamils economically and politically. For example, not only did Sri Lanka move towards being constitutionally a Buddhist state, but the Sinhala political elite introduced a quota system that undermined merit and gave preference to Sinhala students with lower marks, thereby undermining the aspirations of the youth. The Tamils who felt that they were getting politically marginalized and were not even getting equal opportunity in employment took up arms, asking for a separate state. Sri Lanka's democratic dispensation is yet to accommodate the political aspirations of the Tamils and address their fear of being exploited by an unresponsive majoritarian state.

In spite of the democratic transition, South Asian democracy remains a majoritarian construct with institutional biases against minorities ingrained in the emerging political culture. This remains a major challenge for democracy. Weak institutional mechanisms to address grievances have contributed to this decay.

Role of the judiciary and media

In the process of strengthening democracy, the role of an independent judiciary and media is very important. Politicization of the judiciary is one of the major causes for the decay of democracy. This is significant, as many of the countries have recently transited to democracy, and any political differences over interpretation of the constitution are referred to the court. An independent judiciary remains a significant pillar in this transition.

The appointment of judges and their removal is vested with the executive branch of the government. Appointments, promotions and post-retirement benefits are some of the reasons for the judges sometimes to pass orders favouring the incumbent government.[21] Separation of the judiciary from the executive branch remains a lynchpin of the judiciary's independence. The electoral frauds are often referred to the courts to adjudicate. The famous case of the Allahabad High Court's decision that made Indira Gandhi's election void is a case in point.[22] Appointment remains a crucial yardstick to measure the independence of the judiciary. The six-member panel of the National Judicial Appointments Commission (NJAC) Act that was passed by the government of India to appoint judges to the higher judiciary was declared unconstitutional by the Supreme Court. Many feel the collegium system provides arbitrary power to the judiciary, and the judicial appointments are not transparent. It needs to be emphasized that the courts in India have played a decisive role in safeguarding the constitution, and the political interference remains minimal.

The Supreme Court in Pakistan, under Chief Justice Iftekhar Chowdhury, dismissed elected prime ministers for defying the Supreme Court's orders. While the judiciary is expected to provide a level playing field, the Pakistani judiciary acted in a partisan manner against the PPP government from 2008 to 2013. The judiciary-executive tussle created instability in the country at a time when the political government was trying to stabilize the state and overcome the military's interference in the decision-making. In the past, the Pakistani judiciary has legitimized the military rule under the doctrine of necessity. To have the judiciary on its side, the military governments have often made the judges of the Supreme Court and High Court take fresh oaths under provisional constitutional orders that the military regimes implement. The recent verdict on the Panama case, where the Supreme Court decided to overthrow the elected prime minister, Nawaz Sharif, under the controversial Articles 62 and 63 is also a case in point of how the judiciary can be party to the undermining of democracy in Pakistan. It also became an alibi of the military by taking suo motto action against the elected Nawaz Sharif government and effectively sealed the political fate of Nawaz Sharif.

In Sri Lanka, the government of Mahinda Rajapaksa brought impeachment motions against the sitting chief justice, Shirani Bandaranaike, since she allowed a petition challenging a government order, known as the Devineguma bill, and gave an order which did not allow the government to take away rights given to the provincial council under the thirteenth amendment without their consent. The eighteenth amendment to the constitution undermined the appointment of an independent commission, bestowing power in the hands of the president and replacing the Constitutional Council with a Parliamentary Council. The government wanted a pliable judge who would provide legitimacy to various decisions of the Rajapakse government, including some of the high-profile disappearance and assassination cases. After the election of 2015, with the assumption of power of Maithripala Sirisena, the independence of some of these institutions, including that of the judiciary, has been restored through the nineteenth amendment. Independent commissions[23] in Sri Lanka are important pillars of its parliamentary democracy. The media also came under substantial pressure in Sri Lanka. During the civil war, the media was put under the Media Centre for National Security and were supposed to report on the basis of government handouts. Issues of large-scale killings of Tamil civilians went unreported. In the matter of ethnic conflict and Tamil rights, including the disappearances and the occupation of the land by the military, the media remained circumspect during Rajapakse's regime. Those who dared to report were subjected to repression and torture and disappeared. As a result, the government managed to suppress dissent against the government.

In Nepal, the role of the judiciary is still evolving as Kathmandu has only recently passed a new constitution.[24] However, the appointment of judges having affiliation to political parties and some to the foreign-funded civil society groups has dogged the role of the judiciary in Nepal.[25] A judicial appointment during the democratic transition becomes more significant, as the courts are likely to adjudicate some of the problems that arise in the context of implementing the new constitution. A politically biased judiciary in a highly politicized society cannot play the role of neutral arbitrator that, in essence, is a hallmark in any nascent transitional democracy.

In Maldives, the judiciary played a partisan role in the ousting of Nasheed's regime by playing into the hands of Abdullah Yameen's regime and legalizing the overthrow of Nasheed.[26] The Judicial Service Commission (JSC), in 2010, re-appointed all sitting judges despite the procedure laid down in the constitution. Its role in appointing judges remains highly controversial. The Supreme Court of Maldives has vast power that gives the court enormous authority over the lower courts. In January 2016, the Supreme Court took away some power of the JSC and conveyed to the council that they cannot appoint or transfer judges without its approval. This centralized tendency is responsible for the Supreme Court virtually taking over the administrative power of the lower courts, empowered by Article 141(b–d). Communication to the lower courts has to be done through the Supreme Court. The Supreme Court has the power to suspend the chairman of the Election Commission and deputy election commissioner instead of executive. The Supreme Court in Maldives is also playing a controversial role in ordering arrests of the MPs and disqualifying some of the MPs who joined the opposition to sponsor a no-confidence motion against the speaker of the parliament. Reformation of the

Maldivian judiciary is a necessity for the health of its democracy because of the extremely controversial role the judiciary played during the regime of Abdullah Yameen. With the change of the government in Maldives, the repair of institutions has begun.

In Bangladesh, the judiciary (appointment) and separation of the judiciary from the executive branch continues to be a major issue. The High Court in 1999 passed an order for the separation of the judiciary from the executive branch. But the order was not implemented, and the BNP government took twenty-three adjournments to implement the order. Finally, a decision for separation was taken in 2007, when the military-backed CTG took over power. Appointment, promotion and transfer of the judges in the lower judiciary, however, continue to be handled by the Ministry of Law. The government has not restored Article 115, which makes consultation with the Supreme Court mandatory to appoint candidates to the judicial service or as magistrates exercising judicial functions. The government brought change to Article 116 in the fifteenth amendment to the constitution which reads,

> The control (including the power of posting, promotion and grant of leave) and discipline of persons employed in the judicial service and magistrates exercising judicial functions shall vest in the president and shall be exercised by him in consultation with the Supreme Court.

Earlier, this was vested with the Supreme Court. Presently, the power of impeachment of judges on the grounds of misconduct and incapacity is provided to the parliament under the sixteenth amendment to the constitution, striking a blow at the very concept of the independence of the judiciary. However, the sixteenth amendment to the constitution has now been declared as ultra vires, serving a severe blow to the government's design to control the judiciary. The court is not above ideological preferences, and sometimes bail is not granted to people affiliated with the opposition political party. Presidential pardon for convicted criminals is also used for political purposes.

In any democracy, the media plays the role of a watchdog. However, increasingly, the owners of media houses dabble in politics, and some of them openly side with political parties to further their corporate interests. As a result, both the print and the visual media have played a biased role supporting and opposing governments, depending on the ideological orientation of their owners. The government also exerts pressure by withholding advertisement and sometimes persecuting them for their views. This trend is found to various degrees in all the South Asian countries. In Bangladesh, some of the media houses affiliated with the opposition political parties were closed down, and some of the editors, for example, Amar Desh and Mahbubur Rahmar, were arrested. The new broadcasting policy and Digital Security Act of 2018 in Bangladesh places severe restrictions on news that is critical of the government, and all this is done in the pretext of protecting the security and stability of the country. Prominent journalists, like Mahfuz Anam, have been arrested, and around seventy cases were filed by the supporters of the ruling party for admitting his editorial mistake and printing news in the *DailyStar* newspaper of which he is the editor without verifying the content of the news during the military-backed caretaker government's regime.[27] All these act as pressure on the media.

In Sri Lanka though, the media was placed under the Media Centre for National Security during the 2009 war and much after the conclusion of the war; media personnel were routinely harassed and picked up by the intelligence agencies, and some are missing and probably have been killed.[28] The editor of *Sunday*, Lashantha Wickramatunge was brutally killed for his criticism of the Rajapakse regime. Some journalists were picked up in famous "white vans" and tortured, and some journalists, like Prageeth Eknaligoda, went missing after exposing corruption in Rajapakse's family. Some journalists took asylum in foreign countries. Any criticism of the regime and support for the Tamil rights brought the journalists the tag of terrorist and Tiger sympathizer.

In Pakistan, the media people are routinely harassed for criticizing the activities of Pakistan's notorious intelligence agency, the Inter Service Intelligence (ISI). A journalist from *Dawn* was kidnapped and was thrashed in custody and left on the road with his hair shaved off. Another journalist, Selim Sehzad, was tortured and killed by the ISI for revealing the radicalization of some officers in the navy and their links with al Qaeda. Hamid Mir was attacked for his views and criticism of the ISI and Prime Minister Nawaz Sharif's relationship with the military after he went to meet Mir in the hospital.[29] The Urdu media has often been critical of the functioning of the political government and is believed to be conveying the message of the military. Given the role of the powerful military, the media often plays a cautious role and adopts self-censorship in its reporting.

In Nepal, the media was completely divided on the issue of Madhesi representation and their political rights. Instead of strengthening democracy, where all the citizens can enjoy equal rights, the Nepali media, owned by the people of the hill, projected it as an affront to their rights and portrayed the Madhesi and Janajati demands as externally determined and aimed at dividing the country in which India has a role. They not only projected Madhesis and Janajatis as outsiders but also made it an issue of nationalism. Thus, the media's role in creating division and inspiring media nationalism undermines their role in democracy. In India, the powerful business houses that control the media also play the nationalism card in many of the debates in the electronic media. This was evident in the controversy over the Jawaharlal Nehru University incident and also the reporting of various religious and caste conflicts. However, there are media houses that continue to play the role of watchdog by bringing into focus the development and governance lacunae including corruption. Thus media's role in furthering democracy, generating debate and educating public opinion, however, cannot be underestimated.

Emergence of security state and democracy

The states in South Asia, given the eternal security threat and internal political challenges, have emerged as security states. Security states are those where the state security is given primacy over the rights and liberty of citizens. The fundamental rights are suspended and emergency declared to preserve the state. India, in the past, has seen suspension of fundamental rights under the Maintenance of Internal Security Act (MISA) during the emergency imposed by the Congress government. Other acts include the Terrorism and Disruption Act (TADA), which was declared unconstitutional by the Supreme Court; the Internal Security Act imposed in Jammu and Kashmir; and the Arms Force Special Power Act imposed in areas threatened by militancy and terrorism. These acts are considered as restraining people's rights and freedoms. Yet, securing the nation-state and territoriality remains an important component of the state. While asserting diversity is tolerated, secessionist demands are dealt with brute force. If these acts for preserving the state mean the rights of the people are undermined, the government tends to act in securing the state.

In Bangladesh, the government has brought in ICT Amendment Act 2013, which imposes severe restrictions on online activities. Though many consider this as restrictive, the government's justifications for implementing this act are many. The government argues that the bloggers cannot expect leniency if they try to defame Islam and its prophet, which can threaten the law and order situation. Many argue that such actions without corresponding actions against the militants does not serve the purpose. The securitization of the state also imposes various restrictions on individual freedoms, which the fledgling democracies in South Asia confront. The securitization put democracy and the form of government and individual liberty below the security of the state, which is geared towards protecting national interest.

In India, the provision for imposing a national emergency under Article 352, which was imposed in 1975, was made to secure the "nation." Though the reason in 1975 was preservation of Indira Gandhi's government. Similarly, in Pakistan, each time the military took over power, it took over in the pretext of preserving the state from self-serving politicians who put their interests above the interests of the state. Whether it is Bangladesh or Sri Lanka, restrictions on democratic rights are placed on the pretext of securing the state and maintaining internal order.

The state imposes laws like preventive detention and engages in arbitrary arrests to preserve the state. Thus, in the context of South Asia, one perceives the dichotomy between the need to provide rights and various other freedoms through a constitutional arrangement under the democratic regimes and the justification of putting restrictions in the name of law and order, public decency and preventing violence. Constitutional democracy is still evolving in South Asia. Some of the groups within various countries are still fighting for proportional representation and preservation of indigenous rights. While Bhutan is a new entrant to democracy, Nepal continues to face serious constitutional crises as marginalization of Madhesis and Janajatis is yet to be addressed. Here, the securitization assumes a different dimension. The perception of being overwhelmed by the Madhesis in electoral politics has led to the preservation of a system that is loaded against the rights of Madhesis. Preservation of the state is interlinked with nationalism and the character of the state in terms of ethnic preservation of the ruling elite. Thus, electoral politics in essence sometimes get enmeshed with the question of outsiders versus the sons of soil.

The essence of a security state also means that democracy and rights can be sacrificed. It needs to be noted that the South Asian states are still vulnerable to ethno-national forces that continue to demand their separate identity be recognized. Since the 1947 partition divided ethnic groups that had lived together for centuries, the ethno-cultural affinities often clashed with the idea of the nation-state and its territorial boundaries. Cross-border ethnic affinities provided sanctuaries to disgruntled ethnic brethren, often galvanizing support for their political aspirations. Such cross-border affinities added to the security predicament of the new states, which felt preservation of the state was more important than recognition of the rights of the minor ethno-linguistic groups.

India and the process of democratization in South Asia

India has been involved in the process of democratization in some countries. Its role in Nepal after the transition from the Rana regime to a constitutional monarchy in 1950 and later its role in bringing the seven political parties together to bring an end to the Maoist insurgency and help in their political and constitutional rehabilitation are remarkable. It was India that refused to welcome the constitution in Nepal when it realized the political rights of Madhesis and Janajatis were not preserved. This was because India was involved in the political process and was key to the democratic transition in Nepal.

India's decision not to take sides when the problem of the political rights of the Bhutanese of Nepali origin or the Lhotshampas spilled over to India was criticized by Bhutanese refugees as well as the Government of Nepal, which wanted India's intervention to resolve the refugee crisis. India's neutrality or failure to help to establish democracy in Bhutan is often criticized by the Lhotshampas, who were forced into exile by the Bhutan government. Yet India has preferred stability in its neighbourhood over democracy.

India's role in democratization has often faced dichotomical expectations – represented by ruling classes in the neighbourhood that have looked towards India to preserve their power and the civil society that has looked towards India's democratic tradition as an inspiration and wanted India to intervene positively to ensure that democracy is sustained. Such dichotomical expectations are seen in the context of Bangladesh. In Sri Lanka, India's role in midwifing the thirteenth amendment to the constitution to bring in lasting peace in 1987 failed. Yet, India remains engaged with the Sri Lankan government and the Tamils to seek lasting peace in the post-war period. The Tamils have looked towards India to ensure that their rights are preserved in post-war Sri Lanka.

India's effort in Afghanistan is geared towards training young Afghan bureaucrats and providing the wherewithal to hold elections, including building the parliament building. It has insisted on representation of diverse ethnic groups in Afghanistan's power structure for lasting peace.

In Pakistan, the democratic forces do look at India for support and expect it not to get into any kind of rhetorical verbal duel with Pakistan which will strengthen the hand of the army at the cost of fledgling democratic regimes. Both ruling regimes and those who are struggling for autonomy or preservation of their political rights have always looked towards India to take up their political cause at international and regional fora.

India will remain an important factor in South Asia, and there will always be groups in the neighbouring countries which will look towards India for support. As the largest democracy, the civil society members in the neighbouring countries expect India to play a constructive role in promoting democracy and liberal values, often to the dislike of the ruling regimes. There are high expectations of India as far as movement for democracy in the subcontinent is concerned.

Conclusion

The process of democratization is likely to face several challenges. These would range from various ethno-linguistic groups that would draw the attention of the state for the preservation of their rights in the context of majoritarian impulses which would tend to perceive their demands as a challenge to state security. As democracy takes root, the demand for plurality of opinion and political space to ventilate their views will also gain ground. The demand for more democratic space will be part of this democratic transition, as many smaller groups will be drawn to the process of democratization to preserve and further their rights as communities and individuals. Though the tendency of the state would be preservation of the state itself rather than the rights of the groups, such democratic space will often be challenged by arbitrary laws which would deny political space in the name of preserving the security of the state.

While electoral politics will be the most important factor in the democratic transition in South Asia, institutions of democracy like an independent judiciary and election commission, a parliament that provides space for opposition and vibrant media will be significant. The states cannot run away from democratic impulses, as most of them have a large youth population who are social media savvy. Instead of curbing political space to express their views, the state needs to engage them to arrest any youth unrest that can challenge the nascent democracy taking root. Democracy can flourish when the states, instead of overemphasizing state security, place importance on socio-economic development, providing opportunities for employment and guaranteeing individual freedoms that are the essence of citizenship. Given the diversity and plurality that each state of South Asia represents, any attempt to monolithize identity will come with a political price. This will make democracy unsustainable, as the very nature of democracy encourages diversity of opinion. South Asia's march towards democracy will face the challenge from authoritarian leaders who would like to concentrate power in their hands. Yet the yearning for democracy, in spite of institutional and political hurdles, remains strong, and this yearning will prevent authoritarian regimes from consolidating power.

Notes

1 Ayesha Jalal, *Democracy and Authoritarianism in South Asia*, New Delhi: Sage Publication, 1995, p. 35.
2 Bertelsmann Stiftung (ed.), *Transformation Index BTI 2016*, Gutersloh: Verlag Bertelsmann Stiftung, 2016, p. 6.
3 Bertelsmann Stiftung (ed.), *Transformation Index BTI 2018*, Gutersloh: Verlag Bertelsmann Stiftung, 2018, p. 7.
4 Najam Sethi, "Bangladesh Model", 22–28 June 2012, see www.thefridaytimes.com/beta3/tft/article.php?issue=20120622&page=1 (Accessed on 2 September 2014).
5 Editorial, "Failed Bangladesh Model", 15 February 2013, *The Nation*, see http://nation.com.pk/letters/15-Feb-2013/failed-bangladesh-model (Accessed on 15 February 2013).
6 Raza Rumi, "A 'Judicial Coup' Against Pakistani PM Sharif", *DW*, www.dw.com/en/opinion-a-judicial-coup-against-pakistani-pm-sharif/a-39871933 (Accessed on 15 November 2016).
7 "Pakistan's Army Is Using Every Trick to Sideline Nawaz Sharif", *Economist*, 21 June 2018, www.economist.com/asia/2018/06/21/pakistans-army-is-using-every-trick-to-sideline-nawaz-sharif (Accessed on 20 July 2018).
8 The sixth Parliamentary election was held in February 1996. The government of Begum Khaleda Zia was forced to call for a second election (seventh Parliamentary) after passing a constitutional amendment bill that institutionalized the Care Taker government system.
9 The BNP boycotted the election. The credibility of the election is questioned by the EU and the US mainly.
10 See http://eci.nic.in/eci_main1/current/IIIDEM-Files/(Dasho)%20Kunzang%20Wangdi%20-%20SOUTH%20ASIA%20PRESENTATION.pdf (Accessed on 21 June 2018).
11 Michael Collins, "Money power in Indian elections", *The Hindu Businessline*, 29 July 2015, see www.thehindubusinessline.com/opinion/money-power-in-indian-elections/article6261173.ece (Accessed on 30 July 2015).
12 Intikhab Amir, "Money Does Matter in Election", *The Dawn*, 24 April 2013, see www.dawn.com/news/793926/money-does-matter-in-election (Accessed on 27 May 2013).
13 Mahendra Lawoti, "Dynamics of Mobilisation: Varied Tranjectories of Dalit, Indigenous Nationalities and Madhesi Movements", in Mahendra Lawoti and Susan Hangen (eds.), *Nationalism and Ethnic Conflict in Nepal: Identities and Mobilization After 1990*, Oxon: Routledge, 2012, p. 151.
14 See Nira Wikramasinghe, *Sri Lanka in the Modern Age: A History*, London: Oxford University Press, 2014, Chapter V on "Citizens, Communities, Rights, Constitutions, 1947–2000", pp. 169–209.
15 Priya Chacko and Alexander E. Davi, "Myanmar and India: Regimes of Citizenship and the Limits of Geo-Economic Engagement", *European Journal of East Asian Studies*, vol. 14, no. 1, 2015, p. 137.
16 Niraja Gopal Jayal, *Citizenship and Its Discontents: An Indian History*, Cambridge: Harvard University Press, 2014, p. 20.
17 For details see Sadia Saeed, "Desecularisation as an Instituted Process: National Identity and Religious Difference in Pakistan", *Economic and Political Weekly*, vol. 48, no. 50, 14 December 2013, pp. 64–66.
18 Meghna Guhathakurta, "Religious Minorities", in Ali Riaz and M. Sajjadur Rahman (eds.), *Routledge Handbook of Contemporary Bangladesh*, London: Routledge, 2016, pp. 320–321; Bhumitra Chakma, "The CHT and the Peace Process", in Ali Riaz and M. Sajjadur Rahman (eds.), *Routledge Handbook of Contemporary Bangladesh*, London: Routledge, 2016, p. 307.
19 Lok Raj Baral, "Inclusive Democracy and Governance in New' Nepal", in Lipi Ghose (ed.), *Political Governance and Minority Rights: The South and South-East Asian Scenario*, New Delhi: Routledge, 2009, p. 89.

20 Smruti S. Pattanaik, "Ethnic Identity, Conflict and Nation Building in Bhutan", *Strategic Analysis*, vol.22, no.4, July 1998, p. 636.

21 T.R. Andhyarujina, "When the Bench Buckled", *Indian Express*, 8 July 2015, see http://indianexpress.com/article/opinion/columns/when-the-bench-buckled/ (Accessed on 10 July 2015).

22 "Indira Nehru Gandhi vs Shri Raj Narain & Anr", 7 November 1975, see https://indianka noon.org/doc/936707/ (Accessed on 23 May 2018).

23 The appointments to important positions like chief justice and judges of the Supreme Court, the president and judges of the Court of Appeal; chairman and members of the Election Commission, Public Service Commission, National Police Commission, Permanent Commission to Investigate Allegations of Bribery and Corruption, Finance Commission, Human Rights Commission, Delimitation Commission, and Judicial Service Commission; and the attorney general, auditor general, ombudsman and secretary general of Parliament.

24 See www.nbacba.org.np/download/1FINAL_NBA_Position_Paper_on_The_Judicial_System_English_Version.pdf (Accessed on 22 April 2018).

25 Yuvraj Ghimiri, "Cloud Over Judiciary", *Indian Express*, 15 August 2016, see http://indianexpress.com/article/opinion/columns/nepal-judiciary-k-p-oli-prachanda-election-maoist-china-india-2975559/ (Accessed on 17 August 2016).

26 "Maldives Defends Controversial Jailing of Ex-Leader", *Daily Mail*, 15 March 2015, see www.dailymail.co.uk/wires/afp/article-2995501/Maldives-defends-controversial-jail-ing-ex-leader.html (Accessed on 17 March 2015).

27 "Daily Star Editor Mahfuz Anam Admits to Publishing DGFI-fed Baseless Stories", *BDnews34.com*, 4 February 2016, see http://bdnews24.com/media-en/2016/02/04/daily-star-editor-mahfuz-anam-admits-to-publishing-dgfi-fed-baseless-stories (Accessed on 7 February 2016).

28 Sandesen Marasinghe and Irangika Rang, "Slain Journalists' Families Should Be Compensated: PM", *Daily News*, 14 December 2015, see www.dailynews.lk/?q=2015/12/14/local/slain-journalists-families-should-be-compensated-pm (Accessed on 14 December 2015).

29 "PM Inquires After Hamid Mir's Health in Karachi Hospital", *The Nation*, 21 April 2014, see www.nation.com.pk/national/21-Apr-2014/pm-inquires-after-hamid-mir-health-in-karachi-hospital (Accessed on 22 April 2014).

9

PERCEPTION BUILDING IN INDIA–PAKISTAN RELATIONS

The media's agenda

Ramakrishnan Ramani

Introduction

In a democratic political setup, a nation's perception of its neighbours is influenced by many factors, one key element being the role of the national/ regional news media. The role that the news media plays in bilateral relations is all too obvious. Take the case of India-Sri Lanka relations. The Tamil issue in the island nation became a bone of contention in centre-state relations in India, often leading to unfavourable strategic decisions by the central government. The regional news media had a major role to play in influencing the centre's decisions. The same can be said of India-Pakistan relations, where the national media plays a large role in influencing the government in all spheres – military, commerce and trade, sports and cultural and so on. But the question is – what is the media's agenda? A lot of research has been done on what drives the news media and its relationship with the governments and other powers. In the popular book *Manufacturing Consent: The Political Economy of the Mass Media*, Edward S. Herman and Noam Chomsky present in depth the tripartite relationship between the news media, the government and large corporate organizations.

Extending Herman's and Chomsky's propaganda model to the Indian situation, political parties and corporate enterprises with a particular political stance use the news media to publicize their policy concerns. Thus, the news media influences the centre's policy initiatives in certain cases, while it promotes it in other areas. This chapter attempts to study the news media's portrayal of India-Pakistan relations in the light of the five filters of the propaganda model. The article concludes with a few recommendations that the media and government could consider for better outcomes.

India–Pakistan relations in context to "Reimagining Asia in 2030"

South Asia is a region of contrasts. It represents nearly one-fourth of the total global population but is challenged by low GDP, low per capita income and low literacy rates. Economic disparity is glaringly visible with a miniscule minority of the population being rich and the vast majority living below the poverty line. This breeds a number of issues that range the entire gamut of human existence – social, political and economic. The region is also characterized by bilateral disputes and mutual distrust. Despite sharing similarities in culture and experiences, there is a marked absence of regionalism. Conflicts and disputes have pushed the region into backwardness.

SAARC, perhaps the greatest asset of the region, does not seem to live up to its full potential primarily due to the fact that geographical boundaries of the states of this region define not just the physical limits but also national identities. It is important that bilateral relations between every member state of a multilateral organization be good and strong. Every link in the chain of multilateral cooperation is vital to keeping the whole intact. However, in reality, this is far from done – especially in the region. Thus bilateral issues such as the ones between India and Sri Lanka and India and Pakistan foment to destabilize the entire region – and consequently SAARC.

Since the independence of India and the creation of a separate "Islamic" state – Pakistan – in 1947, the two countries have not enjoyed mutually peaceful relations to say the least. Such animosity has been stoked over the past seven decades by four conventional wars and further exacerbated through the innumerable cross-border terrorist attacks that Pakistan has commissioned. Such history has made it very difficult for the countries to see eye to eye in international fora, thus negatively impacting various developmental issues such as people-to-people interaction, trade, energy and environmental security cooperation and so on. The benefits that can be accrued through mutual cooperation and understanding are too great to be ignored, but alas this currently does not seem to be.

In a democratic setup, such as India, where public perception plays a big role in vote bank politics, the perception on India–Pakistan relations has always been poor. The news media plays a big role in building this perception. Observing the current trend, the public's perception of this relationship will continue to be low. The challenges are many and the alternates few unless both governments adopt new redefining policies and – most important – are willing to co-operate with each other, which seems a faint prospect. Given these issues, the perception that the people of these two countries have of each other will continue to remain as it is – and here's why.

The all-powerful news media

The Indian news media, both national and regional, plays a very important role in the country's democratic political setup. The news media does exert an indirect, but definite, influence over the creation or conformity of the central government on bilateral relations through its capability of building and influencing a very powerful democratic force – public opinion. In fact, it would not require any stretch of imagination to state that incidents that are not reported are often treated as if they never happened.

The power of the media stems from the fact that it feeds the people living in democratic societies with information and thus enlightens them. Most often, it also participates as their conduit to share their opinions. On the other end, state authorities also need the support of the news media to propagate policies, understand impact and garner support on policies and actions.

The potency of the news media in India – even regional media – can be well illustrated through the historic example of India–Sri Lanka bilateral relations during the heyday of the Liberation Tigers of Tamil Eelam (LTTE).

In India, the perception the news media created of Sri Lanka was a cause of concern for formulating foreign policies both at the bilateral and multilateral levels. The coverage and impact of the news media ranged from powerful imagery and strong messaging of innocent Tamils and their rightful struggle under the leadership of the LTTE chief, Vellupillai Prabhakaran, to that of matter-of-fact news reporting devoid of any emotional baggage. The former could be noticed in regional Tamil news media and the latter in the larger news publications with greater readership in northern India. However, coverage of the anguish of Tamils in the hands of the oppressing Sinhalese government created unfavourable reception in the state of Tamil Nadu to any national-level bilateral agreement with the island state. However, because of the quasi-federal model of government and the dependence of the centre on regional Tamil politics, the largely negative stand the people of Tamil Nadu, Tamil regional parties and even the Tamil Nadu branches of national parties on any action or policy of the union government that entertained Sri Lanka was looked upon with deep disapproval. This impacts centre–state relations and the position of the party in power at the centre and creates waves of dissonance along the political corridors of the parliament.[1]

What drives the news media, and what does it do?

In India, the news media is driven by two factors: (a) the need to play its role as the fourth estate (b) and the need to survive and thrive in an increasingly competitive and chaotic news media saturated market.

In his book *Military and Media*, Anil Kumar Singh states, "The public has a right to know what the military does. Citizens pay taxes, and an informed public is the key to a democracy, and it allows the military to exist."[2] American journalist and founding director of the Shorenstein Center on Media, Politics and Public Policy, Marvin Kalb, explains the role of the news media:

> From whom, if not from the press, are the American people to get the information on which to base an intelligent decision on the worthiness of a

particular war, or the soundness of their government's strategies and policies, or the actual conditions on and above the fields of combat?[3]

Primarily, the role of the news media, especially in a democracy such as India, is to function as a "feeler" of the society and an instrument to propagate awareness among people. As an institution, the news media's duty is to help strengthen and support democratic processes and national values. Therefore, a responsible news media must play its part effectively in shaping public opinion against atrocities and human rights violations (which are especially prevalent in conflict zones).

As the keepers of the national conscience, the news media has multiple functions, which include its duty as a caretaker and instrument to publicize necessary information and, more popularly, as a manifestation of cultural interests and trends. It is said that the media in India plays many roles, three of which are primary: observer, participant, and catalyst.[4]

In her article, Tanvi Madan quotes C. Raja Mohan: "The media has become the principal theatre for intellectual and policy contestation on the direction of Indian foreign policy."[5] This can be seen in the way debates and discussions happen on this platform. Political parties use this platform and public opinion to influence the centre's stand on bilateral and multilateral security cooperation initiatives.

While the news media's role as the "fourth estate" is more role based and can be thus stated as its reason for existence, the second factor seems more "de facto." The news media industry is business driven, and currently, it seems all segments of the industry are still in the growing phase. The media market as such remains fragmented because of the large number of languages and the sheer size of the country.[6]

Another component of this factor is the concealment of the number of media organizations and media outlets over specific regional and language markets by a few players. The Indian media market is oligopolistic. There is a marked absence of restrictions on cross-media ownership in India. This allows some companies or conglomerates to dominate the different Indian market segments – and even the market as a whole – both vertically (print, radio, television and others) and horizontally (in particular geographical regions).[7] In fact, just like the international scenario, political parties across affiliations and regions increasingly control or own sections of the media.

Also, just like its counterparts across the globe, media publication/broadcast promoters and controllers maintain interests in many other business ventures not aligned to media. They leverage their media assets to promote these other business interests. There are examples of groups moving profits from their media ventures to diversify in other unrelated businesses.[8] The reverse is also witnessed in an increasing manner in the country. This can be seen by the growing corporatization of the media. Large industrial conglomerates show and have invested in media groups. Likewise, there is growing convergence between the creators of media content and distributors (news houses and television channels). These characteristics reveal growing instances of consolidation (concentration of ownership), especially in an oligopolistic scenario that could, over a period of time, lead to loss of heterogeneity and plurality. Thus, despite the massive numbers of publications and radio and television channels across the Indian media market, what is read, heard or watched is influenced, rather dominated, by a few groups with strong commercial bias.

The impact of news media on citizens: building perceptions

How do the two countries view each other? How do they rate their threat perceptions vis-à-vis other existential issues? This is best answered by a few statistical examples.

According to a Pew research report[9] on how people of the Asia-Pacific region perceive each other, Indians were noted to view Pakistan with the least favour amongst other countries. The report states that only eighteen per cent of Indians seek better relations with Pakistan. Over sixty-four per cent feel negative.[10]

Another report by the same research group provides an even grimmer picture. It is of interest to note that the "better educated" segment of the population view Pakistan more critically (seventy-six per cent) than those with lower educational backgrounds (fifty-eight per cent).[11]

The reasons for this stem from the overwhelming picture that the Indian news media paints of India-Pakistan relations, highlighting

- Decades of military tension
- The country as a source of terrorist attacks across Indian cities
- Its "non-cooperative" attitude
- It as a source of "anti-Indian" ideas in other South Asian neighbours

Unfortunately, the picture of India in Pakistan is almost as bad.[12]

Just like the Indian news media, its Pakistani counterpart feeds the minds of the masses with a negative picture based on their "experiences":

- India as hegemonistic
- Perception of being taken over by India – an existential crisis
- Kashmir still remaining an unresolved issue
- India as the source of unrest in Baluchistan

Important topics such as commerce are not highlighted

How much are regular newspaper readers aware of the status of commercial relations between the two neighbours?

According to the Directorate General of Commercial Intelligence and Statistics, Ministry of Commerce and Industry, as of May 2014, trade volumes between the countries witnessed a net increase of $410 million from April 2013 to March 2014. Exports from Pakistan actually grew by twenty-eight per cent while Indian exports went up by nineteen per cent.

The *Express Tribune* reported that there is great optimism for chances that bilateral trade has increased and "may soar to $6 billion in the next two years"[13] if the countries mutually grant each other Most Favoured Nation status – no mean status given the highly competitive global marketplace.

However, the question is except in trade publications, how many times and on how many news media platforms does such good news actually get published? It obviously seems that the media is largely pre-occupied with "national security"–related events to the almost complete exclusion of important non-security issues such as trade. Examples such as given here have limited penetration into popular discourse on India-Pakistan relations. This creates a glaring lack of awareness of positive trade-related activities. This lack of sufficient public awareness may even pose an impediment for governments to invest further resources towards trade normalization, as acceptance among the native population may be cold or lukewarm at the most.

The news dissemination triangle

In traditional news media (as opposed to social media), the flow of information is typically top-down. The type of news, quantity and quality are filtered in two stages – at the source itself (the media elites) and by the gatekeepers – as portrayed in Nidhi Shendurnikar Tere's paper "Bridging Barriers: Media and Citizen Diplomacy in India-Pakistan Relations."[14]

In the context of India-Pakistan relations, the news media's content is believed to be credible. This is primarily due to the absence of any other source of information. The news media often serves as the channel of "authentic" sources, such as governmental departments. This makes the role of the news media very limited in scope – being the mouthpiece of the government. Also, public perception is plagued by an information deficit across borders, as media exchange between the countries is minimal, difficult and hindered by multiple obstacles.

The functioning of this top-down communication paradigm and its effects on the audience are studied in this chapter through the propaganda model proposed by Edward S. Herman and Noam Chomsky.

The news media's agenda: the Herman-Chomsky "propaganda model"

The "propaganda model" was proposed by Edward Herman and Noam Chomsky in their 1988 book *Manufacturing Consent – The Political Economy of the Mass Media*. An overview of this conceptual treatise at this juncture is necessary to get a broader understanding of how news is "manufactured" and undergoes processes – or filters as this model calls them – before publication in any medium – print, television or radio. From the perspective of this study, this model should be scrutinized because of the increasing "corporatization" of the news industry. The model professes that because of the corporate media ownership model, dissident news, or news that is not popular with the wealthy or with the government, is given minimal or no coverage. However, news stories that are in support of either or both get maximum coverage. The propaganda model castigates the news media as a ready propaganda tool in a win–win relationship with the government and wealthy corporations.

According to this study, Herman and Chomsky state that before publication, news stories are passed through five filters.

Filter one

News media are owned by giant corporations; be true to them

The freedom of the press is restricted by the fact that the media are owned by giant corporations with commercial ambitions in focus and driven by free market ideology. Thus, editorial content is shaped based on the dictates of the corporate ownership. Little can be done by the news media considering the fact that they will eventually be put into place by the sheer size and immense wealth of the profit-seeking, capitalist ownership. During the early 1800s, a few radical newspapers brought to the fore the concerns of poor factory workers. However, in conjunction with business entities, the government began levying excessive stamp duties. This restricted newspaper ownership to only the wealthy who could afford them. This, in turn, changed the tone of the press. Today, the media companies are owned by large conglomerates, often in controversial businesses, such as weapons development and nuclear power, and are tied to the stock market. With such loyalties, it is difficult for the press to be truly neutral in their functioning.

In this context . . .

The national and various regional news media play into the popular sentiment on India-Pakistan relations – that of India being a constant victim of terrorism and the cross-border bravado of the Pakistan army. Often being a major factor during elections, they impact the government's effectiveness because of the emotional quotient. Parties align and re-align on this issue. The news media that are in sync with political parties play the "India-Pakistan" card to boost popular support for the parties and in turn boost their business – win–win.

Filter two

Advertisements are the primary source of revenue for news media; don't anger ad sources and cut them off

The second filter for the news media is the source of revenue through advertisements. Advertisements help the news media to cover the costs of production. In fact, they are the primary source of revenue for any news media organization. Thus it is imperative for it to be in the good books of major industry participants to get constant advertisements and tenders. If it is not, it has to hone itself to become sympathetic to business interests. The industry player, in contrast, utilizes such arrangements to propagate its views. In 1999, British Telecom, which was a major advertiser with the *Daily Telegraph*, threatened to withdraw its advertising contracts from the paper, as the latter had published a series of critical articles. The newspaper journalist responsible for the articles was suspended. In a capitalist system, where advertising is a major source of revenue, it is difficult for radical publications to antagonize that source. Thus, advertising, just like corporate media ownership, is a news filter.

In this context . . .

Siding and endorsing popular sentiment is a safe and viable method to increase revenues through advertisements and government tenders. As all political parties take the same stand with regard to this issue in India, there are no news media organizations that are not in line.

Media believes advertisements come from "waging war." Divergent views could ring the death knell to a news publisher.

Filter three

Maintain solid working relations with sources of fresh and authentic news

The third filter relates to the source of news. The news media naturally forms a symbiotic relationship with information sources out of economic necessity. This is a two-way relationship. For example, even major news corporations, such as CNN and the BBC, may not be able to have their report network throughout the world. Thus, they build and maintain relationships in vital news source terminals, such as the Pentagon, major parliaments, ministries, and other major sources. It is important to maintain good working relations with such sources of fresh news.

In this context. . .

Because of the overwhelming popular and political support that an anti-Pakistan stand has across the country, much importance is also given to what the "other side" says (Pakistan news media). However, do constructive debates happen? This is not mostly perceived as popular on television news channels. Information sources apart from governmental bodies continue to be from political parties and from "specialist" spokespersons.

Filter four

Beware of flak; a barrage can bury the news organization

The fourth filter of this model is flak. Noam Chomsky and Edward Herman describe this as the negative responses to a media statement or programme. Such responses may come in any form, ranging from letters to lawsuits and even physical action. Often major industry participants come together in a joint effort of rebuttal. One such example is the United States-based Global Climate Coalition (GCC).

The GCC comprises fossil fuel and automobile companies, such as Exxon, Texaco and Ford to rubbish the credibility of climate scientists and "scare stories" about global warming. The coalition was initiated by Burson-Marsteller, a large global public relations company.

In this context. . .

The Pakistan issue runs very deep in the psyche of the people of India. However, to consider the "other perspective" often results in violent backlash that is often politically driven. This question can stem from questioning the HRD Ministry's policy on raising the tricolour over central universities to supporting broader bilateral discussions.

Being a question of "being incorrectly perceived" and thus inviting flak, not much investigation is usually done to present Pakistan's perceptions. As is popularly viewed on news channels, Pakistan's perceptions are cannon fodder.

Tag along with the winning side. It is safe and ensures cash inflow.

Filter five

The enemy is not permanent, but "enmity" is; demonize the enemy

The fifth news filter is "anti-Communism." However, it can be used to describe demonization of any enemy. Herman and Chomsky's book, *Manufacturing Consent*, was written during the Cold War and hence, was focussed on enemy number one of the period. Today, however, its scope can expand to demonize anybody – Osama bin Laden, Saddam Hussein, Colonel Gaddafi, Slobodan Milosevic or Kim Jong-un. This also can include popular movements that are not conducive to dominant business interests, such as environmental movements. This model is particularly relevant today, as it attempts to bring reason to how and why the status quo of corporate power is maintained in modern society and the roles of the news media. It also studies the relationship between the corporations, the government and the news media.

In this context. . .

This model is particularly relevant in the context of India-Pakistan relations. As witnessed earlier, India's perception of Pakistan is largely unfavourable. The position is clear – with us or against us. There is no in between. Since independence, the relationship has been running high in popular "anti" sentiments, and hence, for the news media, this provides a good cash cow.

How does this impact policy formulation at the centre?

Research reveals that media's role in inter-state conflict is jingoistic and populist.[15] To garner the highest TRPs, objective reporting has taken a back seat. Sensationalism is the norm. This perception is best revealed in the words of the former Indian national security advisor Shiv Shankar Menon: "The 'breaking news model' of 24-hour news networks lent itself to the game of highest TRPs, sacrificing accuracy and credibility in the bargain."[16] This kind of setup often plays into the hands of popular vote-seeking political entities that leverage sentimental foreign policy issues of the larger population to their advantage. This was amply demonstrated in India-Sri Lankan relations during the Sri Lankan civil war. The same can be said of India-Pakistan relations. Political arm twisting of vested parties may not augur well for the centre when it attempts to look deep into strategic issues beyond the limited purview of state-level politics.

If such a political scenario continues, stemming from myopic policies of both the governments, it can be fairly said that the largely negative perception that the public of both these countries have of each other will continue into the future.

What can be done to change this perception?

Is there a possibility to change this perception of the public? Probably there is. However, such a change should begin from the mindset of key influencers – the governments and the news media industry. The latter, in particular, should understand that focus on warmongering alone need not fetch high TRPs and bring in advertisement revenue. In this respect, there should be a larger effort to pursue the opposite route – peace journalism. One popular example is Aman ki Asha – a joint peace promotion campaign of the *Jang Group* in Pakistan and the *Times of India* in India.

In the same vein, the news media could play a big role in promoting Citizen Diplomacy (Track IV Diplomacy) by playing the role of a conduit carrying messages of peace and positive perceptions between both sides. Indians and Pakistanis may leverage such channels to reach out and to promote culture and, in the process, build a strong bridge. The key thing, however, remains the benevolence of the governments and powerful commercial entities. Thus, such initiatives can become sustainable, let alone successful, only if both the governments encourage the news media to initiate such efforts. The governments themselves should take the lead.

Notes

1 Ramakrishhnan Ramani, "India and Regional Security Cooperation in South Asia: Impact of the National Media", Paper Presented at UGC Centre for Southeast Asia & Pacific Studies, Sri Venkateswara University, Tirupati, 22–24 February 2016.
2 Anil Kumar Singh, *Military and Media*, New Delhi: Lancer Publishers & Distributors, 2006.
3 Marvin Kalb, "A View from the Press", in W Lance Bennett and David L Paletz, *Taken by Storm: The Media, Public Opinion, and US Foreign Policy in the Gulf War*, Chicago: The University of Chicago Press, 1994, p. 4.
4 Partha Pratim Basu, *The Press and Foreign Policy of India*, New Delhi: Lancer Books, 2003.
5 C. Raja Mohan, "Rising India: Partner in Shaping the Global Commons", *Washington Quarterly*, vol.33, no.3, July 2010, p. 139.
6 Paranjoy Guha Thakurta, "Media Ownership Trends in India", *Posted Tuesday*, 3 July 2012, see www.thehoot.org/web/home/printstory.php?sid=6053 (Accessed on 12 November 2014).

7 *Ibid.*

8 *Ibid.*

9 Bruce Stokes, "How Asia-Pacific Publics See Each Other and Their National Leaders", *Pew Research Center, Global Attitudes & Trends*, 2 September 2015, see www.pewglobal. org/2015/09/02/how-asia-pacific-publics-see-each-other-and-their-national-leaders/ (Accessed on 12 January 2016).

10 *Ibid.*

11 *Ibid.*

12 *Ibid.*

13 *The Express Tribune*, "Trade Between India and Pakistan Surges 21% to $2.4 Billion", 14 May 2013, see http://tribune.com.pk/story/548768/trade-between-india-and-pakistan-surges-21-to-2-4-billion/ (Accessed on 4 January 2016).

14 Nidhi Shendurnikar Tere, "Bridging Barriers: Media and Citizen Diplomacy in India-Pakistan Relations", see www.academia.edu/3692462/Bridging_Barriers_Media_and_Citizen_Diplomacy_in_India-Pakistan_Relations (Accessed on 14 January 2016).

15 Vanita Kholi Khandekar, *The Indian Media Business*, New Delhi: Response Books, 2006, p. 28.

16 Prashant Jha, "Media's Impact on Foreign Policy 'Short Term,' 'Episodic,' 'Symbolic'", *The Hindu*, 8 March 2013, see www.thehindu.com/todayspaper/tpnational/mediasimpact onforeignpolicyshorttermepisodicsymbolic/article4486591.ece (Accessed on 14 January 2016).

PART 3

Economic cooperation in South Asia

10

RE-ENERGIZING ECONOMIC COOPERATION THROUGH REGIONAL AID FOR TRADE

Lessons from Europe

Kithmina V. Hewage

Introduction

The issue of South Asian regional cooperation has garnered considerable debate, and the future of South Asian regionalism largely hinges on how policymakers respond to the political economy of the region. The path towards stronger relations between members of the region has mostly failed thus far because of the absence of a political will from within. The region, however, faces a crucial period in the immediate future with the rebalance of international trade and investment towards regional efforts. The South Asian region in particular is significant because of the rapid growth of India and the inward flow of investment and trade that may follow.

This chapter explores the prospects of improved regional cooperation in South Asia with the emergence of new trends in trade and investment. While regionalism has gained momentum across the globe over the past few decades, disputes, mistrust, misunderstanding and suspicion have curtailed the prospects of regionalism in South Asia. Consequently, amidst its immense potential, the region accounts for just five percent of global trade and one percent of global investment. One of the main inhibiting factors of intra-regional trade has been the competitive rather than complementary nature of products produced in the region. With the exception of India, the export basket of countries is highly concentrated in labour-intensive goods, such as textiles and agriculture. Consequently, traditional notions of trade, based on competition, have paralyzed the political will to improve intra-regional trade and investment.

However, the production of manufactured goods is increasingly organized through global value or supply chains, with goods being processed (value being added) in multiple countries that are part of the chain. Therefore, new opportunities for regional cooperation have emerged with the possibility of identifying complementarities in order to create regional value chains. In order to create suitable conditions for value chain creation and expansion, it is imperative that South Asia improve its mechanisms for trade facilitation through the reduction of non-tariff barriers and addressing capacity constraints.

The discussion of regional value chains and production networks considers the case study of European enlargement following the Cold War. The comparison is especially pertinent because of the economic power asymmetry that existed between the coreEU and newly acceding countries, similar to that of India and its neighbours. Based on this observation, it is argued that a regional aid-for-trade strategy can provide coherence in directing resources towards investments that are regionally focussed and mutually beneficial. In doing so, the economic power asymmetry between India and its neighbours can be addressed in a positive manner through the emergence of regional production networks.

An extensive literature exists analyzing the relationship between aid and economic growth. The literature fails to provide a conclusive decision on whether a positive or negative relationship exists between aid and growth. Burnside and Dollar[1] argue that aid has no identifiable impact on growth once other factors are accounted for, including economic policies. Contrastingly, Hansen and Tarp[2] find that aid is effective and not dependent on policies. Consequently, significant debate continues to exist on the methods employed to analyze this relationship. Among a variety of factors, the heterogeneity of aid motives, and the complex causality associated with aid and growth are likely to result in divergent findings.[3] Overall, there appears to be considerable influence of particular conditions associated with aid flows such as the absorptive capacity of the recipient country or the type of aid delivered.[4]

At the same time, there is growing consensus that trade policies centred on openness alone are not sufficient to achieve economic growth and development and fail to address poverty reduction concerns. For example, Rodri[5] notes the importance of complementary institutional and governance reforms to realize the benefits of trade liberalization. The impact of increased trade through liberalization in developing countries depends on the structure of the economy and whether the trade-induced growth occurs in sectors where a large number of poor people are active. For instance, the economic structure determines the extent to which trade can lead to job creation and wage increases, whether excess labour can be absorbed and how equipped those in the low-income status are to benefit from the creation of new opportunities.[6]

Moreover, the international community is cognizant of the political-economic implications of trade liberalization, as a well-organized influential segment losing out from liberalization can block reforms that are beneficial to the average citizen.[7] Within this context of shifting perceptions on trade, aid, growth and poverty alleviation, the World Trade Organization (WTO) introduced the Aid for Trade (AfT) initiative to address the "development deficit" in the multilateral trade liberalization process by minimizing the transitional costs of trade liberalization in developing countries.

The global financial crisis and the ensuing demand for austerity in developed nations has resulted in a shift in aid policy, with donors increasingly under pressure to demonstrate immediate impacts in recipient countries. Consequently, the role of AfT has also evolved with changes in the international political economy. Thus, in addition to mitigating the transitional costs of trade liberalization in developing countries, AfT further attempts to address supply-side constraints of trade, such as poor infrastructure.[8] Moreover, AfT is seen as a means to facilitate efforts by developing countries to diversify and reduce output volatility – especially during crises leading to uncertain export demand and fluctuating commodity prices.[9]

Most of the current quantitative research on the effect of AfT disaggregates the flow of aid into six categories, proposed by the Aid for Trade Task Force. The proposed six categories are as follows:

- *Aid directed to trade policy and regulations*, which includes training of trade officials, analysis of proposals and positions and their impact on national stakeholders, technical and institutional support to facilitate the implementation of trade agreements and compliance with rules and standards;
- *Aid directed to trade development*, such as investment and trade promotion, support in different trade sectors and trade finance, market analysis and development;
- *Aid directed to trade-related infrastructure*, including physical infrastructure to connect domestic and foreign markets;
- *Aid directed to building productive capacity*, meaning investments in industries and specific sectors so that countries are able to diversify production and exports;
- *Aid directed to trade-related adjustment*, which comprises complementary measures absorbing some of the costs linked to tariff reductions or declining terms of trade to make developing countries benefit from trade liberalization;
- *Aid directed to other trade-related needs*.

Empirically, research analyzing the effect of AfT on the economic performance of developing countries has found generally positive results, but its impact varies under certain circumstances. Cali and Te Velde[10] find that aid for trade facilitation reduces the costs of trading. In particular, aid to economic infrastructure and aid to productive capacity is seen to have a positive effect with the former particularly benefitting mining and manufacturing exports. Adam and Bevan[11] note that aid channelled through investment and other productive uses can significantly reduce the "Dutch disease" effects of increased aid.

The effect of AfT is also heavily linked to the type of aid provided to the developing country. Collectively, aid for infrastructure, aid for trade development and aid for trade policy are found to reduce worldwide trade costs by 0.2 per cent and generate a total welfare gain of \$18.5 billion. However, among the three categories of aid, aid directed through trade policy is identified as having the greatest impact on lowering trade costs to both exporters and imports; similarly, trade facilitation is observed to have a significant and large impact on the trade costs of exporters.[12] Busse et al.[13] make similar observations regarding the influence of aid categories on trade-related economic benefits. Overall, while AfT accounts for more than one-third of Official Development Assistance (ODA) by traditional donors, the initiative is seen to have succeeded in mobilizing donor resources towards trade-related activities. Moreover, the focussed nature of aid disbursements is seen to generally improve the quality of aid in terms of the ownership and design of programmes and policies.[14]

Notably, much of the existing literature discusses AfT flows from traditional donors (OECD-DAC). However, emerging donors, such as the BRICS (Brazil, Russia, India, China, and South Africa) and oil-producing Middle-Eastern nations have begun to play a strong role in contributing AfT, albeit as "South-South Cooperation." For example, estimates suggest that development assistance from Arab countries between 1974 and 1994 constituted on average 13.5 per cent of all aid.[15] The emergence of new donors has resulted in the exertion of competitive pressures into the aid distribution framework.[16] In fact, emerging donors have taken particular steps to fill a vacuum in diverting aid towards trade-related human capacity development.[17] South-South aid flows are increasingly concentrated within a regional context (with the exception of Chinese aid) and in turn have led to stronger coordination on the trade and investment front between developing countries.[18]

Regional aid for trade

The economic community has generally accepted that developing countries can accrue significant benefits through regional cooperation. Yet, nations fail to utilize these opportunities adequately because of a lack of "groundwork," either in the form of weak infrastructure, human-resource capacity constraints, trade-facilitation-related issues, or policy inadequacies.[19] Whereas traditional aid flows tend to focus on the national level, AfT, by virtue of focussing on trade-related activities, has a cross-border component to it. Resultantly, a growing emphasis has been placed on catalyzing economic growth through a region-focussed AfT strategy.

Currently, regional aid for trade strategies are pursued most aggressively in the Caribbean and Sub-Saharan Africa because of both strong domestic political will for regional integration and economic partnership agreements (EPAs) between traditional donors, such as the European Union (EU) and the respective regional blocs. Regional aid-for-trade flows are small compared to overall flows but have been growing rapidly relative to the baseline. In 2011, regional AfT accounted for roughly $6 billion, and its share in total AfT has grown from about nine per cent in 2002–2005 to twelve per cent in 2006 and eighteen per cent in 2011. Furthermore, while total aid-for-trade flows grew by about 50 per cent in 2006–2011, regional and sub-regional aid for trade increased by 2.5 times as much. Thus, the importance of regional aid for trade is rising in line with the increase in developing-country regional cooperation initiatives.[20]

Theoretically, regional AfT allows partners to pool resources and coordinate activities, leading to more cohesive implementation mechanisms and subsequently, reduced transaction costs. Moreover, regional projects benefit from the ability to replicate best practices from countries within the region that often face similar constraints. Most crucially, a strong overarching rationale exists for regional-level responses where there is a need for harmonizing policies and "unlocking" key cross-border bottlenecks that would otherwise persist in preventing opportunities for trade.[21]

It should be noted, however, that amidst the growing importance of regional AfT, the concept is not well defined. This is mostly since nationally implemented AfT projects can have regional spill-over effects. Consequently, data specific to regional AfT remains vague, as the OECD-DAC Creditor Reporting System (CRS) fails to distinguish between national projects within a broader regional package or AfT given to a specific regional economic grouping.

Production networks

Global production sharing – the break-up of the production process into geographically separated stages – has become an increasingly important facet in modern trade. Through a combination of firms seeking cost advantages, technological advancements and low transport costs and time, trade in parts and components and final assembly within production networks has generally grown faster than total world trade in manufacturing.[22] Often, production networks are established within a regional setting as evidenced in East Asia. A regional presence allows lead firms to organize the production processes according to the comparative advantage of members of a region, minimize transport costs and also benefit from a regional cooperation frameworks, which has the potential of leading to further multilateral liberalization as well.[23]

Regional AfT flows, rather than traditional national-level AfT, facilitate the creation of regional production networks in several ways. One of the key constraints to regional integration among developing countries is the similarity of each other's economy leading to limited opportunities for trade amongst each other. For instance, the export basket of nations is highly concentrated in labour-intensive goods, such as textiles and agriculture. Consequently, through national development programmes, nations are likely to face competing interests with their regional counterparts, and nationally focused AfT flows will be directed towards efforts that further limit the scope of intra-regional trade. Therefore, developing nations continue to be involved in inter-commodity trade (e.g., natural resource exports for imports of manufacturers) and fail to exploit the potential for moving up value chains.

Contrastingly, regional AfT will divert resources towards efforts that create avenues for more dynamic intra-regional trade by addressing regional bottlenecks rather than reinforcing constraining practices. Chief among these bottlenecks is the ability for regional members to direct resources towards developing regional comparative advantages. Even though the overall economic structures of developing countries in a region are likely to be similar, slight variances accommodate the potential for intra-industry trade to occur within a regional setting. In doing so, through participation in regional production networks, diversification proceeds as countries develop and move up value chains.[24] Thus, rather than perpetuate trade friction among regional partners, region-focused AfT can reinforce pathways to stronger intra-regional trade.

Regional political-economy

In addition to the economic benefits of improved trade, regional AfT is also seen as a mechanism through which to improve the political economy of developing regions. As noted previously, the similarity in economic structure leads to a notion that gain by one country in the region will adversely affect another. Thereby, bilateral, regional and multilateral trade and aid negotiations are seen as a "zero-sum game."[25] Through the pursuit of mutually reinforcing economic policies that improve intra-regional trade, AfT could help establish synergies across a plethora of stakeholders. The regional approach, unlike a bilateral or multilateral approach, allows infrastructure investments and trade facilitation measures to be implemented in a coherent, sequenced and coordinated manner.[26] Such an effort requires strong institutional coordination among parties involved. The Caribbean region and East Asia are two distinct examples that have strengthened their respective region's political integration through region-focused trade and aid initiatives.[27]

Furthermore, regional aid for trade has the ability to address trading, investment and negotiating asymmetries that exist within regions as well. Often because of similar-issue salience, developing countries negotiate within regional coalitions during multilateral trade negotiations. The prevalence of regional aid for trade and reinforcing regional priorities through investment, infrastructure development and crucially human capacity development measures, the region gains additional leverage through collective bargaining. It is important to note, however, that such political-economy benefits are not accrued automatically and require leadership and coordinated dialogue within the region. Similarly, the promotion of intra-regional trade, particularly in the form of intra-industrial trade, could align the interests of the "core and periphery" of regions as well. In situations with a dominant partner within the region, other nations that are often on the periphery could benefit by integrating closer to the core.[28]

Regional Aid for trade in Europe

Since the inception of the Marshall Plan, following the Second World War, foreign aid has played a significant role in influencing the economic growth of Europe. Even though the exact nature in which the Marshall Plan stimulated investment and financed infrastructure is debatable, a substantial literature emphasizes the important role of aid in facilitating the economic and political institutional transformation of Western-European nations.[29] The most critical role of foreign aid in spurring economic growth and regional cooperation, however, occurs through regional frameworks for development assistance in a post-Cold War setting. The core-periphery relationship in Europe and the role of aid in addressing this relationship was especially important with the expansion of the EU. This article traces the mechanisms through which regional aid for improving trade networks strengthened cooperation in Europe by discussing a few case studies.

Post-Soviet expansion

Poland acceded to the EU, along with seven other post-communist nations (commonly referred to as the EU-8): Czech Republic, Estonia, Hungary, Latvia, Lithuania, Poland, Slovakia, Slovenia), as well as Cyprus and Malta (collectively referred to as the EU-10). Even though official accession took place in 2004, the path towards accession was initiated in the early 1990s. For example, Poland undertook the process in 1991 upon signing the Europe agreement with the EU. This process is most significant since this was the first instance where EU enlargement addressed the issue of European reunification following the collapse of the Soviet Union.[30] Furthermore, it was during this process that the EU laid out the "Copenhagen Criteria" in 1993. The essential conditions all candidate countries were required to fulfil in order to gain membership included the following:

- Political criteria: stability of institutions guaranteeing democracy, the rule of law, human rights and respect for and protection of minorities;
- Economic criteria: a functioning market economy and the capacity to cope with competition and market forces;
- Administrative and institutional capacity to effectively implement *acquis* and the ability to take on the obligations of membership.[31]

In achieving these requirements, foreign aid had an influential role in facilitating the economic reforms necessary and also had an effect on political and institutional reforms.

Pre-accession aid

The European Union cohesion policy refers to an arsenal of instruments used to address economic and social disparities in Europe. This policy can be broadly categorized into two frameworks. Pre-accession aid, such as the "Phare Programme," is intended to act as a bridge for candidate countries in acquiring the *acquis*. The other form of regional development assistance occurs in a post-accession context through structural funds for areas of member countries that are lagging behind the rest of the region. Cohesion policy was established through the Single European Act (1986). Subsequent reforms in 1989 merged the European Regional Development Fund (ERDF), European Social Fund (ESF) and the guidance section of the European Agricultural Guarantee and Guidance Fund (EAGGF) into a common policy framework, which resulted in the doubling of available funds.[32]

The pre-accession aid programme featured the Instrument for Structural Policies for Pre-Accession (ISPA) that provided funding for environment and transport projects; the Phare programme (Poland and Hungary: Aid for Economic Restructuring) aimed to strengthen economic and social cohesion while developing administrative and institutional capacity; and the Special Accession Programme for Agricultural and Rural Development (SAPARD) focused on a similar role for rural areas. Notably, a single Instrument for Pre-Accession Assistance (IPA) was introduced in January 2007 to replace those instruments that were previously in place.

Phare was first introduced in 1989 and represented the main EU financial aid for Poland and Hungary during their economic restructuring. However, at its inception, the programmes were not targeted towards regional development. The second reorganization of Phare took place in the mid-nineties. Firstly, EU aid was reoriented on investment. It was delivered in the framework of a sectoral and regional programme (PHARE-STRUDER, PHARE-CBC, PHARE-RAPID). Secondly, the available tools and procedures changed as the newly introduced programmes operated on the basis of instruments taken from the structural funds. The third reorganization of Phare took place in 1998 as a result of initiating negotiations with Central and East European countries regarding future members.[33]

The principal objective associated with providing pre-accession aid to candidate nations to the EU was to align the economies of former Soviet nations with the rest of the region. Therefore, as noted earlier, this objective was mainly driven by a strong presence of core-periphery relations within the region with countries formerly isolated from international trade and closed off from private international capital markets embarking on a strategy to dismantle the main obstacles to trade and globalization. As the EU-10 attempted to restructure their economy, the different cost structures in industry between the existing EU and the candidate nations were of significant concern.[34] In essence, similar to the objective of modern regional AfT programmes, the strategy depended on harmonizing the region's trade and infrastructure programmes.

TABLE 10.1 Economic indicators for the countries acceding in May 2004 in comparison to the EU-15

	% of the level in EU-15
GDP (in PPS, 2002)	9.0
Population (2002)	19.7
Total employment (2001)	17.7
GDP per head (in PPP, 2002)	46.4
Labour productivity (GDP per employed persons in PPS, 2001)	52.2

Source: European Commission, *European Competitiveness Report*, Brussels: European Commission, 2003, p. 43

Trade agreements

One of the fundamental policy choices made during the process of accession to the EU was the decision to establish relevant trade agreements between the region and the candidates along with complementary aid disbursements. The Europe agreements – which came into force between 1994 and 1999 – established free trade agreements on the basis of reciprocity but applied in an asymmetric manner and with restrictions in some sectors (e.g., footstuffs, textiles, clothing). For example, a free trade zone was established in the early 1990s that covered eighty-five per cent of bilateral trade. By eliminating tariff barriers among the parties, the regional aid program was better equipped to singularly focus on non-tariff barriers to trade. Moreover, the existence of comprehensive economic cooperation agreements acted as a strong signalling function for foreign investors from the region as well as from outside.

As noted, the level of economic growth in candidate countries was significantly lower than the average of the EU. Similarly, the level of trade intensity was also low because of structural limitations in the periphery nations. Consequently, because of these vast differences, candidate countries are found to be mainly specialized in resource-intensive industries like metals and wood and labour-intensive goods like clothing and textiles. Contrastingly, the core region had already transformed its economy into producing intermediate and high-tech goods.[35]

Moreover, improvements in trade performance by candidate countries occurred prior to official membership in the EU or the European Monitory Union. The availability of suitable trade agreements accommodated the candidate countries and allowed them to benefit from their geographical advantages and gain access to the European market and consequently other markets as well. As discussed in the following section, the availability of complementary trade agreements that opened up trade and investment in candidate nations along with the reduction of capacity constraints (addressed through pre-accession aid) was a significant factor in spurring the creation of regional production networks in Europe. For example, within the mandate of improving intra-regional trade, one of the primary sectors that were focussed on by pre-accession aid was the development of transportation infrastructure between candidate member states (CMS) and old member states (OMS), as well as within each individual CMS. To this end, CMSs were required to create a National Development Plan that was directed towards creating economic and social cohesion.

Regional production networks

As small nations, the CMSs would have experienced considerable difficulties in pursuing their own industrial development because of constraints on access to adequate resources for production as well as limited markets. These challenges are highlighted by the performance of these nations towards the end of the Soviet era. Therefore, close integration with Europe created a context of "regional globalization." Intra-EU-15 trade throughout the 1990s was levelling off whilst intra-EU-25 trade was significantly more dynamic – spurred on by trade between the EU-10 and the EU-15. Foreign direct investments in the EU-10 were particularly important towards this trend, as access to market considerations and strict comparative advantage factors influenced European enterprises to restructure their production processes to benefit from location and cost advantages offered by newly acceding countries.

The EU, before and after formally expanding to the EU-25, has benefitted from a strong growth in technologically sophisticated industries in the EU-10 and a corresponding reduction of specialization in low-skill, labour-intensive products. The corresponding increase in intra-industry trade within the region further reflects the advantages of a narrower scale of development created through vertical specialization. The main influence of vertical specialization, in this instance, is observed to be mainly on the location of production.

Automobile industry

The transformation of production networks in Europe as a consequence of regionally focussed strategies is most pronounced in the automobile industry. The industry expanded from initially servicing the host market to overcoming limitations associated with domestic market size to exporting finished products or tapping into regional production networks in Europe. Among the EU-10, Poland, the Czech Republic, Slovakia and Hungary emerged as the main driving forces associated with this expansion. Through harmonized regional policy frameworks, improved intra-regional transportation infrastructure, and lower non-tariff barriers, these nations were able to offer traditional expertise, cost advantages and proximity to a large European market.

TABLE 10.2 Specialization* of EU-10 in their trade with EU-15

	1993	2003	Change
Furniture and parts	3.1	4.0	0.9
Motor vehicles	-1.7	3.3	5.0
Internal combustion piston engines	0.0	3.0	3.0
Telecommunication equipment	-1.6	1.6	3.1
Television receivers	0.0	1.5	1.4
Equipment for distributing electricity	0.4	1.4	1.1
Wood manufacture	1.5	1.1	-0.4
Automatic data processing machines	-1.2	1.0	2.2
Wood simply worked	1.3	1.0	-0.3
Women's clothing	5.0	1.0	-4.0

Source: Radošević and Sachwald, *Does Enlargement Conceal Globalisation? Location Issues in Europe*, Note de l'ifri 58, Paris: Ifri, 2005.

Note: * Indicator of contributing to trade balance, in %

As noted in the following, the EU-10 have become specialized in automobiles and electronics, sectors in which they were marginal exporters or non-exporters. By joining regional production networks, these nations have consequently broken away from labour-intensive sectors such as textiles and become more specialized in mid- to high-tech industries.

In response to crises faced during the 1990s and an urgent need to pursue cost-effective measures to remain competitive in the global market, the German automobile industry was one of the first to relocate its production network towards the periphery of Europe. These changes were facilitated through the evolution of practices in the industry that depended on modularization and supplier outsourcing.[36] Notably, vertical specialization has allowed R&D and sophisticated production to take place in the EU-15 while automobile assembly was located in plants based in the EU-10. Finally, in addition to cost, market access factors and a rationalization of value chains, the dispersion of the automobile industry has also led to market creation in the EU-10.

Electronics and ICT

In addition to the automobile industry, a region-focussed trade and aid strategy has also benefitted and expanded the ICT sector across Europe. The industry demonstrates a wide degree of specialization between countries, as European countries, especially from the EU-10, specialize in different ICT products. In the EU-10, the Czech Republic and Hungary are leading the path towards rapid specialization in the industry. Radosevic and Sachwald (2005) highlight several factors that have benefitted the nations to benefit from production networks associated with ICT.

Firstly, the manufacture of electronics has moved from a highly localized production pattern to a highly globalized one and a rationalized network of facilities. This has led to an increase in the volume produced in a single factory and is therefore more productive. Secondly, manufacturing has become increasingly decoupled from assembly. Thirdly, in order to solve the paradox between increased concentration and dispersion, firms are keen to reduce costs in the value chain through outsourcing and relocation to low-cost sites. Fourthly, competitive pressures are forcing firms to locate closer to the main market to increase market responsiveness.[37]

Through an emphasis on developing human capacity and reducing institutional barriers to trade through pre-accession assistance and other mechanisms, EU-10 countries have been able to benefit by attracting FDI in the industry. For instance, the availability of a semi-skilled and skilled but cheap workforce along with free-trade zones and close proximity to the greater EU market is seen to be particularly relevant. Therefore, upon reflection, it is evident that the highly cost-sensitive nature of the ICT sector is particularly beneficial to developing nations, such as those of the EU-10, especially when they have access to larger markets.

A Greek tragedy

Comparing the accession of Greece to the EU and the integration of the EU-10 further highlights the importance of development assistance to minimize transitional costs. Whereas the former relied heavily on treaty-based economic liberalization, the latter was relatively more cognizant of subsidizing the costs involved to transform an economy and address the relevant capacity constraints. Greek accession to the EU was based mainly on political factors, as the country shifted away from communism and relied on European regional support to "lock-in" democratic reforms. Consequently, scant attention was paid to the economic distortions that existed between Greece and the main region.

The lack of attention to the transition costs of liberalization and integration to the European model in Greece is seen as a main factor that positions Greece as an outlier to the effects of European expansion with all other countries benefitting through increases in per capita GDP and other economic measures. In fact, on average, studies have found that the per capita incomes of acceded nations would have been twelve per cent lower had they not transitioned into the EU – with the exception of Greece.[38] It is important to note that while membership in the EU is a binary, the process of economic integration is a continuum, and interventions during this process, or the lack thereof, could have significant impacts on the final outcome.

Opening up Greece's uncompetitive market to European competition without facilitating a regionally focussed transition mechanism and assistance is seen to have caused a divergence in Greek economic performance between 1980 and 1995, relative to the region.[39] Interestingly, in 1976, the Council of Ministers extraordinarily rejected the European Commission's assessment, which was against opening accession negotiations with Greece and in favour of delaying entry until Greek producers were deemed capable of competing in the common market. Contrastingly, the provision of greater emphasis to structural limitations associated with transitioning economies resulted in a relatively smoother restructure of economies within the EU-10. Moreover, the emphasis on a regional mechanism prior to accession also enabled the region and its new members to coordinate the reallocation of production networks more efficiently. Consequently, rather than compete amongst themselves in a detrimental manner, the EU-10 was able to establish complementary policy measures that created economic growth in its nations as well as its neighbours.

Opportunities for South Asia

Contemporary South Asian economies and pre-accession Eastern Europe demonstrate considerable similarities in their outlook of intra-regional economic affairs. Factors constraining better regional cooperation and integration are well documented with particular emphasis given to the lack of political will driven by a longstanding trust deficit between South Asian countries, non-tariff barriers, weak regional coordinating mechanisms and similar export baskets.[40] Since many of these factors are inter-linked, continuous efforts in both economic and political fora to address constraints to regional cooperation and integration have failed to successfully materialize. In fact, amidst being recognized as the fastest-going region in the world, intra-regional trade in South Asia accounts for just five percent of its total trade.[41] Therefore, while significant opportunities remain available in strengthening intra-regional trade, proposed policy measures require cognizance of political realities.

Intra-regional trade flows

On the economic front, intra-regional trade in South Asia carries the most significant potential for common growth, especially with the predicted growth of India. In fact, many successful developing strategies, especially in East Asia and Latin America, have paid particular attention to intra-regional trade. Furthermore, while other regions continue to expand their regional trade mechanisms, South Asia continues to lag behind with relatively small gains made over the years (Table 10.3).

Further disaggregation of intra-regional trade in South Asia demonstrates a significant influence of bilateral trade flows between India and its neighbours. While India and its predicted growth provides significant opportunities for the future, particular attention is also required to identify and address constraints prohibiting the expansion of trade between South Asian economies, beyond India. Both historical and structural factors have led to this situation. The region's movement towards trade liberalization has been sporadic, and when faced with restrictive tariff regimes within the region, countries moved towards establishing markets elsewhere, especially in Europe.[42] The absence of a regional market, therefore, negated the necessity to create trade complementarity, and the countries have become competitors across a narrow range of products. As such, South Asian economies are characterized as only moderate "natural trading partners."[43]

TABLE 10.3 Intraregional trade in different trade blocs as a percentage of world trade

Regional bloc	Exports		
	1990	2000	2012
ASEAN	18.9	23.0	26.0
CARICOM	8.0	14.6	14.5
EU	67.6	67.7	61.8
MERCOSUR	8.9	20.0	14.9
NAFTA	41.4	55.7	48.5
SAARC	3.2	4.2	5.8

Source: United Nations Conference on Trade and Development, *Handbook of Statistics*, Geneva: UNCTAD, 2016

Similar production processes, however, should be considered as an opportunity rather than an obstacle. Since countries in the region specialize in similar goods, the region is likely to gain considerably through vertical integration across the region. Lower border costs will facilitate nations to source raw materials and intermediates from their neighbours and thereby expand the export potential of the countries as well. Therefore, while simultaneously addressing non-tariff barriers, the region should also focus on creating regional production networks.

South Asian production networks

Improving intra-regional trade through the creation of regional production networks is a potential opportunity for further engagement since it requires relatively less political capital and is mutually beneficial for all those involved. As noted previously, contemporary trade focuses on "hyper-specialization" whereby the production process emphasizes the manufacture of parts and components. However, with the exception of India and to a lesser extent Pakistan, the manufacturing sectors of South Asian economies are geared almost exclusively towards producing a complete good within its borders. This is due to the orientation of the economy towards import-substitution. Consequently, the production processes based on the comparative advantage in a bygone era has failed to evolve with modern trends in international trade.

As noted in Table 10.4, the share of exports in intermediates is significantly lower compared to that of other regions and country groupings. However, structural characteristics of South Asian economies provide meaningful opportunities to re-orient towards joining and creating regional and global production networks. Firstly, participation in production networks allows countries to specialize in a slice (task) of the production process by maximizing the relative cost advantage in labour-abundant economies, common in South Asia. Therefore, compared to "conventional manufacturing," parts and components trade along with assembly manufacturing tends to be more labour intensive and therefore "pro poor."[44] Secondly, corporations from transitioning and developing economies have accumulated

TABLE 10.4 Share of GPN products in manufacturing exports, 2012–13 (%)

	Parts and components	Final assembly	Total
South Asia	11.2	11.2	22.5
ASEAN	52.5	19.6	71.5
Developed countries	25.2	23.6	48.8
Developing countries	34.1	28.0	62.0
World	29.2	17.9	47.1

Source: Calculations made by Prema-chandra Atukorala using UN Comtrade data for presentation at the Institute of Policy Studies of Sri Lanka, Colombo: IPS, 2015.

sufficient capital, knowledge and know-how to invest abroad by creating emerging multinational corporations (EMNCs).

Currently, regional trade agreements (e.g., SAFTA) focus almost exclusively on reducing tariffs and quotas. Moreover, SAFTA (2004) does not cover liberalization in investment and lists it only as an "Additional Measure" in Article 8. Moreover, bilateral treaties within the region have failed to liberalize investments, and regulatory barriers could curtail the potential for the region to gain from EMNCs. The emergence of EMNCs from India, in particular, bodes well for the region since corporations will look towards creating production networks, especially in terms of reducing transport costs. Thus far, while outward investments of India have steadily increased, investment within the region has failed to match these flows. This trend can be attributed mostly to a restrictive policy framework.[45] In order to facilitate this process, therefore, it is vital that the region adapt its regulatory framework away from their traditional aversion to FDI and towards enabling intra-regional investment.

In fact, the creation of a favourable regulatory framework would incentivize foreign investment in the region. These flows are likely to gain even further prominence with the recent adoption of the "Make in India" policy. Similar to the gains made by Eastern European countries in hosting ancillary investments to the main EU, establishing India as a primary destination of FDI would benefit neighbouring countries by providing opportunities to attract ancillary industries with linkages to the supply chain (i.e., logistics hub). In essence, similar to Europe, the core-periphery dynamic of economic activities in the region could be used to be mutually beneficial to all counties in South Asia. Thus, in order to facilitate this process, regulatory mechanisms should also be complemented with better connectivity and trade facilitation. For example, a study by the ADB and the United Nations Conference on Trade and Development (UNCTAD) in 2008 noted that increasing the scope for intra-regional trade in energy; improving road, rail and air links; developing modern border controls and creating sophisticated telecommunications networks within the region would be crucial towards achieving the benefits of intra-regional trade and investment.

Regional aid-for-trade strategy

The preceding discussion creates a "bottom-up" process of regional integration whereby trade and investment flows create better cooperation and integration within the region. An investment and trade led integration process requires significantly less political capital and could also help reduce the trust deficit that exists in the region. However, in order to fully realize the potential of regional investment and trade, complementary structures are required, especially in terms of creating better connectivity. In order to do so, a regional coordinating mechanism is vital, especially in regard to coordinating resources towards mutually beneficial projects.

A regional aid-for-trade strategy, therefore, would be pertinent to addressing coordination gaps that currently exist in South Asia. Crucially, the policy and institutional mechanisms for such a strategy have already been established through the SAARC Development Fund. However, it is vital that the fund's mandate is strengthened in regard to taking a more prominent role in coordinating trade-related aid towards investments that improve connectivity within the region and address regional barriers to trade.

Therefore, the creation of a regional aid-for-trade strategy will complement a greater emphasis by policymakers towards targeted investment promotion and incentivizing regional off-shoring and regional production networks. In doing so, regional value chains are likely to be created and strengthened while the region is also likely to be better equipped to benefit from increased intra-regional trade and investment.

Conclusion

Obstacles to better cooperation and integration in South Asia are well documented. Political tensions between countries and a resulting trust deficit along with competitive economic structures have become the basis for the creation of other impeding factors as well. While many efforts have been taken to strengthen regional cooperation through political and economic means, the absence of adequate political will continues to undermine any measures. This impediment is becoming even more prominent because of the "top-down" nature of regional integration. Contrastingly, case studies of European integration efforts (especially following the Cold War) and even Latin American integration efforts demonstrate that economic cooperation mechanisms through trade and investment create "bottom-up" integration efforts. Essentially, closer economic ties within a region tend to circumvent the political-economic barriers to regional cooperation.

Cognizant of this trend, future policy prescriptions towards strengthening regional coordination should attempt to create an economic dynamism within the region that evolves from within. Improving intra-regional trade is a key instrument in addressing this concern, and developing regional production networks or value chains requires minimal political capital and is mutually beneficial to all parties involved. While a regional focus is being embraced around the world as a mechanism towards economic growth, South Asia remains stagnant in its regional economic integration efforts. The significantly low intra-regional trade and investment flows in South Asia are a testament to this fact. Moreover, the low levels of intra-regional trade and investment in the region are even more significant when considering the asymmetric economic power relationship between India and the rest of South Asia.

This chapter uses Europe as a case study to observe the use of regionally focussed economic strategies to strengthen cooperation amidst power imbalances. Particular attention is given to the accession of Eastern and Central European nations to the EU following the collapse of the Soviet Union. Notably, it is observed that political integration mechanisms are preceded by regional political strategies underpinned by a regional AfT policy. The combination of economic cooperation, especially through the creation of regional production networks, underpinned by the coordinated distribution of resources towards regionally focussed, mutually beneficial investments in connectivity is of vital significance. The strategy transforms the economic power asymmetry between the core-EU and the newly acceding periphery in a manner that spurs foreign investment, especially in the trade of parts and components.

The adoption of the "Make in India" policy, in particular, provides the region with an ideal opportunity to benefit from the inflow of foreign investment into India. Moreover, the EMNCs also afford an opportunity for South Asia to benefit by joining regional and global production networks. In order to establish ancillary industries and join production networks, however, it is important that nations liberalize their trade and investment regulatory frameworks. Finally, investments should be directed towards improving connectivity in the region and reduce non-tariff barriers to trade. As evidenced by the case study of Europe, a regional aid-for-trade strategy would complement these efforts by directing resources towards regionally focussed, mutually beneficial investments. The successful combination of regulatory and policy mechanisms is likely to create complementarity between the economies of South Asia and thus enable better cooperation.

Notes

1 C. Burnside and D. Dollar, "Aid, Policies, and Growth", *American Economic Review*, vol.90, no.4, 2000, pp. 847–868.
2 H. Hansen and F. Tarp, *Aid and Growth Regressions*, England: University of Nottingham, 2001.
3 F. Bourguignon and M. Sundberg, "Aid Effectiveness – Opening the Black Box", *American Economic Review*, vol.97, no.2, 2007, pp. 316–321.
4 B. Hoekman and J.S. Wilson, *Aid for Trade: Building on Progress Today for Tomorrow's Future*, Washington DC: World Bank, 2010.
5 D. Rodrik, "How to Save Globalization from Its Cheerleaders", *Journal of International Trade and Diplomacy*, vol.1, no.2, 2007, pp. 1–33.
6 J. Hallaert and L. Munro, *Binding Constraints to Trade Expansion*, Paris: OECD Publishing, 2009.
7 E. Basnett, *Increasing the Effectiveness of Aid for Trade: The Circumstances Under Which It Works Best*, London: ODI, 2012.
8 WTO, *Fifth Global Review of Aid for Trade*, Geneva: World Trade Organization, 2015.
9 Hoekman and Wilson, n.4.
10 M. Cali and D.W. Te Velde, *Does Aid for Trade Really Improve Trade Performance?* London: ODI, 2009.
11 C. Adam and D. Bevan, "Aid and the Supply Side: Public Investment, Export Performance, and Dutch Disease in Low-Income Countries", *World Bank Economic Review*, vol.1, no.2, 2006, pp. 261–290.
12 M. Ivanic, C. Mann and J. Wilson, *Aid for Trade Facilitation*, Paris: OECD, 2006.
13 M. Busse, R. Hoekstra and J. Koniger, *The Impact of Aid for Trade Facilitation on the Costs of Trading*, Bochum: University of Bochum, 2011.
14 WTO-OECD, *Aid for Trade at a Glance 2009: Maintaining Momentum*, Geneva: WTO, 2009.
15 E. Villanger, *Arab Foreign Aid: Disbursement Patterns, Aid Policies, and Motives*, Bergen: Chr. Michelsen Institute, 2007.

16 N. Woods, "Whose Aid? Whose Influence? China, Emerging Donors, and the Silent Revolution in Development Assistance", *International Affairs*, vol.84, no.6, 2008, pp. 1205–1221.

17 K.V. Hewage, *Requiem For a Deal: The Influence of Foreign Aid on Cooperation Between Developing Nations at the WTO*, Unpublished Working Paper, 2015.

18 UNCTAD, *South-South Cooperation: Africa and the New Forms of Development Partnership*, Geneva: UNCTAD, 2010.

19 W.M. Hynes, "Regional Aid for Trade – An Effective Crisis Response", *International Trade Forum*, 2013.

20 *Ibid.*

21 B. Byiers and D. Lui, "Enhancing the Regional Dimensions of Aid for Trade", *GREAT Insights*, vol.2, no.5, 2013.

22 P. Athukorala, "Production Networks and Trade Patterns in East Asia: Regionalization or Globalization?" *ADB Working Paper Series on Regional Integration*, vol.56, Manila: Asian Development Bank, August 2010.

23 WTO-OECD, *Aid for Trade at a Glance: Connecting to Value Chains*, Geneva: WTO, 2013.

24 *Ibid.*

25 Hewage, n.17.

26 ODI, *A Regional Approach to Aid for Trade: The Regional Trade Facilitation Programme (RTFP)*, London: ODI, 2009.

27 CARICOM, *Caribbean Community Aid for Trade Strategy 2013–2015*, CARICOM: Caribbean Community, 2013.

28 R.E. Baldwin and R. Forslid, "This Improves the Potential to Harness the Necessary Political Will for Regional Integration as Well", *Economica*, vol.67, 2000, pp. 307–324.

29 B. Eichengree and M. Uzan, "The Marshall Plan: Economic Effects and Implications for Eastern Europe and the Former USSR", *Economic Policy*, 1992, pp. 13–75.

30 E. Balcerowicz, "The Impact of Poland's EU Accession on Its Economy", *Studies and Analyses*, no.335, 2007, pp. 1–31.

31 European Commission, *European Neighbourhood Policy and Enlargement Negotiations*, 7 September 2012, see http://ec.europa.eu/enlargement/policy/glossary/terms/accession-criteria_en.htm(Accessed on 23 November 2015).

32 I. Bache, "Europeanization and Multi-Level Governance: EU Cohesion Policy and Pre-Accession Aid in Southeast Europe", *Southeast European and Black Sea Studies*, vol.10, no.1, 2010, pp. 1–12.

33 ESPON, *Pre-Accession Aid Impact*, ESPON, 2005.

34 W. Jacoby, "Managing Globalization by Managing Central and Eastern Europe: The EU's Backyard as Threat and Opportunity", *Journal of European Public Policy*, vol.17, no.3, pp. 416–432.

35 L. Curran and Z. Soledad, "EU Enlargement and the Evolution of European Production Networks", *Research in International Business and Finance*, vol.26, 2012, pp. 240–257.

36 T. Sturgeon and R. Florida, "Globalization, Deverticalization, and Employment in the Motor Vehicle Industry", in M. Kenny and R. Florida (eds.), *Locating Global Advantage: Industry Dynamics in a Globalizing Economy*, Palo Alto: Stanford University Press, 2004, pp. 52–81.

37 S. Radošević and F. Sachwald, "Does Enlargement Conceal Globalization? Rental Issues in Europe", *Notes de l'Ifri*, vol.58, 2005.

38 N.F. Campos, F. Corichelli, and L. Moretti, *Economic Growth and Political Integration: Synthetic Counterfactuals Evidence from Europe*, Bonn: IZA, 2014.

39 A. Vamvakidis, *The Convergence Experience of the Greek Economy in the EU: Lessons for EU Accession Countries*, National Bank of Poland, 2003.

40 G.M. Llanto, *Binding Constraints to Regional Cooperation and Integration in South Asia*, Manila: Asian Development Bank, 2010.

41 World Bank, *South Asia Economic Focus, Spring 2016: Fading Tailwinds*, Washington, DC: World Bank, 2016.

42 ADB, *Study on Intraregional Trade and Investment in South Asia*, Manila: ADB, 2009; Athu-korala, n.22.

43 N. Pitigala, "What Does Regional Trade in South Asia Reveal About Future Trade Integration? Some Empirical Evidence", *Policy Research Working Paper No. 3497*, 2005.

44 K. Hewage and R. Ekanayake, *Re-Orientation of External Trade Towards Global Production Networks – An Urgent Need for Sri Lanka*, 12 April 2016, see www.ips.lk/talkingeconomics/2016/04/12/re-orientation-towards-global-production-networks-an-urgent-need-for-sri-lanka/ (Accessed on 20 April 2016).

45 P. Athukorala, "Intra-Regional FDI and Economic Integration in South Asia: Trends, Patterns and Prospects", *Background Paper No. RVC 7 – Regional Value Chains*, 2013.

11

COMMON CURRENCY IN SOUTH ASIA

An optimalist assessment

Rahul Tripathi

Introduction

There has been considerable discussion in the policy and academic circles in recent years on the desirability and feasibility of a common currency in South Asia. While, on one hand, common currency rationale is seen as a logical step in cementing regional trade and investment integration, the circumstances surrounding Brexit pose the counter-argument for going slow. The arguments have varied, from pure technical-empirical to the more political-pragmatic, which suggests that the option for going for a common currency in South Asia, with its latent difficulties, may be a desirable but still not feasible one. This chapter tries to discern some of these arguments and to present an optimum position from where South Asia can still embark on monetary cooperation before it sets its sights on a future monetary integration.

The debate on a "South Asian common currency"

In any framework for regional economic cooperation and integration, it is presumed that monetary and financial cooperation should be a logical extension of trade and investment cooperation. An integrated exchange rate and monetary policy is supposed to provide the fundamentals that consolidate the gains made by integration in trade with the overarching objective of an economic union in the region. As the South Asian Association for Regional Cooperation (SAARC) completes three decades since its foundation in 2016, it is imperative to set sights on some grand ideas for the next three. While regional cooperation in trade has been a fairly prominent theme in the discussions of South Asian regionalism, the debate on the feasibility of a common currency in South Asia is one such idea. While recent articulations on common currency have been rather muted in favour of a more cooperative approach on monetary matters, it nonetheless has been an interesting thematic for academics and non-state bodies in SAARC.

While the issue of common currency in SAARC had always had a place in academics, a serious discussion on it in policy circles was initiated only after April 2004, when the then prime minister of India, Atal Behari Vajpayee, announced at the twelfth SAARC Summit at Islamabad that "development of greater economic stakes in each other (i.e., SAARC economies) . . . would pave the way for more ambitious, but entirely achievable, goals such as free trade area and economic union, open borders and common currency for the region."[1] This followed his earlier statement at a public function that "open borders and even a single currency for the region were not unrealistic and utopian if "we can put aside mistrust and dispel unwarranted suspicions" and develop "mutual sensitivity to each other's concerns."[2] The statement not only brought an immediate response from SAARC observers and practitioners, but it also provided a certain impetus to the academic debates on the issue which had preceded the statement – the first of its kind perhaps to come from an Indian prime minister.

The statement definitely had a political context. Vajpayee, the peacemaker at heart, in the final year of his term in office, definitely may have wanted his own mark on the roadmap for a future integration in South Asia. SAARC was about to finish its second decade of creation and the existing mechanisms of regional economic interaction were leaving a less than remarkable impact. Still, the Indian prime minister was prudent enough to put essential preconditions about bridging the trust deficit within South Asia as a precondition for any such eventuality. Besides, India was soon to take over the SAARC chairmanship in a few years' time, which would have given it enough space to test the waters. But as it happened, the idea remained as short-lived as the remaining tenure of the government in terms of its political significance, and six years and three summits later, one does not see the discussion of a common currency for SAARC anywhere closer to where many of the perennial optimists of SAARC would have wanted it to be.

In fact, if one were to do a survey of the SAARC Summit Declarations since 2004, one would see there has not even been a single instance where the idea of common currency in South Asia finds a mention. The only lateral mention comes by way of the declaration in 2007 which talked about the idea of an economic union in South Asia, to be explored with utmost urgency, of which monetary union one would presume is a logical component.[3] In recent years, even the idea of economic union appears to have been put on the backburner, if not discarded. It does appear that the goal of a common currency for South Asia is an idea whose time has not yet come. This chapter tries to attempt unfolding the complexity of the idea by dissecting the political and economic layers that perhaps create more obstacles rather than an enabling environment at this stage as far as adopting a common currency in South Asia is concerned.

The attempt is made by exploring four major propositions. First, what does a common currency imply for South Asia in concrete economic terms? What are the economic prerequisites and consequences if and when the common currency is to become a reality? Second, what are the political imperatives which will need to guide such a landmark economic decision, and will it have a bearing on reshaping the entire discourse on regional integration in South Asia? Third, what are the implications that it has for India vis-à-vis its neighbours, being the largest economy in the region and undoubtedly the fulcrum of any future monetary arrangement? Finally, if we infer that the goal of a South Asian common currency is too distant, is there a more plausible and "optimalist" stepping stone that can make monetary cooperation more meaningful?

The economics of a common South Asian currency

The widely accepted rationale for a common currency, as espoused by the theory of "optimum currency area," tells us that the best candidates for a common currency are those nations which have complete wage flexibility and factor mobility between them so that they do not have to face the pressures of adjusting their monetary and exchange rate policy to maintain price stability.[4] In other words, if a region is to form a monetary union with an ensuing common currency, there should be significant flexibility in other available options so that the use of monetary and exchange rate policy as a tool becomes redundant. Once created, a monetary union with common currency can bring about a host of benefits for the regional economies. First, they can cut down the transaction costs that are involved when one currency is converted into another. Second, it can speed up the time involved in transactions, as there would not be any need to operate through multiple banking channels. Third, a common currency may provide the possibility of creating an enabling environment for reserve pooling, which may be used to finance a temporary balance of payment adjustments at the regional level. Finally, a reserve fund thus created could also be used to fund important infrastructural and developmental projects in a region where regional disparities and imbalances are persistent. The scheme of monetary union fits very well into the broader pattern of regional economic integration where the former is seen as a logical and cumulative progression in a region which may begin first with a preferential trade agreement (PTA), a free trade agreement (FTA), a customs union and an eventual economic union.

Given our South Asian context, where the idea and practice of regionalism has been marked more by extreme gradualism and cautious optimism, it was but expected that the idea of moving into core areas of economic cooperation would come rather late. It was only in the second decade of its evolution in the mid-nineties that SAARC really thought of defining a core economic agenda bordering on trade and investment.[5] This despite the fact that there had already been a number of studies by eminent policy think tanks on how a basic rationale already existed for South Asia to move into core areas of economic cooperation.[6] By the late nineties and at the turn of the new millennium, there was even growing frustration within the policy community that SAARC had not moved ahead in the desired direction. The Eminent Persons Group (EPG), set up by the ninth SAARC Summit, was more direct in articulating its dissatisfaction with the pace of the grouping as it stated,

> Despite the positive developments . . . there are still several economic areas like energy, manufacturing, services, money and finance which are still outside the pale of SAARC cooperation. On the whole the Association has made very little headway in realizing its primary objective "to promote the welfare of the peoples of South Asia and to improve their quality of life."[7]

Besides suggesting a number of obstacles and targets for the medium and short term, the EPG suggested a comprehensive roadmap for future economic cooperation by proposing a South Asian Economic Union by 2010. It stated,

> In the third stage should come the goal of moving towards the establishment of a South Asian Economic Union? The Group suggests that this goal be completed by the year 2020. The first step in this direction will be the establishment of South Asia as a single market . . . With the creation of a single market and harmonization of macroeconomic policies in some areas, particularly exchange rates and interest rates, and common norms for fiscal discipline, it should be possible to put in place a single monetary system, including a common currency.[8]

It was in this context there were a number of studies initiated on themes bordering on the feasibility of a common currency and monetary union in South Asia, using some critical economic parameters, and each of these studies imparted a certain empirical richness to the debate which was still confined in the academic realm but was gaining greater policy relevance. In one of the first such studies, which was based on the assumption that if South Asian countries face similar shocks, then policy response in the form of common monetary and exchange rate policy could also be coordinated, thereby making them better candidates for a common currency. The study inferred that the region is still not ready for a common currency, as it does not face a symmetric pattern of shocks. It concluded that a common currency may in fact end up entailing significant economic costs, as the domestic countries may be forced to go in for a costly adjustment process to stabilize their balance of payments equilibrium.[9] Another study argued that the costs associated with monetary cooperation might decrease as the level of regional integration deepens in South Asia and stated that the long-term goal of a monetary union in the long run shall still remain a desirable one.[10]

Further, in more recent studies that focused on the macro-economic convergence criteria – a prerequisite for an eventual monetary union – it was pointed out that if SAARC member countries could attain low inflation, low interest rates and fiscal discipline and control the volatility of exchange rates, they could be better suited candidates for a common currency. With empirical analysis of the period 1997–2002, the study found out that while there was stability in exchange rates (despite deep differences in values) and inflation rates have been fairly low and converging, fiscal deficits have stood at a fairly high level.[11] In the most recent econometric study based on the theme, it was pointed out that there is evidence of common economic characteristics. There are "dynamic linkages in deviations from the long-term stochastic trend in the growth of industrial production for Bangladesh, India, and Pakistan"; these economies are similar in composition, enjoy considerable labour mobility and engage in substantial amounts of legal and extra-legal trade" and are, therefore, good candidates for forming an optimum currency area.[12] The study, however, makes a rather simplistic assumption that following the peace process initiated between India and Pakistan, the labour mobility between the two countries has improved.

These studies, bordering on the economic logic, therefore, do not totally rule out the feasibility of a common currency over the long term, but at the same time, they do not suggest a probable time frame given the existing realities in the region —which brings us to the other and equally significant political context of a common currency in South Asia.

The political context of the common currency

As mentioned in the initial paragraphs of this article, the debate that really generated a more serious attention on the common currency thematic was actually a political one, with the SAARC platform taking note of the same only when it came from the leader of the largest member country. The political economy of South Asian cooperation has underscored the point time and again that until and unless there is a firm political backing given to the regional economic integration project, the latter may remain a vision devoid of a pragmatic road map. In one of the most significant works on the area, it is pointed out

> (The) political actor's preferences for regional cooperation are determined by the extent to which regional cooperation policies enhance political actors' prospects of retaining power or remaining in office, then these policies are likely to be enthusiastically pursued. Otherwise, political actors will show little preference for these kinds of policies. In addition, externalities, intra-regional and extra regional security consideration and locking are the main motivations that shape political actors' preferences towards regional cooperation . . . Given the weakness of their governments, (South Asian) political leaders are likely to pursue more domestic oriented policies, making regional accommodation a difficult goal.[13]

In the context of such "regional accommodation" required at the political level, the goal of a common currency poses some very significant political barriers, which include the following:

1   Questions of policy autonomy: As stated earlier, an eventual common currency would mean at a very basic level adherence to a set of well-defined,

coordinated economic parameters which may require a kind of surrendering of national policy autonomy. This would imply that member governments would lose their national control over maintaining exchange rate flexibility, manipulating money supply, fixing interest rates and regulating labour flows. Given the incessant instability of the global economy, these are the instruments that member governments would like to preserve rather than give over to a regional mechanism which in any case does not have significantly invested political capital.

2   Lack of political convergence: It has been pointed out that any form of economic integration initiative and more so one relating to a monetary union and common currency requires a certain amount of political convergence. In other words, political union has generally preceded monetary union (with the exception of the euro).[14] Given the present political divergences in South Asia, it remains far too remote a possibility that a common currency will either be preceded by or will lead to some kind of a political conciliation in South Asia.

3   The "India" factor in South Asia: A common currency would certainly need an anchor around which the values of the regional currencies would be converged (such as the German mark during the pre-euro period). Given the size and potential of the emerging Indian economy vis-à-vis South Asia, it is but natural that a potential common currency would have to be streamlined along the weight and the size that the Indian rupee has. While countries such as Nepal and Bhutan with which India has a special currency and trade arrangement may not have an objection to such a convergence, it remains uncertain whether the other members, such as Pakistan and Bangladesh, would agree to the idea. Given the not so accommodative past that the neighbours have with India, it remains to be seen whether they would be willing to be controlled by an Indian-rupee-led common currency. Though in the recent years one has seen some favourable voices for South Asian common currency,[15] in the absence of detailed studies, the prospects remain limited. In fact, there has also been the view within smaller nations as to whether India, under the new regime, will be able to push SAARC forward without a direction to common currency.[16]

4   South Asia factor in India: Looking at it from the other side, there may be problems envisaged on the Indian front as well. Even if we presume that a potential South Asian currency would be synonymous with the strength of the Indian rupee, it remains uncertain whether India would like to be bound by the common monetary regime which an eventual monetary union would pose for its own economic expansion. An India which is at present aspiring for a seat on the high table of the global political economy (with its induction into G20 as an example) would be more comfortable with some globally set rules for monetary and financial expansion rather than becoming constrained by a regional-level binding. Of course, this does not rule out that India's global aspirations can be synonymous with its regional role and responsibility.[17]

It is not surprising, therefore, that the more recent voices on the issue of common currency in South Asia have not been too encouraging. As mentioned earlier, SAARC declarations in recent years have almost forgotten about the idea of the economic union and have focused more on the do-ables, such as harmonization and coordination. A telling statement was made by a person none other than the secretary general of SAARC himself, who stated that South Asia is not yet ready for a common currency and that could come at a more advanced stage of economic development, trade and investment flows in the region.[18] The sentiment is echoed by business leaders as well, with the secretary general of the SAARC Chamber of Commerce and Industry – the apex business body within SAARC – stating,

> SAARC countries were doing only $682 million trade through SAFTA (South Asian Free Trade Agreement) while volume of the total trade through bilateral agreements was $12 billion, which was less than 5% of the total trade of SARRC countries with the rest of the world. For adoption of a common currency in the South Asian region, establishment of a common custom union on the basis of a uniform policy, common stock exchange, monetary union, common monetary policies, common fiscal policies, redressal of transportation and communication issues are the prerequisites . . . On the model of the European Union, the dream of a common currency for SAARC countries – Sarrconomy or Rupee – cannot be realised even in next 20 years keeping in view the ground realities, political and economic problems of the regions.[19]

A more telling and perhaps ironic comment came from the person who had served under the Vajpayee government as the chief economic advisor, though it came when Vajpayee was no more in office:

> Earlier this year, at the twelfth SAARC summit held in Islamabad, then Prime Minister Vajpayee mooted the vision of a common currency for SAARC. Is this a goal worth pursuing seriously? Or is it one of those PMO/MEA "economic initiatives" with low economic rationality and high temporary utility for fleshing out a prime ministerial speech in a regional summit? (Incidentally, it is noteworthy that last autumn's official enthusiasm for free-trade-area initiatives has subsided somewhat in the face of reality and some serious questioning by a new Prime Minister with full command over the economics of international trade.) . . . The advocacy of a common SAARC currency at present is really a case of putting the cart before the horse. We need a far freer movement of goods, services, capital, and people across borders within SAARC before the issue of currency unification can be treated as serious. In any case, there is no real political appetite for a common currency. . . . To sum up, there are compelling economic and political reasons against a common currency for SAARC. It's an idea whose time has not yet come . . . and quite possibly, never will.[20]

An optimalist assessment: the road ahead

It is quite apparent in the light of the preceding discussion that the road for a common currency in South Asia at present appears to be a lot more complicated than it seems in the SAARC declarations and the scholarly as well as popular writings that have appeared on the subject in recent years. The only point of minimum convergence which can be distilled from these articulations perhaps is that the idea of a common currency and monetary union in South Asia may be a desirable one, but at present, the region does not have enough prerequisites, both economic and political, to support the same. Does it imply that the goal of monetary union in South Asia is something that should be dispensed with altogether, and the region should focus on the existing mechanisms on trade and investment first? Or could it possibly use the existing mechanisms in monetary cooperation in the region and still make a case for enhanced monetary interaction in the region, leaving the goal of "monetary integration" for a future time and space?

The author would like to support the latter view, which projects a more "optimalist" view that borders neither on a maximalist nor a minimalist position with regard to monetary cooperation. It is argued that South Asia already has some existing platforms and mechanisms for continuing monetary interaction put in place at times independently or as part of the official SAARC policy. Such mechanisms provide enough space for South Asia to deepen "monetary cooperation" in a more meaningful way, rather than impose a distant "monetary union" framework, which does appear too distant. Such an approach can not only create the much-required building block for existing cooperation in trade and investment cooperation but perhaps lay the blueprint for deeper monetary integration. Some of such existing/ potential mechanisms include the following:

1   Revisit the Asian Clearing Union (ACU): The ACU is a relatively unknown organization created in the 1970s with a membership of six of the eight SAARC members with the primary purpose of clearing and facilitating intra-regional payments transactions and conserving foreign exchange. Over the years, its role has been modified to meet the changing economic requirements, and at present, it serves as a platform for clearing transactions, a short-term credit facility and periodic consultations between central bank governors. There is a strong case for strengthening the mandate of the ACU from a mere procedural body to a more deliberative and policy prescriptive one. The basic unit of account of the ACU, the Asian currency unit, has served as an anchor (from an accounting perspective) and can be modified to play a greater role in providing a unit for exchange and reserve facility.[21]

2   Strengthening SAARCFINANCE: SAARCFINANCE, which is a body of finance secretaries and the central bank governors of the member countries created in 1998 and given official recognition in 2002, is the topmost executive body exchanging views on monetary and exchange rate policy in the

region on a regular basis. The role of the body, however, remains discursive and not policy prescriptive, and there is a strong case for the same to be given an expanded mandate to ensure that the region is better prepared to preempt and confront a regional financial crisis once it unfolds.[22]

3   Creating a Regional Funding Mechanism: South Asia, at present, has a very limited avenue for a regional reserve facility which could be used in financial exigencies. The existing mechanisms, such as the ACU Swap, which is a temporary credit facility under the ACU and the South Asian Development Fund, are too limited and narrow in their scope to be able to meet the significant liquidity requirements of members in need. There is, perhaps, the need for an umbrella fund which could be designed to meet the requirements of both development and infrastructural financing as well as that of meeting liquidity shortfalls on a temporary basis. While there is the existing mechanism of the SAARC Development Fund with a paid up capacity of $300 million, the same is drastically limited in its reach. While India did propose a SAARC Development Bank some years ago, a deeper study of feasibility of the same by an expert committee ruled out the viability of such a bank in view of the limited mobilizational capacity of the same.[23]

4   Greater regional consultation on monetary matters: There is a need to go much beyond SAARCFINANCE in creating networks of exchange in the monetary and financial arena with the involvement of private players. This not only will enable a greater exchange of the banking and accounting practices but would also help in standardizing norms across different financial players in the region. This could also go a long way in building greater confidence beyond the business communities across the region.

Conclusion

It does appear from the preceding discussion that although the debate on common currency in South Asia has certainly entered a realm where it is no more in the exploratory stage, the inferences and the conclusions of the studies conducted does present a not-so-optimistic picture of a common currency in the near future. Because of the British-exit from the European Union, the once SAARC optimists also appear to be unsure of whether SAARC should insist on some other mechanisms rather monetary integration. The reasons for the same range from economic to political. There appears to be a near consensus that South Asia is still not integrated enough to embark on the goal of a common currency and lacks the prerequisites for convergence. Besides, the political will to give up national policy autonomy may also not be strong enough given the present state of political flux that prevails in South Asia. At the same time, there is enough basis for South Asia to build upon an existing monetary interaction within and outside the ambit of SAARC for monetary cooperation in South Asia, even if it does not aim for monetary union at this stage.

Notes

1 For speech of the Indian prime minister at the twelfth SAARC Summit, Islamabad, see www.satp.org/satporgtp/countries/india/document/papers/SAARC_pak.htm (Accessed on 15 November 2018).
2 For speech of the Indian Prime Minister at the Hindustan Times Leadership Summit 2003, see www.hindustantimes.com/PM-prescribes-unified-currency-at-HT-meet/Article1-10791.aspx (Accessed on 10 November 2018).
3 Declaration of the fourteenth Summit of the SAARC held at New Delhi, 3–4 April 2007, see www.satp.org/satporgtp/countries/india/document/papers/sarc14ind.htm (Accessed on 15 November 2018).
4 Robert Mundell, "A Theory of Optimum Currency Areas", *American Economic Review*, vol.51, no.4, September 1961, p. 664.
5 The Colombo Summit of 1991 is credited with injecting a greater urgency into economic deliberations within SAARC, where it approved the setting up of an intergovernmental group on trade liberalization and considered the Sri Lankan proposal to have a South Asian preferential trade arrangement by 1997. See the Declaration of the Sixth SAARC Summit, Colombo, 21 December 1991, *SAARCDeclarations, 1985–2007*, New Delhi: Ministry of External Affairs, p. 72.
6 One such pioneering study is V.R. Panchmukhi, et al., *Economic Cooperation in SAARC Region: Potential, Constraints and Policies*, New Delhi: Interest, 1990.
7 Report of the Eminent Group of Persons in SAARC, *SAARC Vision beyond the year 2000*, New Delhi: Shipra Publications, 1999, p. 16.
8 *Ibid*, p. 56.
9 Nephil Matangi Maskay, "South Asian Monetary Integration in Light of Optimum Currency Area Criterion of Pattern of Shocks", *South Asia Economic Journal*, vol.2, no.2, 2001, p. 205.
10 Sisir Jaysuriya, et al., "Monetary Cooperation in South Asia", South Asia Centre for Economic Policy Studies, *Draft Policy Paper*, July 2003, p. 4.
11 Sweta Chaman Saxena and Mirza Allim Beig, "Monetary Cooperation in South Asia: Potential and Prospects", *RIS Discussion Paper No. 71/2004*, New Delhi, 2004, p. 14.
12 Nilanjan Banik, Basudeb Biswas, and Keith Criddle, "Optimum Currency Area in South Asia: A State Space Approach", *International Review of Economics and Finance*, vol.18, no.3, 2008, p. 19.
13 Kishore C. Dash, *Regionalism in South Asia: Negotiating Cooperation Institutional Structures*, New York: Routledge, 2008, p. 41.
14 Shankar Acharya, "A Common Currency for SAARC?", see www.business-standard.com/india/news/a-common-currency-for-saarc/160623 (Accessed on 15 November 2018).
15 See http://tribune.com.pk/story/870551/economic-bloc-saarc-working-on-single-currency/ (Accessed on 20 November 2018).
16 See the Report, "Can Modi Push SAARC Ahead Without a Common Currency?", www.observerbd.com/2015/06/09/93147.php(Accessed on 18 November 2018).
17 The author has made this point earlier in a paper "Emerging India and Her Neighborhood Policy" (unpublished) at a Seminar on *India and Her Neighborhood Policy*, organized by the Department of Political Science, Osmania University and ICWA, New Delhi, October 2009.
18 "Statement by Sheel Kant Sharma, Secretary General SAARC to the Press", see www.dailymirror.lk/index.php/business/126-economy/3390-south-asia-not-ready-for-single-currency.html(Accessed on 10 October 2018).
19 "Statement by Iqbal Tabish, Secretary General, SAARC Chamber of Commerce and Industry", see www.dailytimes.com.pk/default.asp?page=2010%5C11%5C03%5CStory_3-11-2010_pg5_12 (Accessed on 10 October 2018).
20 Acharya, n.14.

21 For a detailed account of ACU, its functioning and potential role, see, Rahul Tripathi, *Monetary and Payments Cooperation in South Asia: A Case Study of Asian Clearing Union*, New Delhi: Concept Publisher, 2010.
22 Rahul Tripathi, "South Asian Regionalism in the Times of Global Financial Crisis", *Pakistan Horizon*, vol.63, no.3, July 2010, p. 57.
23 See www.livemint.com/Politics/vGeDRynVJ7ziAcgEHA6QNN/NDA-govt-scraps-plan-to-set-up-Saarc-development-bank.html (Accessed on 10 November 2018).

12

REGIONAL IMBALANCES AND IMPLICATIONS FOR SOUTH ASIAN ECONOMIC INTEGRATION

G. Jayachandra Reddy

Introduction

Globalization in the twenty-first century, along with the regional integration of the world brings enormous opportunities to sustain and gain momentum of economic development in different countries. At the same time, such a situation has also been indirectly causing the wide economic gap – regional and intraregional imbalances in general. Of course, the degree of disparity varies from country to country, and it is not restricted to a specific country or a region but is universal. South Asia continues to grow rapidly, and India is becoming its largest partner, being one of the Asian giants. This is a remarkable transformation and welcome scenario, but on the other side, the remaining countries of South Asia have been infamously dubbed as a "basket case" and are known for conflicts, violence and extreme poverty. After independence, the political leadership in the region was motivated by the idealism of balanced growth, commanding heights of the public sector, labour-intensive and low-technology production and self-sufficiency. After thirty years, the outcome of these policies turned out to be very different from what the leadership had in mind. South Asia delivered sluggish growth, continued dependence on low-agricultural productivity and low levels of industrialization. It adopted pro-growth policies, opened up markets, replaced the public sector with the private sector as the engine of growth, increased competition and improved economic management. With the achievement of high growth, the debate has now shifted to the following question: Can South Asia sustain and increase the growth rate further? Rapid growth has already pulled millions of South Asians out of poverty. The average poverty rate has now fallen to around twenty-seven per cent, although there are large inter-country variations. Despite this progress, South Asia still has the largest concentration of poor people in the world. Nearly 400 million people live on less than one dollar a day.

The levels of poverty and intra-regional disparities have serious implications for economic regional integration. Being a South Asian tiger, India's role is very much expected from its neighbouring countries. Unfortunately, India has been experiencing a variety of domestic and socio-economic conditions. The freedom for the Indian political leadership to play a major role in the region has been minimized. It seems to be a one-country show; the others are supposed to be dependents, if not on India, on some other countries.

With this backdrop, this chapter deals with the regional and intra-regional disparities; further, it analyzes how these conditions have been hindering the economic integration of South Asia. An attempt is also made to predict the direction of regional disparities and how the countries will overcome such impediments of regional cooperation in South Asia.

South Asia has a variety of historical legacies with the characteristics of both homogeneity and heterogeneity in different forms – economy, culture, geography, conflicts and rivalry between countries. Of course, these are the common factors of any region with more or less intensity in nature. But in the twenty-first century, the world has been entirely changing from the national perspective to the regional perspective, considering that the globe is becoming very small to access with extraordinary changes in science and technology, which is determining the lives of individuals as well as economies of countries. It is a fact that effective regional and global integration has become an important factor to promote peace and prosperity. Much more effort is being made by the majority of the countries to promote regional integration at different levels. The most significant observation is that the success rate of such efforts is minimal. Of course, there are many factors responsible, either directly or indirectly, of which regional disparities are emerging as an important element to be considered to have a more consolidated and effective regional integration of any region.

The member countries of SAARC are extremely diverse in their natural resource endowment, size, population and economy, as well as many other characteristics. India is the largest country in all respects, and Pakistan is the second largest in terms of size. India occupies over seventy per cent of the landmass of the region, and its territorial and maritime boundary touches all SAARC countries except Afghanistan. Pakistan shares its boundary with Afghanistan.[1]

The South Asian regional group is certainly not a simple one to analyze. India, Pakistan and the other states – Afghanistan, Bangladesh, Bhutan, Nepal, the Maldives and Sri Lanka – are different from other countries of the world in terms of population, territory, military power, technological development, infrastructure and political influence. These countries are either in actual fact small nations, or they are wrongly perceived as such by the rest of the world. Bangladesh, with a population of 160 million, is one of the biggest countries in the world, and even Nepal's population of almost 29 million is larger than that of most EU member states. South Asia as a whole is plagued by extreme poverty, mega-urbanization, immense disparities between rich and poor and fundamental problems in the areas of infrastructure, energy and the environment. On top of this, there are also high levels of internal conflict and political instability within the region.[2]

Disparity between two or more than two objects or countries has been considered as natural phenomena. But it has gained momentum only in recent times to be placed as an important field of study. Along with the significance of the study, the rate of disparities has also been steadily increasing between developed countries and developing countries. Another important dimension in the era of globalization is that most of the developing countries are experiencing more imbalances among their citizens or different regions. Many studies contend that relative and absolute deprivation, or inequality and poverty, are strongly interdependent, making the study of inequality even more important. Inequality is also seen to affect the growth rate of an economy through multiple transmission mechanisms: (i) its effect on redistributive policies and the possible inefficiencies those may bring; (ii) its potential to constitute a cause of socio-political instability or violence; (iii) its detrimental effect on the market size and aggregate demand; (iv) its effect on investment allocations, especially human capital; and (v) even its effect on the fertility rate.[3]

Demography and GDP

The total population in the region has reached 1.721 billion, representing nearly twenty-four per cent of the world's total population spread over less than four per cent of the world's geographical area. From a demographic point of view, South Asia is dominated by India, which alone has a population of 1.295 billion, but there are two other densely populated countries in this region, Pakistan and Bangladesh, with populations of 185 and 159 million respectively in 2014. South Asia also includes countries with small populations, such as Bhutan and Maldives. There are sharp contrasts between these countries in terms of demographic growth, population density, mortality and fertility rates, urbanization and literacy. South Asia is also the second least developed region in the world after Sub-Saharan Africa.[4] India and Bangladesh have been in the forefront with the highest density of population at 1.337 and 1.222 billion respectively. As a whole, there are sizeable imbalances among the countries of South Asia in terms of GDP, purchasing power, gross national income and per capita gross national income (see Table 12.1).

Structural differences of the South Asian economy

All the SAARC countries have been maintaining very good GDP growth rates, ranging between five and seven per cent. A glaring transformation of the economic structure has been recorded from the region. Obviously, the entire region has been identified as developing with an agricultural background. Since the beginning of the twenty-first century, the region has witnessed a shift from agriculture to the service sector. It is surprising that the ratio of agriculture, industry and manufacturing to the GDP has been substantially decreasing, whereas the contribution of the service sector has been tremendously increasing. Except Pakistan and Nepal, all the other countries of the region have their agricultural contribution to GDP as less than twenty-five per cent with a negative growth during 2000–2014. There

TABLE 12.1 Distribution of demography and GDP, 2014

Country	Population	Surface area	Population density	Gross national income, atlas method	Gross national income per capita, atlas method	Purchasing power parity gross national income		Gross domestic product	
	Millions	sq. km thousands	people per sq. km	$ billions	$	$ billions	Per capita $	% growth	Per capita % growth
Afghanistan	31.6	652.9	48	21.4	680	63.2	2,000	1.3	-1.7
Bangladesh	159.1	148.5	1,222	171.3	1,080	529.9	3,330	6.1	4.8
Bhutan	0.8	38.4	20	1.8	2,370	5.6	7,280	5.5	4.0
India	1,295.3	3,287.3	436	2,028.0	1,570	7,292.8	5,630	7.3	6.0
Maldives	0.4	0.3	1,337	2.6	6,410	4.4	10,920	6.5	4.4
Nepal	28.2	147.2	197	20.6	730	68.0	2,410	5.4	4.1
Pakistan	185.0	796.1	240	258.3	1,400	941.1	5,090	4.7	2.6
Sri Lanka	20.8	65.6	331	71.4	3,440	214.0	10,300	4.5	3.5

Source: Extracted from the World Development Indicators, 2014.

TABLE 12.2 Structure of the output of SAARC countries

Country	Gross domestic product $ billions		Agriculture % of GDP		Industry % of GDP		Manufacturing % of GDP		Services % of GDP	
	2000	2014	2000	2014	2000	2014	2000	2014	2000	2014
Afghanistan	2.5	20.0	38	23	24	22	19	12	38	54
Bangladesh	53.4	172.9	24	16	23	28	15	17	53	56
Bhutan	0.4	2.0	27	18	36	43	8	9	37	39
India	476.6	2,048.5	23	18	26	30	15	17	51	52
Maldives	0.6	3.1	9	4	15	19	8	5	76	77
Nepal	5.5	19.8	41	34	22	16	9	7	37	51
Pakistan	74.0	243.6	26	25	23	21	15	14	51	54
Sri Lanka	16.3	78.8	20	8	27	30	17	19	53	62

Source: World Bank Indicators, http://wdi.worldbank.org/tables.

are mixed results from the industry and manufacturing sectors. Exceptional performance of the service sector has been contributing more than fifty per cent to the GDP, except in Bhutan. At the same time, there is a big gap between countries. Being a small country, Maldives has been contributing seventy-seven per cent to the GDP from the service sector. Bhutan shares only thirty-nine per cent and is the only country which contributes less than fifty per cent. India has the bulk of GDP to its credit, with eighty per cent. All the other seven countries are sharing the remaining twenty per cent of the GDP of the region (see Table 12.2).

Millennium Development Goals

The Millennium Development Goals (MDGs) were set in the beginning of the twenty-first century as the ultimate targets by the development community and national governments of developing countries. However, attention has mostly been focused on average achievements, implicitly or explicitly. As a well-known example, South Asia's performance on poverty reduction has been remarkable, but that does not mean the same for India. In fact, South Asia's average performance in all MDGs is largely driven by India. In a similar way, the average performance of a country does not mean the same for everyone. In most countries, urban areas generally achieve more than rural areas, and the affluent communities perform better than the poor. It means that there is a direct influence of well-being with the achievement of MDGs.

Education and gender

Countries in South Asia have achieved impressive progress towards the goal of education for all. The current focus is now on how to reach the children who are still not in school or those who are in school but not learning. The 2010 *UNICEF Progress for Children Report* estimated that there are thirty-three million children of primary school age out of school in South Asia. Most of these children are not in school because they face challenges linked to income, gender, ethnicity/caste, language and where they live. Often, not just one category of disparity keeps a child out of school but a combination of multiple disadvantages.[5] Recent studies in Bangladesh reveal that the number of girls attending school has increased dramatically, but there is an increasing problem of boys' exclusion. Other studies have shown that the rapid rate of urbanization in many countries in the region can mean that an increasing number of children living in large cities now do not have access to school.

Undoubtedly, the educational infrastructure and the budget allocations reflect the levels and indirectly the quality of education. The expenditure on education in terms of percentage of total GDP of the respective countries is less than five per cent with an exception in the case of Bhutan. The percentage of expenditure on education to the total expenditure in different countries has been varying from country to country. It ranges from 8.8 per cent to 22.1 per cent. The size of the population and the percentage of expenditure on education are directly proportional – all the top three countries, like India, Bangladesh and Pakistan, with huge populations, recorded less than fifteen per cent of investment. The same has been reflected in the number of teachers and the student-to-teacher ratio (see Table 12.3).

The enrolment rate of students of pre-primary, primary, secondary and tertiary levels has been exhibiting its variations both in terms of country and age groups. There has been a positive indication in pre-primary and primary sectors but marginal decrease noticed in secondary education. Unfortunately, all the countries of South Asia have recorded very low participation rates in tertiary education. They range from ten per cent to twenty-four per cent. India, with a huge source of human resources, stood on the top of the list with twenty-four per cent. On the other side, India has also been on the top with 5.5 million boys and 0.8 million girls of school age out of school, followed by 2.3 million boys and 3.3 million girls out of school (see Table 12.4).

TABLE 12.3 Education inputs in SAARC countries, 2014

Country	Government expenditure on education		Trained teachers		Pupil–teacher ratio	
			Primary	Secondary	Primary	Secondary
	% of GDP	% of total government expenditure	% of total	% of total	pupils per teacher	pupils per teacher
Afghanistan	4.6	18.4			46	
Bangladesh	2.0	13.8		58.0		35.2
Bhutan	6.0	17.8			27	14.3
India	3.8	14.1			32	30.8
Maldives	5.2	15.3	86.1		12	
Nepal	4.7	22.1	93.6	80.2	24	28.8
Pakistan	2.5	11.3	84.0		47	19.2
Sri Lanka	1.7	8.8	82.4		24	17.3

Source: Extracted from Disparities in Education in South Asia, UNICEF Regional Office for South Asia, Kathmandu, 2014, pp. 1–70.

TABLE 12.4 World development indicators: participation in education

Country	Gross enrolment ratio				Net enrolment rate				Children out of school	
	Pre-primary % of relevant age group	Primary % of relevant age group	Secondary % of relevant age group	Tertiary % of relevant age group	Primary % of relevant age group		Secondary % of relevant age group		Primary school-age children, male	Primary school-age children, female
	2014	2014	2014	2014	1999	2014	1999	2014	2014	2014
Afghanistan	·	112	56		·	·	·	49		
Bangladesh	32	·	58	13	·	·	44	53		
Bhutan	17	102	84	11	56	86	20	63	6,188	4,779
India		111	69	24	80	90		62	5,541,260	860,459
Maldives	·	·			95	·	29	·		
Nepal	86	135	67	16	66	94	·	60	78,173	95,591
Pakistan	70	94	42	10	·	73	·	41	2,311,760	3,300,032
Sri Lanka	95	101	100	21	100	97	·	·	15,796	31,010

Source: Extracted from Disparities in Education in South Asia, UNICEF Regional Office for South Asia, Kathmandu, 2014, pp. 1–70.

South Asia has experienced a positive development in narrowing the gap in gender parity in primary education enrolment, but at the same time, two countries in the region have the steepest gender disparity in the world – Afghanistan with a net enrolment rate for girls of forty-six per cent and Pakistan with a rate of sixty per cent.[6] Girls are also disadvantaged at the secondary education level, particularly in some countries –although in Bangladesh, Maldives and Bhutan, there are more girls than boys in secondary school. However, in all countries, including those where gender parity in education has been largely achieved, another form of exclusion of girls and women exists; gender parity in basic education has not contributed to girls' social and political empowerment.[7]

Different countries in South Asia have different patterns of exclusion. For instance, India and Bangladesh are both facing a vast increase in urbanization, which means that increasing numbers of out-of-school children are to be found in cities, while in Afghanistan and Bhutan, the majority of children who have unequal access to education are in rural areas. It is important that policy makers and planners move away from lists of assumed categories of excluded children and carry out in-depth, country-specific analyses on the actual situation within their own particular country context. This is particularly important considering that the majority of children who are excluded from school experience multiple deprivations. A further key factor in exclusion is discrimination once children are enrolled in school. This includes discrimination both from other children and from teachers, and this reflects the attitudes of the wider community. However, the situation is complex – for instance, while caste is clearly a factor in discrimination in some schools in India and Nepal; in other countries, it is not evident.[8]

Regional trade – economic integration

Historically, South Asia was very much identified as one bloc in many forms. Indeed, countries in South Asia were under the British common rule until they emerged as independent countries. Bangladesh, India and Pakistan were ruled by the same laws and had a common currency; even Nepal and Sri Lanka permitted the Indian rupee to circulate freely. But countries in the region, divided by a common heritage and bondage, quarrels and conflicts, have to reorient their internal and external policies for mutual benefit. Despite the recent success in raising the general level of prosperity, as observed in some of the countries in South Asia, many changes are taking place that are reshaping regional integration in South Asia. The need for economic integration and cooperation leading to a regional economic bloc is much more pressing for the developing nations in a rule-based competitive World Trade Organization environment. Theoretically and practically, justification for stronger economic cooperation among South Asian countries has become substantial beyond their inherent historical, cultural and socio-economic commonalties and geographical and ecological proximity in time and space. It has been decades since the creation of the South Asian Association for Regional Cooperation (SAARC), and regional integration in South Asia is still a long distance from priority for the South Asian countries. The change in the world economic order and recent developments in South Asia make it pertinent to have a re-look at the case of integration in South Asia.

The basic problem of South Asian countries is not cultural or geographical in nature but more economic oriented in the form of poverty. Being one of the poorest regions of the world, it requires more collaboration and cooperation to promote development in the region. Such cooperation should start from the development of infrastructure, which invites more and more investment in the region. When South Asian countries agreed to establish the South Asian Free Trade Area (SAFTA) in effect from 1 January 2006, an important objective was to improve and integrate transport infrastructure to economically help member countries not only to reduce transaction costs but also to generate higher intra-regional trade and promote international market access. Faster progress in infrastructure development will be crucial to sustaining South Asia's competitive advantages. The low quality of infrastructure and high logistics costs for South Asian countries are the result of underdeveloped transport and logistics services and slow and costly bureaucratic procedures dealing with intra-regional trade. Opportunities for improvement of infrastructural facilities are immense in this region.

Trade

Initially, trade has not been recognized as one of the objectives of regional organization, but in the long run, it has the momentum. Currently, trade is considered as an engine for economic cooperation between or among the states. It is generally found that inter-country differences in production and consumption patterns, investment behaviour and tax and non-tax structures leave considerable scope for further regional trade expansion. At present, intra-SAARC trade is quite low as compared to that of regional fora, such as the European Union (EU) and the Association of South East Asian Nations (ASEAN).[9]

There has been a paradigm shift in the world economic and political order in the last three decades, and the world has become increasingly interdependent because of the adoption of globalization across countries of all levels of development. Interestingly,

> the process of "globalization" has been accompanied by the strengthening of economic and financial linkages within geographic regions. Indeed the world economy is simultaneously becoming more "regionalized" and more "globalized." The trend towards regional integration has been supported in many areas by regional policy initiatives, particularly in the field of trade.[10]

SAARC countries have also recognized the significance of trade as an economic growth facilitator. Unfortunately, most of the countries in the region do not have the advantage of a major share of trade in their respective GDP. The proportion of trade in GDP of the SAARC region has had a marginal increase from 15.1 per cent in the 1970s to 51.8 per cent in 2008. For East Asia and the Pacific, however, it soared from 20.9 per cent in the 1970s to as much as 88.6 per cent in 2007 but declined to 64 per cent in 2008 on account of the global financial crisis leading to deceleration in trade. As regards the trend in the share of the SAARC region in total world trade, it witnessed a persistent decline during the 1960s, 1970s and 1980s. However, there has been a gradual pickup in the share of total world exports since the 1990s, but it is still lower than the level of share in 1950. During 2008, the share of the SAARC region in total world exports stood at 1.4 per cent (3.7 per cent in 1950). Similarly, the share of the SAARC region in total world imports declined but picked up in recent years.[11]

The regional trade in South Asia is dismally low at four percent as compared with the regional trade of the European Union at sixty-seven percent, the North American Free Trade Agreement at sixty-two percent, the Association of Southeast Asian Nations at twenty-six percent, the Common Market for Eastern and Southern Africa at twenty-two percent, the Gulf Cooperation Council at eight percent and Latin America and the Caribbean at twenty-two percent.[12] Regional trade among the seven SAARC countries in 2002 was $5 billion, out of which India's share was seventy-six percent ($3.8 billion) and Pakistan's share was eight percent ($0.4 billion). The regional trade among the remaining five countries is limited to around sixteen percent ($0.8 billion) of the total regional trade.[13] There is a divergence of opinions on the prospect of increasing economic integration in South Asia. Some authors argue that unilateral liberalization as is currently underway in South Asia offers greater benefits than regional integration would.[14] Others believe that regional integration will create exciting opportunities and will allow countries to develop a comparative advantage and coordinate programmes to address challenges in governance, environment, social development and other areas that most often spill over national boundaries.[15]

However, the members of SAARC gradually felt their way towards putting the issue of economic cooperation on the association's agenda. The SAARC Preferential Trading Arrangement (SAPTA) was signed in 1993 and entered into force in 1995 with a view to paving the way for increased economic integration in the region, as trade between member states was practically non-existent, apart from a tiny amount of foreign trade. Although four rounds of trade liberalization negotiations were concluded under SAPTA, the agreement had little real effect on increasing trade between SAARC nations. But SAPTA was successful in one respect: the agreement opened the doors to future progress. SAPTA helped to focus the alliance's political leaders on the need for greater economic cooperation in order to achieve real economic integration. Another major development was that the SAFTA, was signed at the 2004 summit of foreign ministers in Islamabad and entered into force on 1 January 2006. By signing this agreement, the governments of the member nations committed to following a concrete road map towards facilitating the cross-border movement of goods.[16] While looking at the track record of the progress, many critics say "not much" has been accomplished. The agreement might have produced better results if it had set tighter deadlines, created a fund

TABLE 12.5 India's trade with SAARC countries (Rs in lacks)

Country	1996		2006		2016	
	Exports	Imports	Exports	Imports	Exports	Imports
Afghanistan	8,073	1,084	63,164	25,866	343,603	202,948
Bangladesh	308,480	22,091	736,872	56,240	3,801,379	431,578
Bhutan	7,803	11,993	43,905	39,302	288,547	181,580
Maldives	3,680	61	29,919	876	117,031	2,814
Nepal	58,830	22,745	380,739	0.31	2,490,306	306,935
Pakistan	55,812	12,836	305,147	79,498	1,388,911	288,450
Sri Lanka	169,479	15,209	896,391	255,768	3,463,996	485,358
Total of SAARC countries	612,157	86,019	2,456,137	457,550	11,893,772	1,899,663
% Share of SAARC countries	5.15	0.621	5.38	0.69	6.94	0.76
India's total exports and imports	**11,881,797**	**13,891,966**	**45,641,786**	**66,040,890**	**171,461,771**	**248,800,747**

Source: Department of Commerce, Ministry of Commerce & Industry, New Delhi: Government of India, 1996–2016, see http://commerce.nic.in/eidb/default.asp.

for the less-developed member states, drawn up a concrete plan for abolishing the non-tariff trade barriers which were such a stumbling block for trade and initiated a clearly defined cooperation on infrastructure projects.[17]

Intra-regional trade in South Asia is relatively low compared with other regions, such as ASEAN in Asia. The South Asian countries exchange goods principally with countries outside the region. SAARC had a slow start but gained momentum with the launch of SAPTA in the mid-1990s. Since the implementation of SAFTA at the beginning of the new millennium, it has begun to perform robustly.[18]

The size of economic integration of any region reflects through its intra-regional trade. Being a major country in the region, India's exports and imports from the other member countries of SAARC are not up to the mark. But there has been marginal growth of India's exports from 5.15 per cent in 1996 to 6.94 per cent in 2016, since the establishment of SAARC in 1985, whereas India's imports from the SAARC countries are very negligible with less than 1.0 per cent (see Table 12.5).

Conclusion

It is important to note that the main idea behind the formation of SAARC was the promotion of political, economic and social interaction; a common vision for using the region's potential; and interdependence to counter threats. Though unsuccessful in some fields, the overall assessment of SAARC's performance shows not very negative trends but emphasizes the need to collaborate further by resolving all outstanding disputes among the member countries and to create mutual trust and understanding. During recent years, realizing the importance of regional cooperation and development, SAARC members have now created a sense of accelerating regional economic development, and they advocate revival of the organization by moving from just the issuance of declarations to practical implementation of the plans and policies to turn this weak region into a potentially developed one. This recognition has led to increasing the pace of cooperation among the member countries. Nevertheless, after more than two decades of its establishment, neither have South Asian nations been able to push the process of integration into full swing, nor has the organization itself become viable enough to promote harmony and economic integration for preventing conflicts in the region.

Though there are many disadvantages with integration, there are greater opportunities for the future of SAARC because both India and Pakistan are now on the way to moving ahead with peace initiatives. Further, this regional organization has enormous potential in the face of changing trends at regional as well as global levels. Member countries of SAARC are well aware of the advantages of closer cooperation between the nations of South Asia. It is, therefore, time to reinvent the wheel of South Asian identity through increased citizen activism, which will lead to a better environment for confidence-building among the formal elites of South Asia and in turn lead to a better South Asia. Despite extremely difficult political circumstances and a more diversified economic character, SAARC has managed to create a variety of institutions and fora where heads of state shake each other's hands. Promoting regional integration in South Asia entails efforts in key areas, such as infrastructure, trade facilitation, investment, governance and implementation. The most critical element of the integration process in South Asia is building confidence and filling the huge trust deficit between the countries. With increased political will and commitment towards integration, greater efforts will have to be made towards integration. In this respect, India will have to take on disproportionately greater responsibility while the other South Asian countries will have to commit to cooperation and openness.

Notes

1 K. Chowdhury, "Convergence of Per Capita GDP Across SAARC Countries", *Working Paper Series*, University of Wollongong, Australia, 2004.
2 Cf. Fischer-Weltalmanach, "Nepal", www.weltalmanach.de/staat/staat_detail.php? staat=nepal and "Bangladesh", www.weltalmanach.de/staat/staat_detail.php?fwa_ id=banglade (Accessed on 13 April 2018).
3 M. Balisacan Arsenio and Geoffrey M. Ducanes, *Inequality in Asia: A Synthesis of Recent Research on the Levels, Trends, Effects and Determinants of Inequality in Its Different Dimensions*, London: Overseas Development Institute, 2006, p. 1.
4 The human development index was introduced by UNDP in 1990. It is a composite index that includes life expectancy, adult literacy rates, and school enrolment ratio, as well as per capita GDP. It ranges from 0 to 1.

5 UNICEF, *Disparities in Education in South Asia: A Resource Tool Kit*, Kathmandu: UNICEF, Regional Office for South Asia, 2011.

6 UNICEF, *The State of the World's Children*, New York: UNICEF, 2011.

7 R. Chitrakar, *Overcoming Barriers to Girls' Education in South Asia: Deepening the Analysis*, Kathmandu: UNICEF ROSA/UNGEI, 2009.

8 UNICEF, *Equity in School Water and Sanitation: Overcoming Exclusion and Discrimination in South Asia*, Kathmandu: UNICEF ROSA, 2009.

9 Rajeev Jain and J.B. Singh, "Trade Pattern in SAARC Countries: Emerging Trends and Issues", *Occasional Paper*, Mumbai: Reserve Bank of India, vol.30, no.3, 2009, pp. 73–117.

10 Julie Mckay, Maria Oliva Armengol, and Georges Pineau (eds.), *Regional Economic Integration in a Global Framework*, Germany: European Central Bank, 2004.

11 Jain and Singh, n.9.

12 World Bank, *South Asia: Growth and Regional Integration*, Washington, DC: World Bank, 2007. Intra-regional trade in South Asian countries was at nineteen per cent of total trade in 1948 and decreased to two percent by 1967 as governments adopted inward-looking policies along with high tariff and non-tariff barriers. The share increased during the 1990s because of the adoption of unilateral trade policy liberalization in the individual countries.

13 World Bank, "South Asia Growth and Regional Integration Report", see http://site resources.worldbank.org/SOUTHASIAEXT/Resources/223546-1192413140459/4281804-1192413178157/4281806-1265938468438/BeyondSAFTAFeb2010 Chapter14.pdf (Accessed on 12 February 2018).

14 J.S. Bandara and W.Yu, "How Desirable is the South Asian Free Trade Area? A Quantitative Assessment", *The World Economy*, vol.26, no.9, 2003, pp. 1293–1323.

15 See UNCTAD and ADB, *Quantification of Benefits from Regional Cooperation in South Asia*, New Delhi: Macmillan India Ltd., 2008.

16 Tomislav Delinić, "SAARC – 25 Years of Regional Integration in South Asia", *KAS International Report*, 2011, see www.kas.de/wf/doc/kas_21870-544-2-30.pdf?110209115423 (Accessed on 15 June 2018).

17 Muchkund Dubey, "Looking Ahead", in Dipankar Banerjee and N. Manoharan (eds.), *SAARC Towards Greater Connectivity*, New Delhi: Anshah, 2008, p. 242.

18 S.K. Mohanty and Sachin Chaturvedi, "Impact of SAFTA on Trade in Environmentally Sensitive Goods in South Asia: Emerging Challenges and Policy Options", *Asia-Pacific Trade and Investment Review*, vol.2, no.2, December 2006, pp. 1–3.

PART 4

Connectivity in South Asia

13

TRANSPORT CONNECTIVITY IN SOUTH ASIAN SUB-REGION

Emerging trends, opportunities and challenges

Indranath Mukherji

Introduction

During the meeting of the Council of Ministers of the South Asian Association for Regional Cooperation (SAARC) in 1996 in New Delhi, the idea of forming a South Asia Growth Triangle (SAGQ) comprising the northeastern parts of India, Bangladesh, Nepal and Bhutan was endorsed for the first time.

At the Ninth SAARC Summit (Male Declaration), the heads of state or government reiterated their determination to reinforce the unity and cohesion of SAARC. With the objective of enhancing regional solidarity and promoting overall development within SAARC, the heads of state or government encouraged, under the provisions of article VII of the charter, the development of specific projects relevant to the special individual needs of three or more member states.[1]

The SAARC Charter (Article VII) provides that the standing committee may set up action committees comprising member states concerned with implementation of projects involving more than two but not all member states.[2] However, the inclusion of any such project under the SAARC umbrella requires the concurrence of all member states under general provisions (Article X) of the SAARC charter.[3]

The example of other growth triangles, like the Johor state of Malaysia, Singapore and the Riau islands of Indonesia (JSRGT) and the South China Growth Triangle, comprising Hong Kong and the Guangdong and Fujian Provinces of China and Taiwan, reinforced the motive for sub-regional cooperation among some SAARC member countries. It was believed this type of cooperation would be both geographically meaningful and economically beneficial.[4]

The SAGQ was seen as a feasible and practical solution to the socio–economic problems of the sub-region which would not compel member states to change their macroeconomic policies and institutional approach to wider issues of governance.

It was also seen as a way of bypassing the political tensions between India and Pakistan. The aim of SAGQ was to integrate the local economies for efficient utilization of manpower, infrastructure, trade opportunities and economic resource endowments. Moreover, the geographical proximity to South East Asia and other Asian countries provided further impetus for cooperation.

At the eighteenth SAARC Summit, the heads of state or government welcomed the significant progress towards finalization of the SAARC Motor Vehicles Agreement and SAARC Regional Railways Agreement and agreed to hold a meeting of the transport ministers within three months in order to finalize the agreements for approval. They renewed their commitment to substantially enhancing regional connectivity in a seamless manner through building and upgrading roads, railways, waterways infrastructure, energy grids, communications and air links to ensure the smooth cross-border flow of goods, services, capital, technology and people. The leaders emphasized the need for linking South Asia with contiguous regions, including Central Asia, and beyond by all modes of connectivity and directed relevant authorities to initiate national, regional and sub-regional measures and necessary arrangements.[5]

A SAARC Motor Vehicle Agreement was on the top of the agenda during the SAARC Summit in Kathmandu in November 2014. Unfortunately, it could not be signed because of the reservations of Pakistan. During this summit, Indian prime minister Narendra Modi stated that regional integration in South Asia would go ahead "through SAARC or outside it, among all of us or some of us."

Disagreements at the Kathmandu Summit only bear testimony to this fact. On top of the agenda were three proposals on road, rail and energy connectivity but consensus emerged only on energy connectivity. The remaining two did not go through, as Pakistan had not completed its internal processes to endorse them. As a result, the Motor Vehicles and Regional Railways Agreement proposed by New Delhi at the summit was blocked by Pakistan. The proposal, initially outlined by India in 2008, intended to connect South Asia with Southeast Asia and other parts of Asia by strengthening the railway. The SAARC declaration at Kathmandu summit also encouraged member states to initiate regional and sub-regional measures to enhance connectivity. Accordingly, it was considered appropriate that a sub-regional Motor Vehicle Agreement among Bangladesh, Bhutan, India and Nepal (BBIN) may be pursued.

Consequently, a meeting of BBIN transport secretaries on Regional Road Transport Connectivity was held in Kolkata (India) during 2–3 February 2015. It was attended by secretaries of transport of the respective countries. The meeting facilitated discussions among senior officials of the Asian Development Bank (ADB) and sponsored the South Asia Sub-Regional Economic Cooperation Programme (SASEC) member states to finalize the draft BBIN Motor Vehicles Agreement (MVA), a transport facilitation framework (similar to the SAARC MVA Draft) that aims to enhance road connectivity in the sub-region by allowing passenger, personal and cargo vehicles to cross international borders and travel along designated key trade routes in the four countries.

The BBIN sub-region constitutes a large share of the overall SAARC region. Further, India constitutes the largest landmass in the BBIN sub-region. In addition, India forms the vital bridgehead for linking the smaller countries in the region with

TABLE 13.1 Select socio-economic indicators of BBIN countries

Country	Population (million)	GNP (PPP) (USD billion)	GDP growth rate over previous year (%)	GNP per capita (PPP) (USD)	Foreign exchange reserves (USD billion)
Bangladesh	163	617.1	7.1	3,790	32.3
Bhutan	0.8	64.0	6.2	8,070	1.1
India	1,324	8594.2	7.1	6,490	361.7
Nepal	29	72.9	0.6	2,520	8.1

Source: World Bank, World Development Indicators, 2017, http://wdi.worldbank.org/table/WV.1. Accessed on 16 May 2019.

each other through its territory, while Bangladesh, in turn, forms a vital bridgehead for India to link up with its northeast through Bangladesh. Thus a cooperative endeavour to link up with each other in this sub-region could yield synergies much beyond their existing bilateral linkages.

Table 13.1 brings out some socio-economic indicators of BBIN member states. It brings to focus the predominance of India in terms of both population and gross domestic product (GDP) in purchasing power parity (PPP) terms. It is also clear that India holds most of the foreign exchange reserves of the sub-region. In terms of GDP growth rate, India and Bangladesh rank the highest (7.1 per cent), followed by Bhutan (6.2 per cent). The literacy rates of all member states remain low.

After a brief introduction to the genesis of sub-regional cooperation in transport connectivity in South Asia and examining the major characteristics of this sub-region, this paper seeks to examine the institutional mechanism for cooperation with the Asian Development Bank's SASEC sub-regional programme providing the platform for BBIN work programmes under different joint working groups (JWG) and transport ministers' meetings. The evolution of JWGs and transport ministers' work programmes on road connectivity is examined next. The chapter subsequently highlights the salient features of the Motor Vehicles Agreement (MVA) that emerged from the transport ministers' meeting in June 2015. The following section deals with intra-BBIN trade (exports) and assesses the market access frontier of Bhutan and Nepal in the Bangladeshi market. The next section examines the likely gains arising from seamless movement of cargo among BBIN countries. The implications of linking South Asian connectivity with Southeast Asia is examined next. This is followed by examining the challenges ahead for implementing the BBIN agreement and its protocols. In the concluding section, a possible scenario is built for the sub-region in 2030.

Institutional mechanism: the Asian Development Bank (SASEC)

The ADB-sponsored SASEC brings together Bangladesh, Bhutan, India, the Maldives, Nepal and Sri Lanka in a project-based partnership to promote regional prosperity in the region. Constituted initially as the South Asia Growth Quadrangle

(SAQG), including Bangladesh, Bhutan, India and Nepal, SASEC was a development plan mooted by the ADB to promote sub-regional economic cooperation among the four countries. Sub-regional cooperation under this framework was targeted towards priority sectors, such as transportation, energy and power, tourism, the environment, trade, investment and private sector cooperation.

In 2001, Maldives and Sri Lanka were welcomed into the group after the initial four countries requested the ADB provide assistance to promote economic cooperation in the sub-region, leading to the creation of the ADB initiative of SASEC with emphasis on private-public partnership with a more project-driven approach, which was a step in the right direction. However, poor infrastructure facilities have delayed and hindered progress in the region.

The ADB, under its SASEC framework, coordinates meetings of joint working groups and the transport ministers of its six member states – Bangladesh, Bhutan, India, Nepal, Maldives and Sri Lanka.

The Institutional Framework for Consultation at the regional level is the establishment of a Joint Land Transport Facilitation Committee (LTFC) to coordinate, implement and monitor the BBIN and IMT MVAs effectively and efficiently. At the national level, the National Land Transport Facilitation Committee (NLTFC) was set up to coordinate and implement transport facilitation activities at the national level; a customs sub-group would also be set up. SASEC of ADB acts as the Secretariat for the BBIN platform.[6]

Evolution of BBIN work programme

First working group trilateral (BBI) meeting (19 April 2015, Dhaka)

The first Bangladesh-Bhutan-India trilateral meeting on connectivity and transit was held on 19 April 2013 in Dhaka. The delegations noted that this trilateral meeting on connectivity and transit was the first initiative of its kind and would pave the way for future comprehensive cooperation in the sub-regional context. The meeting was considered a significant step forward towards materializing the understanding reached among the highest political leadership with regard to concerted efforts towards attainment of the common aspiration of economic development and prosperity of the region for mutual benefit. It was agreed that road, rail and waterways were building blocks to an interdependent and mutually beneficial relationship.

A draft terms of reference (ToR) proposed by the Bangladesh side for the working group was discussed among the parties in the meeting. The meeting also exchanged views on various aspects related to connectivity and transit, including potential benefits in the sub-regional context. It was agreed to continue discussions in this regard at the next meeting of the working group with a view to finalizing the ToR and a framework for facilitating sub-regional connectivity and transit.[7]

Second meeting of the joint working group (30–31 January, New Delhi)

The second meetings of the JWGs on sub-regional cooperation between Bangladesh, Bhutan, India and Nepal (BBIN) on water resources management and power/hydropower and on connectivity and transit were held in New Delhi on 30–31 January 2015.

The JWG on Connectivity and Transit reviewed existing arrangements. It agreed on the significance of BBIN agreements to enable movement of motor vehicles and railways. The meeting exchanged ideas on potential cargo (both roads and railways) and bus routes involving at least three countries, in addition to the existing bilateral routes, and also agreed to share suggestions in this regard. It was also decided to explore the possibility of using multi-modal transport to meet commercial as well as tourist needs.

The JWG deliberated on the need for trade facilitation at land border stations for effective sub-regional connectivity. It exchanged views on the usefulness of sharing trade infrastructure at land border stations and harmonization of customs procedures.[8]

Meeting of transport ministers (15 June 2015, Thimpu)

In a landmark development, the BBIN transport ministers met in Thimphu on 15 June 2015 and endorsed and signed the MVA for the Regulation of Passenger, Personal and Cargo Vehicular Traffic between Bangladesh, Bhutan, India and Nepal (hereinafter referred to as "BBIN MVA"), which was drafted on the lines of the SAARC MVA. They endeavoured to accelerate the preparatory steps for the effective and sustainable implementation of the BBIN MVA, starting with the formulation, negotiation and finalization of the necessary legal instruments and operating procedures, recognizing that the BBIN MVA is a complementary instrument to the existing transport agreements or arrangements at the bilateral levels that the contracting parties would continue to honour. Implementation difficulties, if any, will be resolved based on provisions of the BBIN MVA.

The transport ministers took note of the finding that transforming transport corridors into economic corridors could potentially increase intra-regional trade within South Asia by almost sixty per cent and with the rest of the world by over thirty per cent. They acknowledged that apart from physical infrastructure, the development of economic corridors within and between countries requires the implementation of policy and regulatory measures, including the BBIN MVA, which will help address the nonphysical impediments to the seamless movement of goods, vehicles and people between the four countries.[9]

The BBIN transport ministers later acknowledged the technical and facilitating role played by the ADB in taking the BBIN MVA initiative this far and requested ADB to continue providing much-needed technical support and other related arrangements necessary to ensure the effective and efficient implementation of the work plan. They noted that thirty priority transport connectivity projects with an estimated total cost of over $8 billion have been identified; these projects will rehabilitate and upgrade remaining sections of trade and transport corridors in the four countries. These corridors and associated routes were determined based on analysis of patterns of regional and international trade.[10]

Salient features of MVA

Signing of the BBIN agreement will promote safe, economical, efficient and environmentally sound road transport in the sub-region and will further help each country in creating an institutional mechanism for regional integration. BBIN countries will benefit from mutual cross-border movement of passengers and goods for overall economic development of the region. The people of the four countries will benefit through seamless movement of goods and passengers across borders.

All the vehicles of the contracting party (CP) will require a permit for plying through the other CPs. Apart from a valid permit, the driver of the vehicle should be in possession of a number of other valid documents, such as registration and a fitness certificate. Crew members will carry passports or relevant accepted documents which will be issued to facilitate frequent endorsement of visas and will be granted multiple entry visas, valid for at least one year, by the CP(ies) concerned.

Under the agreement, vehicles registered in one CP and operating under this agreement will not be permitted to transport local passengers and goods within the territory of other contracting parties (Article VI). In relation to border, land-port/dry-port formalities, customs and quarantine formalities, taxations and fees, the provisions of internal laws or agreements between CPs will be applied in deciding matters which are not regulated by this agreement (Article VII).[11] The salient features of the agreement are presented in Table 13.2.

TABLE 13.2 The conditions required to operate the BBIN-MVA

Permit requirement	All vehicles
Quota restriction	Unrestricted
Cabotage operation	Prohibited
Special traffic exemption	No special consideration
Third country traffic	Allowed
Routes of operation	Prescribed route
Vehicle registration	Registration in home country
Driver licensing	National/international driving permit
Passenger identification	Internationally recognized travel document
Visa for crew members	Multiple entries valid for at least one year
Prohibited goods	Restricted/prohibited list of travelling country
Fees and charges	To be decided by contracting parties

Source: Abstracted from http://morth.nic.in/showfile.asp?lid=1715, accessed on 16 May 2019.

Intra-sub-regional trade in BBIN countries

This section examines intra-sub-regional exports among BBIN member states, particularly among the least developed ones.

Bhutan's exports

It will be observed in Table 13.3 that between 2009–12, Bhutan's exports to other BBIN member states increased significantly. Bhutan's exports were predominantly to the BBIN region, accounting for as much as ninety-eight per cent of its global exports in 2012. India was Bhutan's predominant market in the region. The second most important market for Bhutan in the sub-region was Bangladesh. Bhutan's exports to Nepal in this sub-region were minimal.

Bangladesh's exports

Table 13.4 illustrates Bangladesh's exports to the BBIN region. The country's exports to the region as per cent of world exports comprised less than two per cent in 2014, having declined from 2.36 per cent in 2011. Again, India has been the predominant market for Bangladesh in the sub-region. The next most important market for Bangladesh has been Nepal. Its bilateral exports to Nepal, even though modest, have been increasing during this period.

TABLE 13.3 Bhutan's exports to BBIN countries ($ million)

BBIN member states	2009	2010	2011	2012
Bangladesh	15.67	19.81	26.40	21.91
India	463.64	340.82	343.02	497.72
Nepal	1.75	0.87	1.64	2.01
Total BBIN	481.06	361.50	371.06	521.64
Total World	495.85	413.48	452.96	531.23

Source: IMF Direction of Trade Statistics, https://data.imf.org/regular.aspx?key=615458706, accessed on 19 February 2016.

TABLE 13.4 Bangladesh's exports to BBIN countries ($ thousand)

BBIN Member States	2011	2012	2013	2014
Bhutan	4.24	4.19	1.76	3.40
India	523.02	519.97	472.98	432.00
Nepal	16.96	18.18	18.56	20.50
Total BBIN	544.21	542.33	493.30	455.90
World	23100	22251	25913	28434
BBIN as % World	2.36	2.44	1.90	1.60

Source: IMF Direction of Trade Statistics, in, http://dhttps://data.imf.org/regular.aspx?key=61545870, accessed on 19 February 2016.

India's exports

Table 13.5 shows the growing importance of BBIN markets for Indian exports during 2011–2014. During this period, the sub region's share in India's world exports increased from 2.17 per cent to 3.55 per cent. The most important market for India has been Bangladesh, followed by Nepal. India's exports to the world have been less modest.

Nepal's exports

Table 13.6 shows Nepal's exports to BBIN countries. During the period 2011–14, Nepal's exports to BBIN member states were stagnant, being around half a billion US dollars. Its share in global exports has also remained stagnant, varying from sixty to sixty-three per cent. Nepal's major market in the sub-region has been India, followed by Bangladesh.

Additional market access frontier (AMAF)[12] of select products in intra-BBIN trade

In this section, a match-making exercise has been done to match the supply potential of Bhutan and Nepal as sub-regional suppliers with Bangladesh as the market.

TABLE 13.5 India's exports to BBIN countries ($ million)

BBIN member states	2011	2012	2013	2014
Bangladesh	3765	5018	5710	6580
Bhutan	220	229	297	303
Nepal	2687	3059	3439	4405
Total BBIN	6672	8306	9446	11288
World	307071	297261	315127	317733
BBIN as % World	2.17	2.79	3.50	3.55

Source: IMF Direction of Trade Statistics, http://dhttps://data.imf.org/regular.aspx?key=61545870ee; http://data.imf.org, accessed 19 February 2016.

TABLE 13.6 Nepal's exports to BBIN countries ($ million)

BBIN member states	2011	2012	2013	2014
Bangladesh	25.78	33.72	19.83	17.67
Bhutan	2.94	3.06	3.22	3.38
India	489.72	515.75	458.77	547.31
Total BBIN	518.44	552.53	481.82	568.36
World	822.72	865.73	807.62	917.64
Total BBIN as % world	63.02	63.82	59.65	61.94

Source: IMF Direction of Trade Statistics, see http://dhttps://data.imf.org/regular.aspx?key=61545870, accessed on 19 February 2016.

The objective is to examine how the least developed countries (LDCs) of this sub-region could expand trade among themselves, thereby reducing their excessive trade with one dominant country in the region. Could the smaller LDCs in this region (Nepal, Bhutan) find a market in the growing market of an LDC (Bangladesh) poised to emerge in a non-LDC status in the coming years? In Table 13.7, Bhutan is the supplier and Bangladesh is the market.

In Table 13.7, data on Bhutan's additional market access frontier (AMAF) with Bangladesh reveals that in 2011, Bhutan exported 183 products to the world that were also being imported by Bangladesh from the world. However, only two of the matched products were actually being exported by Bhutan to Bangladesh. Bhutan had revealed comparative advantage (RCA)[13] in all the matched products. The export potential of Bhutan in terms of AMAF was substantial, being $43 million on all matched products in 2011.

Table 13.8 shows Nepal's AMAF World Bank, World Integrated Trade Solution (WITS), available at http://wits.worldbank.org/ith Bangladesh. Data reveals that in 2011, Nepal exported 1,496 products to the world that were also being imported by Bangladesh from the world. However, only one of the matched products was actually being exported by Nepal to Bangladesh. Nepal had RCA in all the matched products. The export potential of Nepal in terms of AMAF was substantial, being $256 million on all matched products.

This section demonstrates that considerable market potential exists for exports from Nepal and Bhutan to find a market in Bangladesh to justify the investment made to build better connectivity between these countries. The cost saving that could accrue from reduced transport costs could possibly induce exports, currently with the rest of the world, to be channelled to meet the sub-regional demand at much lower cost.

Major gains from BBIN road transport connectivity

The agreement provides a framework for the seamless flow of goods and passengers across these countries' borders. With effective implementation, it will promote safe, economical and efficient road transport in this sub-region and will also generate new economic opportunities, particularly in border areas.

The BBIN MVA is expected to bring three potential benefits to BBIN countries. First, the agreement will substantially reduce the cost of doing cross-border trade by shelving the time-consuming exercise of unloading and loading goods at border points. This will help countries realize their trade and investment potential. Improved connectivity will contribute to the development of regional and bilateral value chains in the sub-region.

Second, the agreement will open new opportunities for investment in trade and transport-related infrastructure in the sub-region, which will have a positive impact on the local economy through employment generation and business activities.

Third, it will facilitate economic integration among member states of the BBIN region and could be expanded to other SAARC countries and also to Myanmar and Thailand.

TABLE 13.7 Top ten products of Bhutan as supplier having AMAF with Bangladesh as market (2011: US$ thousand)

HS code	Description in brief	Bhutan's export to world (supply)	Bangladesh's import from world (demand)	Bhutan's existing exports to Bangladesh (existing exports)	Additional Market Access Frontier (AMAF) min (supply, demand)- existing exports	Revealed Comparative Advantage (RCA)
252010	Gypsum; anhydrite	10,558	19,791	351	10,208	81
441011	Particle board	5,496	3,714	0	3,714	4
720719	Other	3,526	3,221	0	3,221	10
090831	Neither crushed nor ground	8,271	17,701	5,395	2,877	57
252329	Other	21,990	2,051	0	2,051	10
284910	Of calcium	19,863	2,043	0	2,043	144
252020	Plasters	1,544	2,094	0	1,544	9
720410	Waste and scrap of cast iron	1,378	1,676	0	1,378	2
740819	Other	42,940	1,270	0	1,270	37
391740	Fittings	999	1,500	0	999	1
	Top 10 products	**116,566**	**55,060**	**5,746**	**29,305**	
	All matched products (183 products at HS-6 digit)	**250,075**	**4,104,854**	**15,319**	**42,674**	

Source: Author's estimate from UN Comtrade data using World Bank World Integrated Trade Solution (WITS) Platform, https://wits.worldbank.org/WITS/WITS/Restricted/Login.aspx, accessed on 8 February 2016.

Notes:

(i) Data for 2011 have been taken as these were the latest data available for the two countries at the time of accession.

(ii) For a complete description of products, see Harmonized Commodity Description and Coding Systems (HS), which can be found at the World Customs Organization website at www.wcoomd.org/home_wco_topics_hsoverviewboxes.htm accessed on 17 May 2019.

TABLE 13.8 Top ten products of Nepal as supplier having additional market access frontier with Bangladesh as market (2011: US$ thousand)

HS code	Description in brief	Nepal's export to world (supply)	Bangladesh's imports from world (demand)	Nepal's existing exports to Bangladesh (existing exports)	Additional Market Access Frontier (AMAF) min (supply, demand-existing exports)	Revealed Comparative Advantage (RCA)
090831	Neither crushed nor ground	21,603	17,701	0	17,701	718
392690	Other	39,833	12,765	0	12,765	18
540233	of polyesters	10,055	91,841	0	10,055	2
721049	-- Other	41,618	9,871	0	9,871	4
080270	Kola nuts (Cola spp.)	9,588	21,768	0	9,588	212
550931	Single yarn	9,405	69,956	0	9,405	334
090240	Other black tea (fermented) and other partly fermented tea	12,949	8,530	1	8,529	106
740921	In coils	9,182	7,620	0	7,620	49
392020	Of polymers of propylene	6,641	37,402	0	6,641	9
550951	Mixed mainly or solely with artificial staple fibres	6,887	6,521	0	6,521	620
	Top 10 products	**167,761**	**283,975**	**1**	**98,695**	
	All matched products (1,496 products at HS-6)	**795,069**	**14,458,278**	**110**	**264,372**	

Source: Author's estimate from UN Comtrade data using World Bank World Integrated Trade Solution (WITS) Platform available in https://wits.worldbank.org/WITS/WITS/Restricted/Login.aspx, accessed on 9 February 2016.

Notes:

(i) Data for 2011 have been taken as these were the latest data available for the two countries at the time of accession.

(ii) For a complete description of products, see Harmonized Commodity Description and Coding Systems (HS), which can be found at the World Customs Organization website at www.wcoomd.org/home_wco_topics_hsoverviewboxes.htm, accessed on 17 May 2019.

A revised India Bangladesh Trade Agreement signed on 6 April 2015 has been considered to be groundbreaking in terms of initial steps in improving connectivity in the region. Article VIII of the agreement states,

> The two Governments agree to make mutually beneficial arrangements for the use of their waterways, roadways, and railways for commerce between the two countries and for passage of goods between two places in one country and to third countries through the territory of the other under the terms mutually agreed on. In such cases, fees and charges, if leviable, as per international arrangements, conventions or practices, may be applied, and transit guarantee regime may be established through mutual consultations.[14]

Under the agreement, Bangladesh will now be able to use Indian roads, railways and waterways in transhipment of goods to Bhutan and Nepal. Under the deal, India would also be able to send goods to Myanmar through Bangladesh. It incorporated a provision that the deal would be renewed automatically after five years if either of the countries did not have any objection. It is notable that Kathmandu and Thimphu already had identical agreements with India, but Bangladesh's trade with Nepal and Bhutan were being hindered for want of such a treaty with New Delhi.[15]

As Nepal is a landlocked country, the Nepal-Bangladesh corridor via India is not only important for trade between Nepal and Bangladesh but could be relied upon by Nepal for its overall trade, beyond Dhaka to the Hatikumrul sector, which extends to Mongla and Chittagong ports in Bangladesh. At Kakarvitta/Panitanki and Phulbari/Banglabandha border posts, cargo is required to be trans-shipped from Nepali/Bangladeshi registered vehicles to Indian registered vehicles. This activity adds to costs and causes delay.[16]

The BBIN MVA signed by the transport ministers of the four countries in June 2015 makes a further advance, since it moves on to transit replacing transhipment. The MVA benefits not only India directly in linking with its northeast through Bangladesh territory but further all other BBIN countries by helping them to transit to each other through India. Thus, the MVA benefits all the countries in this sub-region, and this is one rare example in which India is not perceived as "winner takes all" but as bridgehead that integrates all countries in the region for mutual benefit. The uninterrupted flow of activities that promote this integration illustrates this.

We first examine the benefits that accrue to India by transiting from Agartala to Kolkata via Bangladesh. It is well known that the Chittagong port in Bangladesh is only around seventy-five kilometres from the southern border of the northeastern Indian state of Tripura, but the goods have to travel from the capital Agartala to Kolkata port, which is more than 1,600 kilometres and from there through the Siliguri corridor, better known as the "Chicken's neck."

Given transit facilities, India's current road route from Agartala to Kolkata (via Badarpur, Shillong, Guwahati, Siliguri), which is 1,650 kilometres, can be drastically reduced to 646 kilometres when transiting through Bangladesh.[17]

It will be apparent that under the current situation, if Bangladesh seeks to export to Nepal, it would have to transship at two border points, Phulbari (India) and Kakarvitta (Nepal). Similarly, if Bangladesh wishes to export to Bhutan, it will be required to transship at Chandrabhanga (India) and Phuntsholing (Bhutan). In the case of India-Bangladesh trade, the two countries will be required to transship only once at the Petrapole (India) Benapole (Bangladesh) border points and at Tambail (Bangladesh)-Dawki (India)border points. These transshipments involve loading and unloading at multiple border points, which adds considerably to freight costs in bilateral trade between countries of this region. Transit traffic between these countries under the MVA is thus expected to considerably reduce the cost of freight movement among these countries. It is notable that since the smaller countries in this region, having to pass through India, involving two transit points at the borders, are likely to generate greater savings per tonne of freight moved.[18]

The benefits of extended connectivity with Southeast Asia

The BBIN MVA will enter into force on its ratification and issue of notifications by all the four countries. Negotiations for finalizing a similar MVA among India, Myanmar and Thailand (IMT) for enhanced regional connectivity through road transportation have been held and consensus on the text of the MVA evolved by the three countries. For finalizing the text of protocol and its schedules which would be part of the IMT MVA, negotiations are required to be concluded among the three countries. Tentatively, the three countries had agreed during the IMT transport secretary level meeting in Bangkok on 13–14 July 2015 that the IMT MVA could be signed during a transport ministers' meeting of the three countries in Myanmar in November 2015 when the respective governments would complete their internal approval process. This agreement will facilitate movement of cargo and passengers (including personal vehicles) on the India-Myanmar-Thailand road corridor, enhancing intra-regional and inter-regional trade and commerce in Southeastern Asia. There is no proposal at present for signing a separate MVA with Sri Lanka.[19]

Considering the importance of closer regional economic cooperation and integration through enhanced regional connectivity by road for cross-border travel to improve connectivity and people-to-people contact and further the shared goal of overall economic development, a meeting of the secretaries of transport of IMT on 13–14 July 2015 was held to reach a consensus on signing and operationalizing the IMT MVA, which has been under negotiation since March 2015.

The meeting at Bangkok was attended by delegations from the IMT countries, comprising secretaries of transport and other transport and customs officials, and was supported by staff and consultants of the ADB. The meeting emphasized the importance of the IMT MVA and its critical role in realizing the seamless movement of passenger, personal and cargo vehicles along roads linking the IMT countries. The initiative will also establish road connectivity between South Asia and Southeast Asia, which will strengthen economic integration and cooperation between the two sub-regions and boost their collective economic progress and development.

The transport secretaries' meeting was preceded by the IMT customs sub-group meeting on 13 July 2015 to address the various customs-related issues in the protocol to be finalized under the IMT MVA, and consensus was reached that the customs issues identified would be incorporated into the protocol(s). Various non-customs-related issues for the protocol were also negotiated, and a largely agreed-upon text of draft protocol(s) was developed in the meeting.

The meeting recognized the importance of carrying out necessary actions to ensure speedy finalization of the text (protocol/schedule) as part of the IMT MVA. It was decided that the IMT MVA would be signed during a proposed transport ministers' level meeting of three countries in Myanmar in November 2015. The signing of the agreement and its implementation were planned to occur by December 2015, and it was expected to be operational in 2016, opening the way for movement of cargo and passengers (including personal vehicles) on the India-Myanmar-Thailand road corridor.

The India-Myanmar-Thailand Trilateral Highway, which is expected to become operational by 2018, could bring about a sea change in regional connectivity and accelerate India's economic integration with the ASEAN. The trilateral highway has been a key component of the National Democratic Alliance (NDA) government's "Act East" policy and is designed to promote trade, investment, culture and historical linkages between India, especially its northeastern region, and Southeast Asian countries.[20]

BBIN also needs to work and coordinate with other sub-regional groupings, such as the Bangladesh, China, India, Myanmar Economic Corridor (BCIM-EC) and the Bay of Bengal Initiative for Multi-Sectoral Technical and Economic Cooperation (BIMSTEC), that operate beyond South Asia.

The challenges ahead

Protocols for regulating movement of passenger and cargo vehicles need to be implemented. Protocol 1 requires designation of corridors, routes and points of entry and exit (border crossings). Protocol 2 relates to the fixing of charges concerning transit traffic. Protocol 3 deals with the frequency and capacity of services and issuance of quotas and permits. For this purpose, standard operating procedures (SOPs) need to be designed in a manner that facilitates the implementation of all protocols under BBIN.[21] The MVA is only one step forward – though undoubtedly an important one – to facilitate seamless cross-border movement of cargo and passengers among BBIN countries. However, this will need to be followed up by other trade facilitation measures, including reduction/removal of non-tariff barriers (NTBs) and para-tariff barriers (PTBs); streamlining the excessive documentation required for cross-border movement; improvements in hard and soft infrastructure (e.g., road infrastructure); streamlining technical regulations, standards and conformity assessment procedures; facilitating investment cooperation; promoting transport facilitation; and streamlining legislative, regulatory and institutional dimensions.

All the aforementioned measures would involve massive investment in infrastructure. Investment costs in Bangladesh alone for establishing closer connectivity with India for roads, rail, inland water transport and ports is estimated to cost $8.0 billion.[22] Besides, as noted earlier, the ADB estimates that the thirty identified transport connectivity projects would cost over $8 billion.

A scenario for 2030

With the seamless movement of cargo among BBIN countries, one could legitimately expect intra-BBIN trade to at least double itself in relation to the sub-region's world trade. Along with increases in the goods trade, the services trade will similarly expand to facilitate the movement of goods. Accordingly, the trade corridors would take the shape of economic corridors, as services trade in travel, freight forwarding and insurance and construction also increases in response to the increase in goods traffic. The border areas of the sub-region have the highest density of impoverished people. The absorption of this population through gainful employment would help bring down the incidence of poverty in the border areas and help control illegal migration and trafficking.

Presently, the sub-regional trade is dominated by India's trade with the least developed countries – Nepal, Bhutan and Bangladesh. As noted earlier, the seamless flow of cargo is likely to benefit the least developed countries more, as they are currently required to do multiple transshipments through Indian territory for their bilateral trade with each other. These countries, when enabled by the seamless movement of goods traffic through Indian territory, would be benefitting from relatively greater cost reduction for their cargo movement and may find it more profitable to import from each other rather than from India or from the rest of the world. Besides, both Nepal and Bhutan, by having further access to the sea via Chittagong/Haldia, could diversify their markets with the rest of the world as well. It would thus help them in reducing their excessive dependence on India for sub-regional trade.

This chapter has demonstrated that the investment required for the transport infrastructure, even though high, would be justified given the market access potential that exists even for trade among the least developed countries in the region. With the support of the ADB, and with public – private partnerships, the mobilization of the required resources should not pose a formidable problem that cannot be overcome.

It can be anticipated that following the benefits of BBIN, a SAARC-level MVA would also come into force along with IMT MVA. The BBIN framework would then be merged under the SAARC Motor Vehicles Agreement. From being one of the least integrated regions in the world, this region would become much more integrated, much beyond what it was during the pre-partition days. This integration would spill over to both South and Southeast Asia. As the integration efforts of BCIM, BIMSTEC and One Belt One Road (OBOR) regional arrangements mingle, we may expect a landscape in which South Asia would be fully integrated with the larger Asian Community.

Notes

1 See South Asian Association for Regional Cooperation, Male Declaration, see www.ciel. org/Publications/Male_Declaration_Nov07.pdf (Accessed on 16 May 2019).
2 For SAARC Charter, see on www.saarc-sec.org/SAARC-Charter/5/ (Accessed on 16 May 2019).
3 General Provisions of (Article X) of SAARC Charter requires (i). Decisions at all levels shall be taken on the basis of unanimity; and (ii) Bilateral and contentious issues shall be excluded from the deliberations, see www.saarc-sec.org/SAARC-Charter/5/ (Accessed on 16 May 2019).
4 For details see Asian Development Bank, http://www.adb.org/themes/regional-cooperation/features (Accessed on 16 May 2019).
5 For Kathmandu Declaration, see, https://mea.gov.in/bilateral-documents.htm?dtl/24375/KATHMANDU+DECLARATION+Eighteenth+SAARC+Summit+Kathmandu+Nepal+2627+November+2014 (Accessed on 16 May 2019).
6 See presentation by S.P. Choudhury at *Regional Meeting on Harmonisation of Legal Instruments and Documentation for Cross-Border and Transit Transport by Road*, 16–17 December 2015, www.unescap.org/sites/default/files/India_11.pdf (Accessed on 16 May 2019).
7 See Joint Press Statement on the 1st meeting of Bangladesh-Bhutan-India trilateral Joint Working Group on Connectivity and Transit, www.hcidhaka.gov.in/pages.php?id=559.
8 For Joint Press Release – The Second Joint Working Group (JWG) Meetings on Sub-Regional Cooperation between Bangladesh, Bhutan, India and Nepal (BBIN) in New Delhi, 30–31 January 2015, https://mea.gov.in/press-releases.htm?dtl/24746/Joint_Press_Release__The_Second_Joint_Working_Group_JWG_Meetings_on_Sub Regional_Cooperation_between_Bangladesh_accessed (Accessed on 16 May 2019).
9 For Press Information Bureau Government of India Ministry of Road Transport & Highways, 15 June 2015, see http://pib.nic.in/ErrorPage.html?aspxerrorpath=/newsite/mainpage.aspx (Accessed on 16 May 2019).
10 See Asian Development Bank, *South Asia Sub regional Economic Cooperation*, www.adb.org/countries/subregional-programs/sasec (Accessed on 15 May 2019).
11 See MVA for the regulation of passenger, personal and cargo vehicular traffic between Bangladesh, Bhutan, India, and Nepal, http://morth.nic.in/showfile.asp?lid=1715 (Accessed on 16 May 2019).
12 Additional Market Access Frontier (AMAF) for Product i:

$AMAFi = Min(SEi, MIi) - EEi$

Where for product i, SEi = Supplier's Global Exports; MIi = Market's Global Imports; ETi = Supplier's Existing Exports to Market; Min = minimum.
13 The *revealed comparative advantage* is defined as the ratio of two shares. The numerator is the share of a country's total exports of the commodity of interest in its total exports, and the denominator is the share of world exports of the same commodity in total world exports. The RCA takes a value between 0 and (infinity). A value of more than 1 reveals the product's comparative advantage.
14 Government of India, Ministry of External Affairs, Trade Agreement between India and Bangladesh, www.mea.gov.in/Portal/LegalTreatiesDoc/BG15B2412.pdf (Accessed on 17 May 2019).
15 See presentation by Mustafizur Rahman, https://cpd.org.bd/wp-content/uploads/2015/06/Trade-Facilitation-South-Asia-Transport-Connectivity-Operationalising-Motor-Vehicle-Agreements-MVAs (Accessed on 16 May 2019).

16 Trade Buzz, *E-Newsletter*, n.5, November 2015-February 2016, see www.cuts-citee.org/pdf/Trade_Buzz-Nov2015-Feb2016.pdf (Accessed on 16 May 2019).

17 *The Indian Express*, 16 May 2019, https://indianexpress.com/article/explained/through-bangla-a-development-shortcut-for-northeast/ (Accessed on 16 May 2019).

18 *The Independent*, 29 March 2016, www.theindependentbd.com/printversion/details/38836 (Accessed on 16 May 2019).

19 This information was given by Minister of State for Road Transport and Highways P. Radhakrishnan in a written reply to a question in the Lok Sabha on 6 August 2015, see p://inbministry.blogspot.com/2015/08/motor-vehicles-agreement.html (Accessed on 16 May 2019).

20 See Government of India, Press information Bureau, nhttp://pib.nic.in/newsite/mbErel.aspx?relid=123623 (Accessed on 16 May 2019).

21 Rahman, n.15.

22 *Ibid.*

14

LINKAGES BETWEEN ELECTRICITY CONSUMPTION AND ECONOMIC GROWTH

Evidence from South Asian economies

Kamal Raj Dhungel

Introduction

Researchers have options when choosing a model to assess the exact relationship between electricity consumption and economic activity. One can use the model based either on the demand side or supply side. This chapter considers electricity as an essential factor of production. Thus, it uses the demand side model to reexamine the association and determine the causality between the variables of electricity consumption (EC) and gross domestic product (GDP) in five South Asian countries during the period 2000–2011. A panel unit root test and panel co-integration test are used to determine the long-run equilibrium. The fully modified ordinary least square method was applied to estimate the panel electricity elasticity coefficient. Granger causality based on the vector auto regression model was then applied to determine the direction of causality. The data are found stationary at first difference but are found non-stationary at their level. A co-integration test confirmed the long-run relationship or equilibrium between the variables EC and GDP. The electricity elasticity coefficient (EEC) is 1.31. It reveals that a one per cent increase in electricity consumption would lead to an increase in the GDP by 1.31 per cent, indicating a highly responsive electricity demand. In the spontaneous process of economic development of South Asian countries, there is a significant impact of EC on GDP. The value of EEC is self-spoken. A large change in GDP would be expected from a small change in EC. It has a big implication of bringing rapid economic progress within a short span of time, and any shortage of electric energy would retard economic progress. Electricity consumption is found to cause GDP. This unidirectional causality running from electricity consumption to GDP has important policy implications – electricity consumption leads economic growth, which has two policy implications. One, reduction of electricity consumption through bringing domestic energy prices in line with market prices would lead to a fall in GDP or employment. Two, electricity consumption bears the burden of short-run adjustment to reestablish the long-run equilibrium.

South Asia is home to over one billion people. A majority of them are living without access to electricity. Modern technology is based on the availability of electricity. Electricity is an essential prerequisite not only for modern life but also to power machines to produce goods and services.[1] Most of the South Asian countries obtain electricity from both non-renewable sources, such as nuclear, coal and natural gas, and from renewable sources, such as hydro, solar and wind power. Both of these sources, to some extent, are home-grown. All countries in the region are endowed with one source or another. Coal is available in India. Bangladesh and Pakistan are rich in natural gas, while Nepal and Bhutan have in hydropower. There is a golden opportunity to produce electricity from these indigenous sources. Among the potential sources, coal is highly exploited. It has been a major source of power for nearly a century and is expected to remain so in the days to come. Hydro and natural gas are untapped. These resources, if developed wisely, would be a boon for the development of South Asian countries.[2] They would provide ample opportunity for South Asian countries to exchange power with each other, plugging a particular country's demand and supply gap. It would help to ensure energy security and provide scope for regional market integration. Also, almost all the countries have hydropower potential, but to some extent, the degree of availability varies. This represents a renewable source of energy. Obtaining a higher economic growth rate to the extent of it being in the double digits is the primary goal of the South Asian countries. However, a double-digit growth rate requires huge units of electricity. Presently, this is constrained by inadequate power supplies. Thus, the goal is conditional upon an adequate and uninterrupted power supply. Electricity consumption and economic growth are closely interrelated. This chapter aims to investigate the causal relationship between economic growth and electricity consumption in five countries of the region.

Hydropower potential

Like coal and natural gas, the region possesses immense hydropower potential to the extent of 103 TWh, which would comprise 1.5 per cent of the global total. The South Asian region is fortunate to have such vast potential because hydropower is a renewable and non-polluting source of energy. Currently, the region has only harnessed 28 GW (see Table 14.1). Despite the potential, the region depends on petroleum products from Gulf counties in order to achieve targeted economic growth.

TABLE 14.1 Hydropower potential in South Asia in TWh

Potential	South Asia	Global	Percent
Theoretical	3635	40784	8.9
Technical	948	13945	6.8
Economic	103	6964	1.5
Installed (gigawatts)	28	655	4.3

Source: World Energy Assessment 2000, New York: UNDP, p. 154.

In the process, there are intangible costs of pollution stimulating climate change. From this perspective, the benefit of the exploitation of hydropower is manifold. It facilitates the following:

1 Utilizing the region's untapped resources;
2 Ensuring energy security;
3 Holding energy trade across the regional countries;
4 Creating an environment in which to integrate the regional market;
5 Reducing the import bill for petroleum products;
6 Reducing greenhouse gas emissions in the atmosphere.

Electricity production

Five countries of South Asia produce 1374.693 billion KWh of electricity. Coal is the major source of electricity. It contributes more than fifty-two per cent to the total electricity production. The share of hydro, natural gas and renewables in electricity production is 12.22 per cent, 12.83 per cent and 16.03 per cent respectively. India alone produces 86.1 per cent of the total followed by Pakistan (9.01 per cent), Bangladesh (3.1 per cent), Sri Lanka (1.2 per cent) and Nepal (0.48 per cent).

Development indicator

Electricity is the major source of power. The nation's economic activities depend on its availability. Per capita electricity consumption, in modern usage, is taken as one of the measures of development. Higher per capita electricity consumption shows the better development of a nation. The per capita electricity consumption of selected countries is given in Table 14.3. India's highest per capita electricity consumption (684 KWh) indicates that it is a relatively more developed country in the South Asian region. The second highest is Sri Lanka, with per capita electricity

TABLE 14.2 Source-wise electricity production in billion KWh in 2011

Source	Bangladesh		India		Nepal		Pakistan		Sri Lanka	
	Value	Percent	Value	Percent	Value	Percent	Value	Percent	Value	Percent
Coal	0.78	0.06	714.95	52	0	0	0.096	0.007	1.04	0.08
Hydro	0.872	0.06	130.67	9.51	3.31	0.24	28.52	2.07	4.62	0.34
Natural gas	40.31	2.93	108.53	7.89	0	0	27.65	2.01	0	0
Nuclear	0	0	33.29	2.42	0	0	5.26	0.38	0	0
Oil	2.1	0.15	12.22	0.89	0.003	0	33.73	2.45	5.85	0.43
Renewable	0.872	0.06	183.33	13.3	3.31	0.24	28.62	2.08	4.76	0.35
Total	44.934	3.21	1182.99	86.1	6.623	0.48	123.9	9.01	16.27	1.2

Source: www.nationmaster.com/index.php, accessed on 5 July 2014.

TABLE 14.3 Per capita electricity consumption in 2011 (KWh/annum)

	Bangladesh	India	Nepal	Pakistan	Sri Lanka
Electricity consumption	259	684	104	471	490

Source: www.nationmaster.com/index.php, accessed on 5 July 2014.

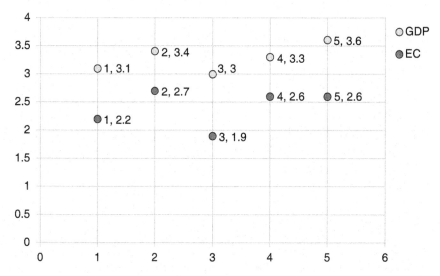

FIGURE 14.1   Graphical view of the mean value of GDP and EC

Source: Author's estimation (original data are taken from World Bank and Asian Development Bank)

consumption (490 KWh), followed by Pakistan (471), Bangladesh (259 KWh) and Nepal (106 KWh).

Data and variables

The study period depends primarily on the availability of data for all the selected five South Asian countries – Bangladesh, India, Nepal, Pakistan and Sri Lanka. For data processing purposes, these countries are numbered 1, 2, 3, 4 and 5 respectively. On the basis of the availability of annual time series data for all the countries under consideration, this study covers the time period from 2000 to 2011. Gross domestic product (GDP) and electricity consumption (EC) are the variables included in the study. Annual data of per capita GDP in PPP US dollar and EC in per capita KWh are obtained from key development indicators and World Development Indicators of the Asian Development Bank and World Bank respectively, and then they are expressed in logarithm. The average values of both the variables are plotted in Figure 14.1. The distribution of the pair match observations has a trend with long-run positive movement. It is observed that GDP growth is thinly associated with electricity use in Nepal over the years as compared to the rest of the countries under consideration.

Theoretical structure

Traditional production function models do not consider energy (electricity) as an input to produce output. The knife-edge growth theory of Harrod-Domer and Solow Swan growth model claim that energy has no significant role in the production function. However, Stern (1997), among others, takes the view that energy is the major input which plays a crucial role in the production process. It can directly be used as a final product. Pokrovski (2003) puts forth that tools and machinery, which are considered as capital input, are used in lieu of manual labour and require electricity for their operation. Thus, in this sense, energy is the primary factor of production. The output is the result of the combined effort of labour, capital and energy. A number of studies, such as Sharma and Dhakal,[3] Nourzad,[4] Paual and Rabindra,[5] Beaudreau,[6] Lee,[7] Thompson[8] and Sari and Soytas,[9] have shown strong evidence of internalization of the role of technology in the production function. Thus, in this respect, their argument to internalize the role of energy in the production function seems justifiable.

The model

This chapter aims to establish the relationship between GDP and EC by using Pedroni's[10] fully modified ordinary least square (FMOLS) method and thereby investigate the Granger causality. FMOLS corrects biases of estimators with fixed effects arising from the problems of autocorrelation and heteroscedasticity and allows considerable heterogeneity among the individual cross sections.[11] It considers possible correlation between the differences in constant term, dependent variables and error term. For this purpose, the following type of equation is used to determine the relationship between the variables under consideration.

$$GDP_t = b_0 + b_1 EC_t + \epsilon_t \qquad\qquad [1]$$

Where, GDP_t = Per capita gross domestic product at PPP dollars,
EC_t = Per capita electricity consumption in KWh,
ϵ_t = error term and
b_0 and b_1 are the parameters to be estimated.

In order to apply, FMOLS to estimate equation (1), there are some pertinent issues to be addressed. Investigation of panel co-integration is a must. Co-integration requires a panel unit root test that can determine whether the series are stationary or non-stationary. Thus, in this respect, this study investigates the panel unit root test and co-integration test before applying the FOMLS to establish the inter-relationship between GDP and EC. Four methods,[12] Im, Pesaran and Shin W-stat,[13] ADF – Fisher Chi-square and PP – Fisher Chi-square) are employed to determine the panel unit root in the series. Pedroni[14] and Kao[15] panel co-integration test methods are used to investigate the long-term relationship between the variables under consideration.

Finally, the Block Exogeneity Wald test based on VAR is applied to determine the causal relationship between the variables. If unidirectional causality runs from EC to GDP, reduction of electricity consumption through bringing domestic energy prices in line with market prices would lead to a fall in GDP or employment. However, if unidirectional causality runs from GDP to EC energy conservation policies, such as phasing out energy subsidies or elimination of energy price distortions, it will have little adverse or no effect on economic growth.[16]

Empirical finding

Unit root test

Four types of test statistic (see Table 14.4) were chosen to test the null hypothesis of unit root or I(0) in the variables GDP and EC. Lags are chosen automatically. These tests at level accept the null hypothesis of unit root. It means both the variables GDP and EC contain unit root, indicating they are non-stationary in the data. But they become stationary at first difference in all the chosen test methods. It indicates that they are in the same order I(1). It is the precondition to conduct a panel co-integration test, which determines the long-term relationship between the variables under consideration.

Panel co-integration test

The unit root test fulfills the precondition of no unit root in the series to conduct a panel co-integration test between the variable GDP and EC. Under this test, no

TABLE 14.4 Panel unit root test summary

Method	GDP				EC			
	Level		First difference		Level		First difference	
	Stat	Prob	Stat	Prob	Stat	Prob	Stat	Prob
Levin, Lin & Chu t*	0.15473	0.5615	-4.25194*	0.0000	1.19115	0.8832	-5.17742*	0.0000
Im, Pesaran and Shin W-stat	2.73337	0.9969	-2.39899*	0.0082	2.53013	0.9943	-3.54111*	0.0002
ADF – Fisher Chi-square	2.77183	0.9863	22.2478*	0.0139	3.12672	0.9783	29.5989*	0.0010
PP – Fisher Chi-square	1.08232	0.9998	27.2810*	0.0024	4.51619	0.9211	45.2122*	0.0000

Source: Author's estimation (original data are taken from World Bank and Asian Development Bank).
Note: * significant at 1% level

TABLE 14.5 Results of panel co-integration test

Method	Pedroni within dimension			
	t-stat	Prob	Weighted t-stat	Prob
Panel V-stat	3.4231*	0.0085	3.6041*	0.0002
Panel rho-stat	−3.8650*	0.0003	−2.3446*	0.0006
Panel PP-stat	−1.9424*	0.0260	−1.9833*	0.0346
Panel ADF-stat	−1.9402*	0.0262	−1.2817	0.0536
	Pedroni between dimension			
Group rho-stat	0.6494	0.7420		
Group PP-stat	−2.8812*	0.0022		
Group ADF-stat	−1.1673	0.1215		
	Kao residual			
ADF	−1.938326*	0.0263		

Source: Author's estimation (original data are taken from World Bank and Asian Development Bank)
Note: * significant at 5% level

co-integration within the variables GDP and EC is the null hypothesis. There are eleven test outcomes, of which eight are within dimension and the rest are between dimensions. Eight test outcomes are statistically significant at the 5 per cent level (see Table 14.5). It indicates that the null hypothesis of no co-integration is rejected through the majority test outcomes and ensures that the variables are co-integrated. In a similar fashion, the Kao residual test of co-integration also confirms that the variables are co-integrated. This evidence proves that the variables GDP and EC have a long-term equilibrium relationship.

FMOLS estimation

The estimation results of FMOLS are presented in Table 14.6. The electricity elasticity coefficient (EEC) is 1.31, which is greater than 1 in panel FMOLS estimation. It implies that the demand for electricity is elastic and indicates that electricity consumption has a positive impact on economic growth. A one per cent increase in EC led to a 1.31 per cent increase in GDP. The implication is that the economies of South Asian countries will grow at a faster rate if they supply adequate units of electricity. The same is true for individual countries. The EEC is greater than one, except for Bangladesh, and ranges from 0.81 in Bangladesh to 1.69 in Pakistan. All the respective coefficients are statistically significant, revealing that a one per cent increase in electricity consumption would lead to an increase in the GDP by 0.81 per cent, 1.51 per cent, 1.10 per cent, 1.69 per cent and 1.53 per cent in Bangladesh, India, Nepal, Pakistan and Sri Lanka respectively.

TABLE 14.6 Estimated results of FMOLS (GDP is dependent variable)

Countries	EC is independent variable			
	Coefficient	Standard error	t-stat	Prob
Panel	1.31	0.072228	18.21097★	0.0000
Bangladesh	0.81	0.063137	12.84932★	0.0001
India	1.51	0.076244	19.76911★	0.0000
Nepal	1.10	0.081592	12.84862★	0.0001
Pakistan	1.69	0.279670	6.001975★	0.0018
Sri Lanka	1.53	0.189083	8.100650★	0.0005

Source: Author's estimation (original data are taken from World Bank and Asian Development Bank).
Note: ★ significant at 1% level

Granger causality

All sample countries

The Granger causality based on the vector auto regression for all the countries under consideration shows the causality running from electricity consumption to GDP, or EC to GDP. The value of Chi-square is 9.344 with probability 0.0094, which is significant at the five per cent level (see Table 14.7). It rejects the null hypothesis: EC does not cause GDP. The implication is that the causality is running from EC to GDP. The theory suggests that if causality is running from electricity consumption to income, the shortage of electricity may negatively affect GDP. It implies that these countries are struggling with the shortage of electricity, on the one hand, and their economic development is highly dependent on the adequate availability of electricity, on the other. It implies that all countries included in the analysis are suffering from the shortage of electricity. Shortage of electricity negatively affects the GDP growth. Thus, they should put great effort into generating electricity from the region's indigenous sources.

Individual country

The statistically significant coefficients of the Chi-square test statistic (see Table 14.7) reject the null hypothesis: EC does not cause GDP. It implies that the unidirectional causality is running from EC to GDP for Bangladesh, India and Nepal. It indicates that these economies are electricity dependent. Pakistan is just the opposite. The statistically significant coefficients of the Chi-square test statistic reject the null hypothesis: GDP does not cause EC. It implies that the causality is running from GDP to EC. It implies that the economy of Pakistan is less dependent on electricity. It suggests that energy conservation policy may be implemented with little adverse or no effect on GDP. The estimated results for Sri Lanka are unique. There is bidirectional causality between EC and GDP. It implies that there is a feedback effect on the economy.

TABLE 14.7 Results of VAR Granger Causality/Block Exogeneity Wald Test

Country	Regression on			
	ΔEConΔGDP (EC causing GDP)		ΔGDPonΔEC (GDP causing EC)	
	Chi-square	Prob	Chi-square	Prob
Panel	9.343684★	0.0094	1.0555	0.5899
Bangladesh	16.46118★	0.0003	4.463314	0.1073
India	21.01098★	0.0000	1.224171	0.5222
Nepal	15.43043★	0.0004	5.179362	0.0750
Pakistan	1.464394	0.4001	15.42777★	0.0004
Sri Lanka	8.727284★	0–0000	10.07727★	0.0005

Source: Author's estimation (original data are taken from World Bank and Asian Development Bank).
Note: ★ significant at 1% level

Conclusions and policy implications

The exact relationship between electricity consumption and economic activity can be assessed using a model based either on the demand side or on the supply side. Considering electricity as an essential factor of production, this chapter has used the demand side model to reexamine the association and to determine the causality between the variables EC and GDP in five South Asian countries during the period 2000–2011. A panel unit root test and panel co-integration test are used to determine the long-term equilibrium. The fully modified ordinary least square method was applied to estimate the panel electricity elasticity coefficient. Granger causality based on the vector auto regression model was then applied to determine the direction of causality.

The data were found to be stationary at first difference but were non-stationary at their level. A co-integration test confirmed the long-term relationship or equilibrium between the variables EC and GDP. The electricity elasticity coefficient is 1.31, meaning that a one per cent increase in electricity consumption would lead to the increase of GDP by 1.31 per cent. Electricity consumption is found to Granger cause GDP. This unidirectional causality running from electricity consumption to GDP has important policy implications. Electricity consumption leads to economic growth, which has two policy outcomes. One, reduction of electricity consumption by bringing domestic energy prices in line with market prices would lead to a fall in GDP or employment. Two, electricity consumption bears the burden of short-term adjustment to reestablish the long-term equilibrium. Thus, in this connection, it can be concluded that energy conservation policy may harm economic growth in the South Asian countries. Hence, in general, electricity is an important ingredient for economic growth. In order to meet this requirement, it is necessary to put effort into generating electricity from their untapped resources.

Notes

1 K.R. Dhungel, "Income and Price Elasticity of the Demand for Energy: A Macro-level Empirical Analysis", *Pacific and Asia Journal of Energy*, vol.13, no.2, 2003, pp. 73–84; K.R. Dhungel, "A Causal Relationship Between Energy Consumption and Economic Growth in Nepal", *Asia Pacific Development Journal*, vol.15, no.1, June 2008, pp. 137–148.

2 K.R. Dhungel, "Regional Energy Trade in South Asia: Problems and Prospects", *South Asia Economic Journal*, vol.9, no.1, 2008, pp. 173–193.

3 S.C. Sharma and D. Dhakal, "Causal Analyses Between Exports and Economic Growth in Developing Countries", *Applied Economics*, vol.26, 1994, pp. 1145–1157.

4 F. Nourzad, "The Productivity Effect of Government Capital in Developing and Industrialized Countries", *Applied Economics*, vol.32, 2000, pp. 1181–1187.

5 S. Paul and R.N. Bhattacharya, "Causality Between Energy Consumption and Economic Growth in India: A Note on Conflicting Results", *Energy Economics*, vol.26, 2004, pp. 977–983.

6 B.C. Beaudreau, "Engineering and Economic Growth", *Structural Change and Economic Dynamics*, vol.16, 2005, pp. 211–220.

7 C.C. Lee, "Energy Consumption and GDP in Developing Countries: A Co-integrated Panel Analysis", *Energy Economics*, vol.27, 2005, pp. 415–427.

8 H. Thompson, "The Applied Theory of Energy Substitution in Production", *Energy Economics*, vol.28, no.4, 2006, pp. 410–425.

9 R. Sari and U. Soytas, "The Growth of Income and Energy Consumption in Six Developing Countries", *Energy Policy*, vol.35, no.2, 2006, pp. 889–898.

10 P. Pedroni, "Fully Modified OLS for Heterogeneous Co-integrated Panels", *Advances in Econometrics*, vol.15, 2000, pp. 93–130.

11 C.C. Lee and C.P. Chang, "Energy Consumption and Economic Growth in Asian Countries: A Comprehensive Analysis Using Panel Data", *Resource and Energy Economics*, vol.30, 2007, pp. 50–65.

12 A. Levin, C.F. Lin, and C.S.J. Chu, "Unit Root Tests in Panel Data: Asymptotic and Finite Sample Properties", *Journal of Econometrics*, vol.108, 2002, pp. 1–22.

13 K.S. Im, M.H. Pesaran, and Y. Shin, "Testing for Unit Roots in Heterogeneous Panels", *Journal of Econometrics*, vol.115, 2003, pp. 53–74.

14 P. Pedroni, "Panel Co-integration: Asymptotic and Finite Sample Properties of Pooled Time Series Tests with an Application to the PPP Hypothesis", *Econometric Theory*, vol.20, no.3, 2004, pp. 597–625.

15 C. Kao, "Spurious Regression and Residual-Based Tests for Co-integration in Panel Data", *Journal of Econometrics*, vol.90, 1999, pp. 1–44.

16 G. Abdoli, Y.G. Farahani, and S. Daston, "Electricity Consumption and Economic Growth in OPEC Countries: A Co-integrated Panel Analysis", *OPEC Energy Review*, vol.39, no.1, 2015, pp. 1–16; Y. Bayer and H.A. Ozel, "Electricity Consumption and Economic Growth in Emerging Economies", *Journal of Knowledge Management, Economics and Information Technology*, vol.10, no.4, 2014.

15

CONNECTIVITY BETWEEN INDIA AND SRI LANKA

A model for South Asia

N. Manoharan

Introduction

No two countries enjoy bilateral relations as unique as India and Sri Lanka with differing characteristics. India is not only Sri Lanka's closest but also most important and powerful neighbour. Relations between the two neighbours stretch back more than two millennia in wide-ranging areas – political, economic, socio-cultural and security.[1] A common colonial experience under Great Britain led the two countries to have similar worldviews, yet certain strategic imperatives and national interests dictated differing policies, at times conflicting with each other. India has always stood by Sri Lanka in its difficult times and again has reiterated its unambiguous support for safeguarding the latter's unity, territorial integrity and sovereignty.[2] India has also been assisting in Sri Lanka's development, both at bilateral and multilateral levels. Despite witnessing various ups and downs, the bilateral relations between the two countries have never descended to a level of confrontation. They have, in fact, matured over a period of time and serve as a model of good neighbourly interaction. Hence, it is pertinent to take the case of connectivity between India and Sri Lanka as a model for South Asia.

Located strategically in the Indian Ocean, Sri Lanka is at the cross-regional transit point between Africa and Europe on the one side and Asia and the Pacific on the other.[3] In other words, it is a maritime transit hub of the Indo-Pacific region with over 60,000 ships crossing the Indian Ocean each year, including nearly half of the world's containerized cargo. Sri Lanka has emerged as one of the most popular tourist destinations of the region, attracting over eight times the numbers since the end of the ethnic war in 2009.[4] With a literate and affable population, Sri Lanka has a good appetite for economic development. Its economic system is business-friendly, and the present political-security environment is conducive for both regional and global connectivity.

Model of connectivity

Among South Asian countries, connectivity between India and Sri Lanka is at an all-time high if not at its best. Connectivity between the two countries could be analyzed in four broad areas: physical, cultural, information and communication technology (ICT) and economic.

Physical connectivity

Given the interjection of waters between India and Sri Lanka, connectivity through land is absent. However, historical evidence indicates that Adam's Bridge was acting as land connectivity between the two countries. The idea of the Indo-Ceylon Bridge goes back to 1894 when a land route connecting Madras with Colombo through Rameshwaram (in India) and Mannar (in Sri Lanka) was proposed.[5] Reviving this idea had been explored way back in 2003. Dubbed as "Ram Sethu" or the "Hindu–Buddhist Bridge," the proposal originated from Sri Lanka to construct a combination of a sea-bridge and underwater tunnel linking Talaimannar and Dhanushkhodi, the two nearest points between Sri Lanka and India respectively.[6] A feasibility study conducted by the Board of Investment of Sri Lanka looked at three financial options: a build-operate-transfer model, co-financing between the two governments and bilateral and multilateral financing as part of a critical link in the Asian Highway Concept.[7] The report recognized that such a land link would "strengthen the growth prospects in both the regions."

Presently estimated to cost around INR 23,000 crores, such a link will facilitate the effective movement of both passengers and cargo, resulting in increased economic opportunities for both countries, and it "would also help in increasing the trans-SAARC road and transport network."[8] It also goes well with the UNESCAP (United Nations Economic and Social Commission for Asia and the Pacific) initiative of the Asian Highway and the Trans-Asian Railway, which presently intends to connect India and Sri Lanka through ferry service.[9] A memorandum of understanding (MoU) was indeed signed between India and Sri Lanka in 2011 on commencing a ferry service connecting Tuticorin and Colombo. But the mode of transport is yet to materialize because of a lack of abiding interest in both countries.

The land bridge will also offer tremendous scope for industrial linkage, especially between southern parts of India and Sri Lanka. If a railway is also added to the corridor, the connection will have a competitive advantage for high-volume traffic, in which case Sri Lanka will benefit more than India in terms of industrial development in the island state. India is already involved in developing certain rail lines in Sri Lanka.[10] That way, a railway interlinking the two countries would be easier. Freight originating from Chennai, Bangalore, Hyderabad and other major South Indian industrial enclaves could be routed through Sri Lankan trans-shipment hubs like Colombo and Hambantota for rapid connections to the rest of the world. It will create an opportunity for developing ports in northeast Sri Lanka, like Kankesanthurai and Point Pedro.[11] Also, Sri Lanka will immensely benefit from the easy access to the large domestic consumer base in India in general and South India in particular.

Interestingly, India did not show much interest when the idea of a land bridge was first floated by Sri Lanka, mainly for security reasons. Now, after the ethnic conflict, when India shows interest, the project seems to have lost traction in Sri Lanka. The present government in Colombo has not been able to sell the idea to its critics, who argue that Sri Lanka would face threat of invasion from India if linked by land, and "the seas around Lanka is also a moat around the Lankan citadel and forms the first formidable defence against any invader."[12] The argument is amusing because, in modern-day warfare, a twenty-kilometre sea divide is not a big obstacle for a military power like India. Apprehensions about "hostile elements from Tamil Nadu storming North Lanka or infiltrating into Lanka" and that "Tamil Nadu could well use Tamil-speaking North Lanka as a rear base to the detriment of Lanka's interests" using a land link are unwarranted.[13]

It should be realized that Sri Lanka will benefit more than India from such land connectivity. In addition to the advantages identified earlier, the land bridge would also hook Sri Lanka to India's Southern Region Electricity Grid with the Kudankulam Nuclear Power Plant serving as a base load station. India is already involved in enhancing the power generation capacity of Sri Lanka in the Sampur Coal Power Plant.[14] Given the fact that Sri Lanka has been facing severe power shortages, India could act as a transit country for excess power from countries like Bhutan. Given Sri Lanka's potential in excess of 40,000 MW of wind energy, there is a scope for the island state to export power to India.[15] But that requires a grid connection across the Palk Straits. Setting up a South Asian or SAARC grid could be explored in due course.[16]

As far as air connectivity is concerned, both India and Sri Lanka have been following an "open skies" policy since 2003. Sri Lanka is one of the few countries which has utilized its entitlement of flights to the maximum. Colombo is a major air hub in the region. The number of Indian airports from which flights to Sri Lanka take-off and land is around twenty-five, including both metropolitan and secondary destinations. With more than 150 flights every week between India and Sri Lanka, tourist arrivals to Sri Lanka from India are the highest. With the extension of the facility of the "Tourist Visa on Arrival – Electronic Travel Authorization" Scheme to Sri Lankan citizens, the tourist flow between the two countries is expected to go up.[17] Revival of the "Buddhist Circuit" in India and the "Ramayana Trail" in Sri Lanka will further boost tourist flow between the two countries. In 2017, out of the total tourist arrivals, about 384,628 were from India, constituting about 18 percent of the total number of tourists in Sri Lanka. In comparison, 268,952 Chinese travelled to Sri Lanka during the same period. The annual growth rate of leisure travel from India to Sri Lanka is about 15–20 percent. Sri Lanka too is among the top ten sources of tourists to India. Sri Lankan Airlines operates over 100 weekly flights covering twelve cities.[18] In 2016, around 215,000 visas were issued by the High Commission and other posts in Sri Lanka to facilitate travel between India and Sri Lanka.[19] In the absence of effective surface connectivity, air connectivity has, to an extent, supplemented the need for linkage. This applies not only to passenger transport but also cargo. Interestingly, India is considering a possible joint venture to operate the loss-making Mattala International Airport in southern Sri Lanka.[20] In that case, India-Sri Lanka air connectivity will increase further, apart from solidifying the connectivity ties between the two countries.

Cultural connectivity

During his meeting with the Sri Lankan president, Prime Minister Narendra Modi observed, "The timeless links of history, religion and culture provide a solid foundation of partnership" between India and Sri Lanka.[21] Though cultural connectivity between the two countries dates back centuries, the Cultural Cooperation Agreement signed in 1977 forms the basis for periodic cultural exchange programmes. With that framework, the Programme of Cultural Cooperation is implemented every three years to enhance cultural cooperation in several broad areas: performing arts, visual arts, exhibitions, museums, libraries, archives and cultural documentation, archaeology, publications and professional exchanges.[22]

To give an institutional framework, the Indian Cultural Centre was established in Colombo in 1998. It was aimed at building bridges of cultural exchange and interaction between the two countries; to revive and strengthen cultural relations and mutual understanding; and "to promote India-Sri Lanka cultural cooperation by building on cultural commonalities and creating an awareness of Indian culture in all its facets."[23] The Centre offers classes in Indian classical dances like Bharatanatyam and Kathak, Indian classical music forms like Hindustani and Carnatic and instruments like the violin, sitar and tabla, apart from teaching Hindi language and yoga. Interestingly, to conduct these classes, the centre draws on a talented and committed group of Sri Lankan teachers. Over time, the centre has gained tremendous popularity, with nearly 1,500 students enrolled in the various classes conducted at the centre. Not limiting itself to coaching, the centre is involved in the outreach by organizing performing art shows, visual art exhibitions, seminars, workshops and lecture demonstrations at its auditorium. The centre also screens Indian films and documentaries every month. The centre maintains a well-equipped library and reading room with a large collection of books, newspapers, periodicals, CDs and DVDS and so on. However, the main issue is making the cultural and art forms appealing, especially to the Sri Lankan youth, in terms of employment opportunities.

Apart from the Indian Cultural Centre, the India-Sri Lanka Foundation was setup in December 1998 as an inter-governmental initiative aimed "towards enhancement of scientific, technical, educational and cultural cooperation through civil society exchanges and enhancing contact between the younger generations of the two countries."[24] The activities of the foundation include the following:

- Financing higher studies, research and other education activities at institutes of learning located in India and Sri Lanka;
- Facilitating visits and exchanges between India and Sri Lanka for scholars, academics, professionals, artists and experts involved in areas of activities covered by the foundation;

- Assisting activities such as seminars, symposia, colloquia and workshops on subjects of common interest;
- Extending financial support to those non-governmental organizations both in India and Sri Lanka whose work facilitates achievement of the objectives of the foundation;
- Contributing towards publication of standard works on India-Sri Lanka relations in specified fields;
- Encouraging the translations of the standard works of Sri Lankan literature into Indian languages and viceversa and arranging for their publications;
- Promoting awareness of yoga by observing International Yoga Day annually in various parts of the island since 2015.[25]

Education is an important component of cultural cooperation between the two neighbours. As part of the "India Sri Lanka Knowledge Initiative," announced on 19 January 2012, the number of scholarships and self-financed slots for undergraduate/masters/PhD courses were increased from 113 slots to 270 per year and later to 290. This apart, 370 scholarships are offered annually to Sri Lankan nationals under the Indian Technical and Economic Cooperation Scheme (ITECS). In addition, scholarship support to deserving students pursuing their GCE "A" level and university degrees in Sri Lanka was expanded to cover about 500 students annually.[26] The Indian Council for Cultural Relations (ICCR) has its own set of SAARC and Commonwealth scholarships for Sri Lankans. Establishment of the Centre for Contemporary Indian Studies at the University of Colombo in February 2012 was a good move in enhancing the cultural linkage and popularizing Indian studies in Sri Lanka. Similar centres could be considered in other South Asian countries. But the principal query that should be addressed is whether there are career opportunities after completion of courses on India studies. If this is taken care of, then the popularity of India studies could be established in the neighbourhood.

Interestingly, the two countries have also been collaborating on the use of technology in education. In January 2018, Colombo and New Delhi agreed to partner in introducing a model e-office application for the government of Sri Lanka under the Sri Lanka Education and Research Network (LEARN) and the connectivity for academic and research institutes under the National Knowledge Network (NKN) of India. The total number of academic institutions that would benefit from this technological linkage is about 2,000 in both countries.[27]

The most important cultural cord connecting the two countries is in the form of Buddhism. Both countries commemorated the 2600th year of the attainment of enlightenment by Lord Buddha (*Sambuddhatva Jayanthi*) through activities like the exposition of Sacred Kapilavastu Relics in Sri Lanka (August – September 2012) in which about three million Sri Lankans participated and paid respects to the Sacred Relics. In December 2013, the Indian Gallery at the International Buddhist Museum, Sri Dalada Maligawa, Kandy, was inaugurated. The two countries also jointly celebrated the 150th Anniversary of Anagarika Dharmapala, a famous Buddhist revivalist, in 2014.[28]

ICT

ICT linkage between the two neighbours is also at a reasonably good level. Interestingly, both public and private players of India are involved in this linkage. At the government level, a MoU signed between the two sides in 2003 for cooperation in the field forms a basis for cooperation in the ICT sector. Another MoU was signed in January 2018 in the field of information technology and electronics (IT&E) to several areas of future collaboration. Some of them included e-governance with special focus on rural areas, cooperation in the area of cyber-security, B2B partnerships and collaboration between industry associations, development of digital talents and enhancement of digital/ICT literacy and cooperation in R&D and innovation in ICT, the sector between private and public institutions.[29] It should be noted that India has been extending strong support towards expanding the network of Nenasalas (Telecentres) across Sri Lanka.[30]

It is important to note that Sri Lanka's geographical location makes it a natural nexus for communications in the Indian Ocean region and helps ensure that the country plays a key role in the process of unfolding new technologies across the region.[31] Sri Lankan government-owned Sri Lanka Telecom (SLT) has partnered with SEA-ME-WE, a twenty-member consortium, right from the inception and currently connects globally via SEA-ME-WE 3, SEA-ME-WE 4 and two other private cables to India and Maldives. With SLT's investment in the new SEA-ME-WE 5 cable, the country's global connectivity capacity will move to the next level with the capacity of twenty-four terabytes and 100G technology. This has made Sri Lanka future ready to take on the envisaged data explosion.[32]

As a result, not surprisingly, Sri Lanka has emerged as one of the most preferred destinations in the region for BPO or data centre operations. Significantly, instead of considering Sri Lanka as a competitor in the BPO sector, India has encouraged Sri Lanka to take advantage of the expertise of the Indian IT sector. For instance, New Delhi has offered Colombo use of 200 training slots offered by the Indian IT giant Infosys for the training of Sri Lankan IT professionals at Mysore.[33] SLT has developed important partnerships through its relationships forged with Indian companies like Bharti Infotel and Tata Communications. This is a good model to extend to countries like Pakistan, Bangladesh and Maldives, where English education is at a reasonably good level.

Economic connectivity

Economic connectivity between India and Sri Lanka is appreciable. India is Sri Lanka's largest trading partner, and Sri Lanka is India's second largest trading partner in South Asia. A significant amount of bilateral trade takes place under the framework of the India-Sri Lanka Free Trade Agreement (ISLFTA), which went operational in 2000.[34] According to Sri Lanka, bilateral trade in 2017 amounted to $5.3 billion. Of this figure, exports from India to Sri Lanka were about $4.5 billion (up by 2.1 percent), while exports from Sri Lanka to India were $789.5 million (up by 3.2 percent).[35] The trade may appear to be in India's favour; however, close reading of figures reveal that the deficit has been closing annually. In terms of ratio of trade by each country, it is 1:7 (Sri Lanka: India); it was 1:10 in 2011. Significantly, about seventy percent of Sri Lanka's exports to India continue to be under the ISFTA. India's exports to Sri Lanka under the ISFTA remain only around 25 percent. This clearly proves who is benefitting from the FTA.[36]

Thus, ISLFTA is considered as "one of the few South-South Agreements that is working credibly and could be an example for other South-South Agreements to emulate."[37] In specific terms, the agreement serves as a model ("spaghetti bowl" model in economic parlance) of developing such arrangements in South Asia as a precursor for a successful South Asian Free Trade Agreement (SAFTA). Bangladesh has realized this and emerged as India's largest trading partner in South Asia.

Not limited to ISLFTA, India and Sri Lanka share membership in other regional and multilateral trading arrangements like the *Asia-Pacific Trade Agreement (APTA)*, the *South Asian Free Trade Area (SAFTA)*, the Bay of Bengal Initiative for Multi-Sectoral Technical and Economic Cooperation (BIMSTEC), the Global System of Trade Preferences among Developing Countries (GSTP) and the *World Trade Organization (WTO)*. India could utilize this route for enhancing economic connectivity if there is an issue at the bilateral level.

Given the robust improvement in trade relations, both countries wanted to take the economic ties to the next level through the Comprehensive Economic Cooperation Agreement (CECA). The proposed CECA aimed "at promoting trade in both goods and services, facilitating greater investment flows and enhancing mutual cooperation in the sphere of overall economic relations."[38] But there has been opposition against such a comprehensive framework from the Sri Lankan side, principally due to political reasons. Now both countries have decided to negotiate the Economic and Technology Cooperation Agreement (ETCA) instead of the CECA. Yet, the ETCA is being opposed in Sri Lanka by certain professional bodies, fearing that it would pave the way for Indian professionals and semi-skilled and unskilled persons to "flood" Sri Lanka's labour market.[39] There is also no political consensus on the benefits of the deal. The present government has to take both the opposition and professional bodies into confidence while finalizing the deal. Given the economic situation of the island state, autarchic economic policies would hamper the much-needed development. A closed economy cannot create the promised one million jobs; neither could it become the Singapore of South Asia.

Economic connectivity also includes investments apart from trade. As per the Indian Ministry of External Affairs, India is among the top four investors in Sri Lanka with cumulative investments of over $1 billion since 2003. The investments are in diverse areas, including petroleum retail, IT, financial services, real estate, telecommunications, hospitality and tourism, banking and food processing (tea and fruit juices), metal industries, tires, cement, glass manufacturing, and infrastructure development (railway, power, water supply).[40] The investments are not one way. In recent years, an increasing trend of Sri Lankan investments is flowing into India.

Important investors include Brandix (about $1 billion to set up a garment city in Vishakapatnam), MAS holdings, John Keels, Hayleys and Aitken Spence (Hotels), apart from other investments in the freight servicing and logistics sector.

The way ahead

After a slight dip, India-Sri Lanka relations are back on track in a positive direction. There seems to be a perfect political alignment between the pro-business regime in Colombo and the pro-development government in Delhi for enhancing connectivity between the two countries. There are indeed certain challenges in terms of unwanted apprehensions, especially in Sri Lanka, due to India's largeness. But what has not been appreciated by India's neighbours is India's magnanimity and good intention for regional development. Connectivity in the SAARC region hinges on this realization. For small island countries like Sri Lanka, connectivity is all the more crucial in its growth and prosperity.

Even ten years after the termination of the armed component of the ethnic conflict, the Sri Lankan economy is still reeling from the after-effects of the three-decade war. But, of late, it is doing better. As per Asian Development Bank, the GDP grew at 3.1 percent in 2017, a dip of more than a percentile from 4.5 percent in 2016.[41] In the preceding three years, the growth rate was around seven percent. Though Sri Lanka has been pushing ahead in the transition to a middle-income economy, it has to face "additional pressure on already stretched resources and economic opportunities, from greater urbanization, environmental degradation, changes in aspirations on the type of employment sought by young people, and changes to the country's epidemiological profile."[42]

Inflation has come down appreciably, but it is still a cause of concern to the common man, whose real income has not kept pace with it. The government is counting on aid flows meant for post-war reconstruction to bail itself out of the crisis. The overall development, however, depends on three factors: how well the global economy revives itself from the current slowdown, how well Sri Lanka is connected to the outside world and political stability. The present pro-market government in Colombo has been trying its best to enhance the economic connectivity. But the connectivity has to be looked at in a comprehensive sense — not just economic but also cultural, ICT and physical. Being an island, Sri Lanka has to reach out to its immediate neighbourhood first, especially India.

For India, the best way to secure the neighbourhood is to improve connectivity with the SAARC countries. India has the advantage of centrality and proximity. To step up intra-regional trade, an increase in intra-regional connectivity is important. Market forces may be given free hand and in fact could be encouraged and incentivized. Demographic dividends could be harnessed better by connectivity.

Threats could be addressed effectively through connectivity. People-to-people contacts will have spill-over effect on politics and the economy. The cultural component is presently underutilized. India is doing its bit in harnessing the culture, but the effect has not been optimal.

When it comes to economic engagement, India has to learn from China. Beijing places no conditions in terms of "structural adjustments, policy reforms, competitive biddings, or transparency attached to their loans" or even human rights, except bringing in some off their own labourers.[43] Indian companies have certain inherent disadvantages compared to their Chinese counterparts. While most Indian companies are privately owned, Chinese ones are state-owned and supported by state financial institutions, like China Development Bank Corporation, the Industrial and Commercial Bank of China (ICBC), China International Trade and Investment Corporation (CITIC), China Export and Credit Insurance Corporation (CECIC) and China Export-Import Bank. Profit motive comes last for the Chinese companies. Their priority is to look towards aspects like strategic advantages, diplomatic mileage and goodwill gained through projects.[44] Most important, in the Indian case, the private sector and the government do not seem to complement each other's efforts and gains. Risk-averse Indian companies care less about the projection of Indian "soft power" without much state support and motivation.[45] This point should be taken into consideration by the government of India in its economic diplomacy. The Indian private sector could be encouraged through various incentives to project India's soft power in the neighbourhood. Simultaneously, New Delhi has to work on relaxing visa rules that are considered as "tedious and cumbersome," not only by the common man but also the business sector of South Asian countries.

Notes

1 For the official Indian version of the state of India-Sri Lanka relations, see Ministry of External Affairs, "India-Sri Lanka Relations", January 2016, see www.mea.gov.in/Portal/ForeignRelation/Sri_Lanka_09_02_2016.pdf (Accessed on 20 February 2018).
   For the official Sri Lankan version of the state of India-Sri Lanka relations, see www.mea.gov.lk/index.php/en/foreign-policy/historical-context (Accessed on 25 February 2018).
2 When JVP militants attempted to the depose Sri Lankan government in April 1971, then Prime Minister Sirimavo Bandaranaike pleaded for external military assistance from various countries. The first to reach Sri Lanka was India. While Indian paratroopers and infantry regiments were rushed by air, the Indian Navy patrolled Sri Lankan maritime borders just to block possible foreign assistance to insurgents by sea.
3 Lucien Rajakarunanayake, "New Focus on Sri Lanka's Rise: The Strategic Hub of Indian Ocean Maritime Security", in *News Line*, Colombo: Policy Research & Information Unit of the Presidential Secretariat of Sri Lanka, 21 September 2014.
4 Central Bank of Sri Lanka, *Annual Report 2015*, Colombo: Central Bank of Sri Lanka, 2016, pp. 149–152.
5 Willie Mendis, "The Indo-Lanka Land Bridge: Reviving the Proposal", *The Island*, 7 August 2009.
6 "Ram Sethu" is a stretch of limestone shoals that runs from Pamban Island near Rameshwaram in South India to Mannar Island off the northern coast of Sri Lanka. Some Hindus believe it as the structure built by Lord Rama and his army of monkeys led by Hanuman to reach Lanka.
7 Anto T Joseph, "Myth and Match: Lanka Completes Hanuman Chain", *The Economic Times*, 7 January 2003.
8 "India-SL road link in works: Union Minister", *The Daily Mirror*, 17 June 2015.

9 The Asian Highway network is a regional transport cooperation initiative aimed at enhancing the efficiency and development of the road infrastructure in Asia, supporting the development of Euro-Asia transport linkages and improving connectivity for landlocked countries. The Trans-Asian Railway network now comprises 117,500 km of railway lines serving 28 member countries. It aims to serve cultural exchanges and trade within Asia and between Asia and Europe. For details see, www.unescap.org/our-work/transport (Accessed on 1 March 2018).

10 India's IRCON completed three lines: the Medawchchiya – Talaimannar and the Omanthai-Jaffna lines in the north and the Kalutara – Galle – Matara-Colombo line in the south of Sri Lanka.
     See High Commission of India in Sri Lanka, "Agreed Minutes of the 9th session of the India-Sri Lanka Joint Commission", 5–6 February 2016, Colombo.

11 Sri Lanka Ports Authority, "Port Development in Sri Lanka Towards a Maritime and Logistics Hub", see www.unescap.org/sites/default/files/Sri%20Lanka-DP-WGM-1.pdf (Accessed on 7 March 2018).

12 Don Manu, "India's New 5-billion-dollar one-way Hanuman Bridge to Lanka", *The Sunday Times*, 27 September 2015.

13 P.K. Balachandran, "Sri Lanka Scuttles Gadkari's Plan for Bridge Over Palk Strait", *The New Indian Express*, 19 December 2015.

14 Located about 275 km from Colombo in the Eastern Province of Sri Lanka, the Sampoor power plant is coal fired with a capacity of 500 MW. It has been proposed as part of a joint venture between the Ceylon Electricity Board (CEB) and the NTPC of India on a 50:50 basis, costing about $512 million.
     T. Ramakrishnan, "Sri Lanka-India Power Project to Get Green Nod Soon", *The Hindu*, 14 October 2015.

15 Ministry of Commerce & Industry, "India Sri Lanka CEO's Forum Identifies Potential Areas for Strengthening Bilateral Ties", New Delhi: Government of India, 5 August 2012.

16 The Asian Development Bank has done a detailed study on this. For details, see Priyantha Wijayatunga, D. Chattopadhyay, and P.N. Fernando, "Cross-Border Power Trading in South Asia: A Techno Economic Rationale", *ADB South Asia Working Paper Series, No. 38*, August 2015.

17 "PM Modi Announces Visa on Arrival for Sri Lankans from April 14", *The Financial Express*, 13 March 2015.

18 V. Sajeev Kumar, "Sri Lankan Airlines Expands India Operations", *The Hindu Business Line*, 30 May 2017.

19 Ministry of External Affairs, "India-Sri Lanka Relations", January 2016, see www.mea.gov.in/Portal/ForeignRelation/Sri_Lanka_November_2017_NEW.pdf (Accessed on 20 March 2018).

20 PTI, "India Wants to Operate World's Emptiest Airport in Sri Lanka", *The Economic Times*, 4 July 2018.

21 Government of India, Press Information Bureau, "Text of Statement to Media by the Prime Minister, Shri Narendra Modi, During the Visit of President of Sri Lanka", Shri Maithripala Sirisena, to India, 16 February 2015.

22 For full text of the current agreement covering the period 2015–2018, see www.india-culture.nic.in/sites/default/files/cultural_rel/MX-M452N_20150409_143910_0.pdf (Accessed on 25 March 2018).

23 For details, see Indian Council for Cultural Relations, http://iccr.gov.in/content/indian-culture-center-colombo.

24 High Commission of India in Sri Lanka, "India-Sri Lanka Foundation", see www.hcicolombo.org/hpages.php?id=77 (Accessed on 1 April 2018).

25 *Ibid.*

26 High Commission of India in Sri Lanka, "Agreed Minutes of the 8th session of the India-Sri Lanka Joint Commission", 21–22 January 2013, New Delhi, para 29.

27 PTI, "India's NKN, Sri Lanka's LEARN Connect with High Capacity Net", *The New Indian Express*, 15 January 2018.

28 Government of India, Ministry of External Affairs, "India-Sri Lanka Relations", November 2017, www.mea.gov.in/Portal/ForeignRelation/Sri_Lanka_November_2017_NEW.pdf (Accessed on 4 April 2018).

29 "India, Lanka ink MoU on ICT", *Daily News*, 16 January 2018.

30 Government of India, Ministry of External Affairs, "Agreed Minutes of the 7th session of the India-Sri Lanka Joint Commission", 26 November 2010, para 23.

31 Sri Lanka Telecom, "SLT Significantly Strengthened Its Multiple Global Connectivity Options", 22 June 2015, see www.slt.lk/en/content/slt-significantly-strengthened-its-multiple-global-connectivity-options (Accessed on 10 April 2018).

32 Sri Lanka Telecom, "Consortium Starts Deployment of SEA-ME-WE 5 Cable System", see www.slt.lk/en/content/consortium-starts-deployment-sea-me-we-5-cable-system (Accessed on 13 April 2018).

33 High Commission of India in Sri Lanka, "Agreed Minutes of the 8th Session of the India-Sri Lanka Joint Commission", 21–22 January 2013, New Delhi, para 29.

34 For full text of the Agreement and other pertinent documents, see http://commerce.nic.in/trade/international_ta_indsl.asp (Accessed on 15 April 2018).

35 Global Business Edge, "Sri Lanka: Trade Statistics", https://globaledge.msu.edu/countries/sri-lanka/tradestats (Accessed on 22 April 2018).

36 Saman Kelegama, "India-Sri Lanka Free Trade Agreement: Sri Lanka Reaping the Benefits from Preferential Trade", *Asia Pacific Brief No. 50*, Bangkok: United Nations Economic and Social Commission for Asia and the Pacific, 5 July 2017.

37 Vivek Joshi, "An Econometric Analysis of India-Sri Lanka Free Trade Agreement", *HEID Working Paper No: 04/2010*, Graduate Institute of International and Development Studies, March 2010, p. 4.

38 Sri Lanka Deputy High Commission in Southern India, "Indo-Sri Lanka Trade Relations", www.sldhcchennai.org/node/106 (Accessed on 26 April 2018).

39 T. Ramakrishnan, "Storm Over Sri Lankan Deal with India", *The Hindu*, 21 February 2016.

40 A number of new investments from Indian companies are in the pipeline or under implementation. Notable among them are proposals of Shree Renuka Sugar to set up a sugar refining plant at Hambantota ($220 million), South City, Kolkata for real estate development in Colombo ($400 million), Tata Housing Slave Island Development project along with Urban Development Authority of Sri Lanka ($430 million), 'Colombo One' project of ITC Ltd. (ITC has committed an investment of $300 million, augmenting the earlier committed $140 million). Dabur has already set up a fruit juice manufacturing plant ($17 million) in May 2013.

41 Asian Development Bank, "Sri Lanka: Economy", see www.adb.org/countries/sri-lanka/economy (Accessed on 1 May 2018).

42 Institute of Policy Studies of Sri Lanka, *Sri Lanka: State of the Economy 2013*, Colombo: Institute of Policy Studies, October 2013.

43 Patrik Mendis, "The Colombo-Centric New Silk Road", *Economic and Political Weekly*, vol.97, no.49, 8 December 2012, p. 69.

44 Some refer to the working relation that exists between Chinese companies, the state and quasi-commercial lending institutions as the "Golden Triangle" that provides the Chinese companies with cheap finance to undercut their Western competitors. See, in the African context, Executive Research Associates, China in Africa: A Strategic Overview (Chiba: Institute of Developing Economics & Japan External Trade Organization), October 2009.

45 Some of the Indian companies present in Sri Lanka are IOC, Tatas, Bharti Airtel, Piramal Glass, Life Insurance Corporation of India (LIC), Ashok Leyland, Larson & Toubro (L&T), ICICI Bank and Taj Hotels.

INDEX